Drift from the Churches

Religion, Culture and Society

Religion, Culture and Society is a new series presented by leading scholars on a wide range of contemporary religious issues. The emphasis throughout is generally multicultural, and the approach is often interdisciplinary. The clarity and accessibility of the series, as well as its authoritative scholarship, will recommend it to students and a non-specialist readership alike.

Drift from the Churches

Attitude toward Christianity during Childhood and Adolescence

by

WILLIAM K. KAY

and

LESLIE J. FRANCIS

UNIVERSITY OF WALES PRESS
CARDIFF
1996

© William K. Kay and Leslie J. Francis, 1996

British Library Cataloguing in Publication Data
A catalogue record for this book is available from
the British Library.

ISBN 0-7083-1330-2

Cover design by John Garland, Pentan Partnership, Cardiff
Typeset at the University of Wales Press
Printed in Great Britain by Dinefwr Press, Llandybïe

Contents

Preface

The scientific study of religion is a slow and painstaking business. Theories may be easy to generate, but the collection and analysis of real data strong enough to test those theories is expensive in time and resources. The data presented in this book have taken twenty-five years to assemble.

The component parts of these data would never have been assembled without the industry and commitment of many colleagues and friends. The contribution of each is made clear in the references. Nor would the data have been available without the willingness and help of many teachers and thousands of pupils. We stand greatly in their debt, and in the debt of the various groups who have, at different stages, helped to fund the research.

The fact that we have now been able to draw together the threads of twenty-five years of research is due to the initiative of the Principal and Governors of Trinity College Carmarthen, in the establishment of the Centre for Theology and Education. We hope that the present study makes a worthy contribution to fulfilling the vision which they hold for the Centre for Theology and Education as a place of excellence for promoting research in religious education and practical theology.

Finally, we record our gratitude to Dr Oliver Davies, who commissioned and restructured this volume, to Ms Anne Rees, who shaped the manuscript, and to Ms Diane Drayson and Ms Mandy Robbins for help with editing the text.

William K. Kay
Leslie J. Francis
December 1995

The authors

William K. Kay is Senior Research Fellow at the Centre for Theology and Education, Trinity College, Carmarthen.

Leslie J. Francis is D. J. James Professor of Pastoral Theology, Trinity College, Carmarthen, and University of Wales, Lampeter.

1
Introduction

The first seeds of this book were sown twenty-five years ago, when Leslie J. Francis began to search the available literature, in books, journal articles and unpublished dissertations, to discover what was known about the pattern of attitude toward Christianity during childhood and adolescence. In particular, there were three kinds of questions which he had hoped this literature would answer. The first set of questions was concerned with providing an accurate description of how attitude toward Christianity changes during the years of childhood and adolescence. Is it true that attitude toward Christianity becomes less favourable as children grow up and, if so, are there any particular stages associated with this trend? The second set of questions was concerned with identifying the causes or precursors of changing attitude toward Christianity during childhood and adolescence. For example, how important is parental example? How important is the influence of school? How important is the young person's personality in shaping attitude toward Christianity? The third set of questions was concerned with identifying the correlates and consequences of changing attitude toward Christianity during childhood and adolescence. For example, does religion in fact make any difference to the lives of young people? Are religious young people more or less happy than those who reject religion? Do religious young people espouse different moral values, or hold a different outlook on life?

That initial review of the literature twenty-five years ago led to two fundamental conclusions. The first conclusion suggested that considerably less was known about the development of attitude toward Christianity during childhood and adolescence than had been anticipated. If the three sets of questions could not be answered satisfactorily from existing research, the only sensible solution was to begin to plan a research strategy which could discover the answers. The second conclusion suggested that one of the major weaknesses with the field stemmed from the lack of integration between the existing studies. Each piece of work seemed to have been set up in isolation from the others, which meant that it was very difficult for an overview to be constructed from the disparate research initiatives. If existing studies could not be integrated satisfactorily, the only sensible solution was to plan a research strategy on to which other studies could build in a flexible and open way.

At that stage, the essential key to integrating the findings from a range of studies concerned with attitude toward Christianity during childhood and adolescence seemed to concern reaching basic agreement about how attitude toward Christianity is defined and assessed. If a number of studies could agree on employing the same scale of attitude toward Christianity, then the findings of these studies would begin to hang together. If different pieces of the jigsaw puzzle agreed to hold a measuring instrument in common, then it would become possible to fit pieces of the jigsaw puzzle together.

From this starting point, Francis set out to develop a scale of attitude toward Christianity to high psychometric standards. The scale was designed to function reliably and validly among children and young people from the age of eight upwards.[1]

After conducting a series of studies of his own, using this scale, Francis wrote a paper entitled, 'Measurement reapplied: research into the child's attitude toward religion',[2] in which he invited other researchers to collaborate with him in adding to the developing jigsaw of studies employing the scale. William K. Kay was among the first colleagues to collaborate in this way, when he designed a significant study among young people in England and Ireland.[3] Since then, a number of other colleagues have joined in the enterprise. Now over a hundred studies have been published using the Francis scale of attitude toward Christianity. Taken together, these studies enable a much fuller and more detailed picture to be constructed regarding attitude toward Christianity during childhood, adolescence and adulthood than was the case twenty-five years ago.

The aim of the present book is to unfold part of that story of research which has occupied the past twenty-five years. By the end of the book it will be possible to claim that something is known about the changing pattern of attitude toward Christianity during childhood and adolescence, that something is known about the causes or precursors of attitude toward Christianity during these years, and that something is also known about the correlates and consequences of attitude toward Christianity during these years. By chronicling what is known about these issues, it is also easier to see what is not yet known, or not yet known with sufficient clarity or certainty. A clear research agenda remains for the next twenty-five years as well.

The programme of research outlined in this book is firmly grounded in one particular approach to the scientific study of religion. This approach involves some clear assumptions about the nature of knowledge and how certain kinds of *truth* can be established. It also involves making use of a range of technical terms grounded in the languages of social psychology and statistical analysis. Some readers will be thoroughly familiar with this approach, while others may not be so familiar with it.

For this reason, appendix 1 discusses the wider context of the *scientific study of religion*, in which the programme of research needs to be placed. The first part of this appendix discusses broad issues of objectivity and subjectivity. After evaluating the strengths and weaknesses of both approaches, we define our preference for an approach to the scientific study of religion based on objectivity and measurement. The second part of this appendix discusses those key concepts employed by the objective approach to the scientific study of religion and assumed in subsequent chapters. Readers not already thoroughly familiar with such concepts as measurement, probability, correlation, factor analysis, causation, reliability, validity, variance, models and path analysis would be advised to linger over this discussion before encountering the concepts at work in later chapters.

The findings from empirical research integrated in this book are derived from studies using the Francis scale of attitude toward Christianity. The scientific evaluation of these studies needs to draw both on knowledge about the wider field of attitude measurement and on information about the development of this specific instrument. Once again, some readers will be thoroughly familiar with these issues, while others may not be so familiar with them.

For this reason, appendix 2 discusses the wider context concerned with *assessing attitudes* and draws attention to the way in which the Francis scale of attitude toward Christianity was developed. This appendix discusses the various principles involved in different techniques of attitude-scale construction and illustrates how each of these techniques was tested, before selecting the method chosen to construct the scale used in the rest of the book. The resulting scale is a twenty-four-item instrument, arranged for scoring by the Likert method. This means that the respondents are invited to respond to each item on a five-point scale, ranging from 'agree strongly', through 'agree', 'not certain' and 'disagree', to 'disagree strongly'. Appendix 2 concludes by presenting detailed information about the reliability and validity of the scale among different age groups of children and young people and in different cultural contexts.

Chapter 2 begins to unfold the findings which have emerged from the programme of research by discussing the question of *sex differences*. The chapter begins by looking at the range of reasons advanced by other researchers to account for the regular finding from research that women are more religious than men. These arguments fall into two basic categories. The first category of argument accounts for sex differences in religiosity in terms of sociological theories concerned with sex-role stereotyping or with women's distinctive location in society. The second category of arguments accounts for sex differences in religiosity in terms of psychological theories. Studies using the Francis scale of attitude toward Christianity are employed to adjudicate between these two types of theory. As a consequence of these studies, a psychological account is preferred to a sociological account. It is concluded that the general finding that women are more religious than men can be adequately accounted for in terms of the psychological characteristics of femininity and, to a lesser extent, masculinity. While, as might be expected, women record higher scores of femininity than men, both men and women vary considerably in levels of psychological femininity. Both women and men who score high on femininity are more religious than women and men who score low on femininity.

Chapter 3, on *age trends*, assesses the changes which take place in attitude toward Christianity over the whole age range from eight to sixteen years. Previous theory had suggested that deterioration in attitude toward Christianity, assumed to take place during childhood and adolescence, was associated with specific social or development stages, like the move from primary to secondary school, the transition from concrete to abstract operational thinking, or the preparation to leave school for the adult world. By administering the Francis scale of attitude toward Christianity to several cohorts of young people, throughout the age range from eight to sixteen years, it has been possible to assess the power of these theories. Contrary to prediction, the data made available from these studies reveal a consistent and persistent decline in attitude toward Christianity throughout the whole age range.

Chapter 4, on *generational trends*, provides a detailed picture of the way in which attitude toward Christianity has been changing among young people over a twenty-year period. Back in 1974, Francis conducted a systematic survey, using the scale of attitude toward Christianity, throughout two secondary schools. Since then, the survey has been repeated at four-yearly intervals, in 1978, 1982, 1986, 1990 and 1994, to the successive generations of pupils sitting at the same school desks. While limitation on resources has meant that only two schools were involved in the study, nevertheless the data provide a unique insight into the changing climate in which Christianity is received among young people. The results of these surveys indicate a consistent and persistent decline in attitude toward Christianity between 1974 and 1986. At the same time, however, scores recorded in 1994 are neither lower nor higher than those recorded in 1986.

Chapter 5, on *school influence*, discusses a series of studies which have employed the Francis scale of attitude toward Christianity to assess the impact of church schools on the pupils who attend them. To begin with, a set of four studies all confirm that church primary schools, within the state-maintained sector, exert an identifiable influence on their pupils' attitude toward Christianity, even after taking into account the influence of home and church. Roman Catholic primary schools consistently exert a positive influence on their pupils' attitude toward Christianity and are, therefore, to be seen to be making a positive contribution to the religious development of young people, which would not be made if the Catholic church were not sponsoring such schools. The major puzzle, and point of controversy, emerging from these four studies is the finding that Church of England schools either make no contribution to their pupils' attitude toward Christianity, or make a negative contribution. A second set of studies conducted among Roman Catholic secondary schools draws particular attention to the way in which these schools make a significant positive contribution to the development of a positive attitude toward Christianity among practising Catholic pupils, but may be serving less well pupils from lapsed Catholic backgrounds, or pupils from practising Christian backgrounds of other denominations. Another strand of research examines the influence of different approaches to religious education on pupils' attitude toward Christianity. It is shown that approaches which concentrate specifically on multi-faith religious education can lead to the development of a less positive attitude toward Christianity among pupils.

Chapter 6, on *home influence*, draws together findings from three types of studies, using the Francis scale of attitude toward Christianity. The first type of study scrutinizes conflicting theories about the relative influence of mothers and of fathers on the religious development of their sons and daughters. In relation to adolescent religious practice, the findings demonstrate that parental influence is important for both sexes and for the two age groups studied, namely eleven- to twelve-year-olds and fifteen- to sixteen-year-olds. There is little difference in overall parental influence on sons and daughters, although this influence increases rather than decreases between the ages of eleven to twelve and fifteen to sixteen. The influence of mothers is stronger than the influence of fathers among both sons and daughters. At the same time, the comparative influence of the father is weaker among daughters than among sons, while the comparative influence of the mother is stronger among daughters than among sons. The second type of study scrutinizes conflicting theories about the influence of social class on religious development. The data from these studies demonstrate that, although more frequent church attendance is associated with the higher social classes, a more positive attitude toward Christianity is associated with the lower social classes. The third type of study compares attitude toward Christianity among children from homes where the parents were in various degrees of accord, from happily married to divorced. Children from homes where the parents had divorced had a lower attitude toward Christianity, while children from homes where the parents had separated had a higher attitude toward Christianity.

Chapter 7, on *personality and religion*, explores the extent to which attitude toward Christianity can be predicted from knowledge about the young person's personality. The chapter begins by discussing different traditions in personality theory, and then presents the results of a series of studies designed to assess the usefulness to the psychology of religion of theories of personality advanced by Freud and by Eysenck. It is concluded that there is little empirical support for theories generated from Freud's model of personality. On the other hand, there is much more support for theories generated from Eysenck's model of personality. Eysenck's model of personality proposes the three major dimensions known as introversion–extraversion, neuroticism–stability, and tender-mindedness–tough-mindedness (psychoticism). Repeated studies among primary school children, secondary school children, under-graduates and adults, using the Francis scale of attitude toward Christianity, demonstrate that it is the personality dimension of tender-mindedness–tough-mindedness (psychoticism) which is fundamental to individual differences in attitude toward Christianity. On some accounts, introverts may also be more religious than extraverts. On the other hand, there is no evidence to suggest a relationship between neuroticism and religiosity on the basis of these studies.

Chapter 8, on *science and religion*, reviews the popular notion that there is radical conflict in the mind of young people between the claims of science and the claims of religion. A series of studies employing the Francis scale of attitude toward Christianity has begun to unravel this relationship, on data collected from young people both in the UK and in Kenya. These studies point to the importance of two key variables in generating the conflict between science and religion. These variables are scientism and creationism. For example, while the view that Christianity necessarily involves creationism may be helpful in promoting a positive attitude toward Christianity at the beginning of the secondary school, by the end of the secondary school this view is detrimental to the development of a positive attitude toward Christianity. Scientism, also, militates against the development of a positive attitude toward Christianity.

Chapter 9, on *religious experience*, turns attention to two types of question concerning the part played by religious experience in the development of a positive attitude toward Christianity among young people. The first type of question concerns the broader notion of religious experience. Two studies carried out among Catholic and Protestant pupils in Northern Ireland demonstrate that, within both faith communities, the naming and valuing of religious experience makes a significant and positive contribution to the development of a positive attitude toward Christianity. The second type of question concerns the specific notion of religious conversion, which is particularly relevant among some Protestant churches. Again, this kind of religious experience is shown to be associated with the development of a positive attitude toward Christianity.

Chapter 10, on *religion and life*, moves attention from the factors which may influence individual differences in attitude toward Christianity to the factors which may themselves be influenced by individual differences in attitude toward Christianity. Three different types of studies using the Francis scale of attitude toward Christianity are discussed in this chapter. The first set of studies explores the influence of attitude toward Christianity on the development of attitude toward other people. The data demonstrate that a positive attitude toward Christianity promotes the development of empathy, a key psychological precursor to pro-social behaviour. Another study, conducted among both Protestant and Catholic adolescents in Northern Ireland, shows that a positive attitude toward Christianity engenders greater openness to members of the other religious community. The second set of studies explores the influence of attitude toward Christianity on the development of attitude toward the self. Studies, conducted both among primary school pupils and among secondary school pupils, demonstrate that a positive attitude toward Christianity promotes the development of a more positive self-concept and the development of a higher self-esteem. Another study, conducted among sixteen-year-olds, shows that a positive attitude toward Christianity engenders greater personal happiness. The third set of studies explores the influence of attitude toward Christianity on the shaping of moral values. The data demonstrate a highly significant link between a positive attitude toward Christianity and the espousal of traditional Christian moral values.

Chapter 11, on *conclusions*, draws together the findings of the previous chapters and assesses the significance of these findings for understanding the drift from the churches.

Finally, the section headed *references* lists the published studies and unpublished dissertations which have employed or critiqued the Francis scale of attitude toward Christianity.

By demonstrating how the various studies employing the Francis scale of attitude toward Christianity integrate to begin to produce a cumulative picture, it is possible to see how interrelated studies can, when put together, provide a picture larger than the sum total of the individual parts. At the same time, it is possible to see more clearly the gaps in the picture, where other studies are needed to clarify the situation. From this review, it is also possible to see how even the small-scale study, possible within the context of an undergraduate dissertation, can contribute to the overall picture, if that study is designed with sufficient clarity and focus. Our hope is that, over the next twenty-five years, a new generation of students and scholars will join our quest to map in greater detail the correlates of attitude toward Christianity among different age groups. After all, the work has only just begun.

By concentrating on the measurement of attitude toward Christianity, the present book has deliberately restricted its focus to one religious tradition. The findings cannot, therefore, as yet be generalized beyond this tradition. Again, our hope is that scholars working in other religious traditions will wish to extend our quest by both replicating some of our earlier studies and developing new studies with comparable instruments designed to measure attitude toward other religions. Such collaboration is already well under way in Israel and in relationship to the Jewish tradition.[4]

2
Sex differences

Introduction

This chapter sketches many of the main religious differences between males and females. After this it describes the main explanatory theories put forward to account for these differences. These theories have been drawn from psychological and sociological disciplines and may be grouped under two main headings. The first set of theories deals with social or contextual influences which shape responses to religion among men and women, while the second set of theories concentrates on personal and individual psychological characteristics. Under the first heading are sex role socialization theories and structural location theories. Under the second heading are gender orientation theories, depth-psychological theories and personality theories. We conclude by reviewing the contribution of attitude toward Christianity to this debate and comment on its significance to the explanatory theories put forward earlier.

Briefly, a large body of research demonstrates that women attend church more often than men and in greater numbers.[1] Women are more likely than men to claim for themselves denominational membership,[2] to pray,[3] to read their bibles,[4] to report religious and mystical experiences,[5] to watch religious television programmes[6] and to express belief in God.[7] They are also more likely to hold traditional religious beliefs,[8] to report feeling close to God,[9] to believe in spirits[10] and to report deriving comfort from religion.[11] These sex differences are well established and found in, among other places, England, Ireland, Wales, Japan, New Zealand, Canada, the United States, Australia, Scotland and western Europe generally.[12]

Sex-role socialization theories
Sex-role socialization theories begin from the different social experience of men and women.[13] They argue that men and women in westernized societies are brought up with distinct

ideals and values. Men learn to set goals and compete aggressively without being concerned to resolve interpersonal conflicts peacefully. The socialization of women emphasizes gentleness, nurturance, the resolution of interpersonal conflicts and expressive values that easily fit a religious life style. In the USA a national sample of thirteen- to eighteen-year-old adolescents showed that parents placed greater emphasis on the religiousness and conformity of girls.[14]

Structural-location theories
Structural-location theories also begin from a sociological rather than a psychological basis. There are two main forms of structural-location theory advanced to account for greater religiosity among women. The first form emphasizes the child-rearing role of women. The family-centred role of women encourages dependence on personal influences. Religion, therefore, which addresses the dynamics of relationships within the home, is more appreciated by women than by men.[15] Additionally, parents feel that the church is good for their children.[16] As the primary care-takers, mothers attend church to encourage their children's involvement. In favour of this structural-location theory, it is argued that men and women have different social roles: the mother takes a family role and the father an economic role. As the bonds between family and church are still relatively strong, in comparison with the bonds between economy and church, females who are more heavily involved in the family role may be expected to be more church-oriented.[17] In a similar vein it has been argued that women are 'expected to be the prime socializers of their children and as part of this to teach their offspring morals'. This they accomplish in part by being examples themselves, attending church and evincing religious interests.[18]

De Vaus formulated a set of specific hypotheses on the basis of this form of structural location theory.[19] He argued that the theory implies that mothers will attend church more than childless women; that having children will lead to greater church attendance for women than for men; and that the difference between church-attendance rates of men and women *with children* will be greater than between *childless* men and women. Testing these hypotheses on data derived from the National Opinion

Research Centre general social survey data between 1972 and 1980, De Vaus found that mothers attended church more than childless women. On the other hand, having children led to an equal impact on church attendance among men and women. Moreover, the difference in church attendance between mothers and fathers was no greater than between men and women without children.

The second form of structural-location theory advanced to account for the greater religiosity of women emphasizes the different place of women in the workforce. One strand of this argument is a development of the more general secularization thesis.[20] According to this argument, religious involvement declines with participation in the modern secular world. Since women are less likely to be fully a part of the ongoing secular world, at least in terms of outside-the-home employment, they are also likely to be less secularized than men.

A second strand of this argument suggests that women seek social support from religion to alleviate the greater isolation they experience as a consequence of not benefiting from the social contacts of the workplace and that women seek comfort from religion to compensate for not benefiting from the more socially valued role of the wage earner.[21] A third strand of this argument suggests that women are more likely than men to avoid the conflicts between the competitiveness of the workplace and the essence of Christian values which in turn leads to a greater distance from the churches.[22] A fourth strand of this argument simply suggests that lower commitment to the workplace releases more time for women to devote to the church.[23]

De Vaus formulated a set of specific hypotheses on the basis of this form of structural-location theory.[24] He argued that the theory implies that when level of workforce participation is held constant the gender difference in religiosity should evaporate; that women who are in employment should be less religious than women who are not in employment, and that men who are not in employment should be more religious than men who are in employment. Testing these hypotheses on data derived from the National Opinion Research Centre general social-survey data between 1972 and 1980, De Vaus found that, even when level of workforce participation is held constant, more women attend church than men. Indeed, contrary to the hypothesis, men who were not working full-time were *less* likely to attend church regularly than men who were working full-time. Other empirical studies also contradict these hypotheses. For example, working women attend church as frequently as non-working women, and unemployed young people were less likely to attend church than those in employment.[25]

Finally, a contrary argument is raised by a group of studies which suggest that any correlation between levels of religiosity and participation in the workforce by women should be explained by a different causal model according to which women who are more committed to religion should be less willing to enter the workforce, preferring to maintain more traditional family-oriented roles.[26]

Gender-orientation theory
Gender-orientation theory accounts for gender differences in religiosity by building on the notions of feminine and masculine orientations of personality. This is well illustrated by the Bem Sex Role Inventory.[27] According to Bem's conceptualization, masculinity and femininity do not simply belong to the biology of gender. They are ways of behaving, ways of living, ways of understanding oneself. Bem's Sex Role Inventory shows that there are considerable variations in the masculinity and femininity of men and in the masculinity and femininity of women.

Using this theory, Thompson argued that individual differences in religiosity should be affected more by gender orientation than by being male or female.[28] According to this account, being religious is a consonant experience for *people with a feminine orientation* and that men as well as women can have a feminine orientation.

In order to test this theory, sex-role orientation needs to be separated from gender itself. Multiple regression is very helpful here because, if the biological sex of the respondent is entered into the equation first, any variance it accounts for will be removed. If sex-role orientation is entered to the equation next and can account for no further variance, then it becomes clear that gender is the crucial variable. If, on the other hand, sex-role orientation makes a significant contribution, even after the effects of gender have been subtracted, then sexual orientation will be shown to be an important variable in relation to religiosity. Thompson's empirical analysis, using data from 358 undergraduate students in New England who completed the Bem Sex Role Inventory together with five measures of religiosity, provided clear support for the view that being religious *is* a function of gender orientation.

The view that there is a positive relationship between religiosity and *psychological* femininity is also supported, in a different way, by a study which invited a heterogeneous sample of 95 males and 105 females to rate a religious or non-religious prototype target on the Australian Sex Role Inventory.[29] They found that more positive feminine characteristics were assigned to the religious targets and more masculine characteristics were assigned to the non-religious targets.

In the UK, Francis found that male clergy and ordinands recorded a characteristically feminine profile on the Eysenck Personality Questionnaire.[30] This finding, in this context, may support the sex-role theory because many of the traditional clergy tasks, involving caring for people and reducing interpersonal tension, are characteristic of the feminine orientation.

Depth-psychological theories

Depth-psychological theories appropriately find their 'father figure' in Freud. Freud thought that in monotheistic religions, especially in the Judaeo-Christian tradition, God is in every case modelled after the father and that personal relationships with God depend on our relationships with physical fathers.[31] Consequently girls and boys form different relationships with God. Boys have ambivalent feelings toward their fathers because the father is a more powerful competitor for the affections of the mother. Girls have less complicated feelings toward their fathers as the love object of their infantile sexuality.[32] In subsequent development women smoothly transfer their love for their fathers on to God. Men have greater obstacles to overcome, and their concept of God is formed from the superego and becomes the bearer of standards and values rather than an object of love.

Freudian theory suggests that the Virgin Mary of Catholicism is a female projection close to God to whom men may be attracted. Protestant men have no comparable female figure, and this difference is employed by some commentators to explain why

there are proportionately more Catholic than Protestant men in their respective churches.[33]
When thorough attempts have been made to test Freudian theories of religion, the results are far from conclusive. In an American sample both males and females emphasized the paternal rather than the maternal image of God, and this tendency was even stronger in males than in females.[34] In a Scottish sample boys and girls were both more likely to think of God as being like a father than a mother.[35] Freudian theory would anticipate that the girls' image of God would be more masculine and the boys' image more feminine, but these were not the reported findings.

In another group of studies males and females were tested to see how closely their concept of God matched the image of the mother or the father. Both sexes recorded a strong relation between the concept of God and the mother image.[36] These findings are not supportive of the Freudian position on two counts: they fail to differentiate between males and females, which is crucial to the psychodynamic notion of religious origins, and they show a mother image, rather than a father image for God, which is contrary to the basic presumptions of the theory.

Personality theories
Personality theories make use of the differences between males and females in areas indirectly related to religion. Argyle and Beit-Hallahmi suggest that women feel more guilt than men and that religion is used as a mechanism for controlling guilt.[37] The rationale for this is that the ratio of women to men rises in Protestant groups that lay great stress on sin and guilt and falls in Catholic groups where sin and guilt are less emphasized. Other female characteristics may also be utilized in the same way. Studies showing that women experience greater frustration or are more submissive and passive than men can also be turned to account for greater female involvement in religion. In each case the characteristic is minimized by, or consonant with, the effects of religion. Frustration is reduced while submissiveness and passivity are rewarded. Similarly, dependency needs are met and, for this reason, that lower value women are considered as placing on independence and autonomy is reflected in their greater dependence on religion.[38] In a nutshell, it is argued that 'whereas

a relationship with Christ may fulfil a woman's desire for relationship, it directly confronts a man's desire for independence.'[39]

If Eysenckian personality theory is used, the focus of attention moves from male–female differences in traits to male–female differences on broad dimensions. The psychoticism dimension of personality can be shown to be fundamental to religiosity. Psychoticism is consistently related negatively to religion (see chapter 6). Women show lower psychoticism scores than men.[40] Therefore women are more likely to be positive about religion.

Findings

The findings in this chapter are presented in two groups. First we present the findings relating to sex differences in attitude toward Christianity where the only relevant variable is the biological gender of the respondent. Then we present findings relating to the Bem Sex Role Inventory where biological gender and sex role are tested against each other.

The first set of findings confirms that girls demonstrate more favourable attitude toward Christianity than boys at every age level and in several cultures. For example, in an English sample made up of 200 boys and 200 girls from each of nine year groups between the first year of junior education (year three) and the last compulsory year of secondary education (year eleven), it was evident that the overall mean score for girls of 84·3 was significantly higher than the overall mean score of 74·6 for the boys. It was also clear that in each year group taken separately the girls registered higher scores than the boys. Moreover, although, in both cases, a decline in scores took place during the years of compulsory schooling, the decline was steeper for boys than it was for girls. The girls dropped by 19·6 points and the boys by 32·2 points.[41]

Similar results are found among Protestant pupils in Northern Ireland,[42] Roman Catholic pupils in England,[43] non-denominational secondary pupils in Scotland[44] and secondary pupils in Kenya.[45]

The second set of findings are derived from studies which employed the Francis scale of attitude toward Christianity alongside the Bem Sex Role Inventory. In the first study in this series, Francis and Wilcox explored Thompson's hypotheses, using data from seventy-nine male and eighty female students in Wales who completed the Bem Sex Role Inventory together with the Francis scale of attitude toward Christianity.[46] In this study Francis and Wilcox employed a more stringent use of multiple regression than that employed in Thompson's original study. With attitude toward Christianity as the dependent variable, femininity and masculinity were entered into the equation first. Then, after controlling for these expressions of gender orientation, sex was entered into the equation. As with Thompson's original analysis, this study demonstrated that the significant relationship between religiosity and being female disappeared after controlling for individual differences in masculinity and femininity.

In the second study in this series, Francis reported on findings based on two samples of adolescents.[47] The first sample comprised 340 male and 347 female pupils, aged between thirteen and fifteen years, in the year-nine and year-ten classes of two secondary schools. The second sample comprised fifty-nine male and 233 female pupils, aged between sixteen and eighteen years, attending a sixth-form study programme. The Bem Sex Role Inventory and the junior and adult forms of the Francis scale of attitude toward Christianity were completed by the respondents.

All three measuring instruments achieved satisfactory reliability coefficients within both samples, producing the following alpha coefficients for the younger and older groups respectively: attitude toward Christianity, 0·96 and 0·97; femininity, 0·75 and 0·78; masculinity, 0·80 and 0·84. The slightly lower reliability of the femininity scale is consistent with the findings of Francis and Wilcox in the study mentioned earlier and suggests that femininity is less satisfactorily operationalized by the Bem Sex Role Inventory among adolescents and undergraduates in the UK than is the case for masculinity.

The correlations between masculinity, femininity, sex and attitude toward Christianity among the sixteen- to eighteen-year-olds, are presented in full in table 2.1 in the appendices. All the predicted relationships hold true in this sample. The female pupils score higher on femininity and on attitude toward Christianity. The male pupils score higher on masculinity. Masculinity and femininity are uncorrelated orthogonal factors. Higher scores on femininity predict a more positive attitude toward Christianity, while masculinity scores are unrelated to attitude toward Christianity.

The multiple regression significance tests exploring the influence of masculinity, femininity and sex on attitude toward Christianity, entered into the equation in that order, among the sixteen- to eighteen-year-olds, are presented in full in table 2.2 in the appendices. These statistics confirm that femininity is the key predictor of attitude toward Christianity and that sex contributes no additional predictive power after taking femininity into account. In other words, these data among sixteen to eighteen year olds replicate the findings of Thompson among undergraduate students.

The correlations between masculinity, femininity, sex and attitude toward Christianity among the thirteen- to fifteen-year-olds, are presented in full in table 2.3 in the appendices. The picture here is more complex than the situation among the sixteen- to eighteen-year-olds. In accordance with the predictions, the female pupils score higher on femininity and on attitude toward Christianity; the male pupils score higher on masculinity; masculinity and femininity are uncorrelated orthogonal factors; higher scores on femininity predict a more positive attitude toward Christianity. Contrary to the predictions, however, masculinity is also a significant predictor of a less positive attitude toward Christianity.

The multiple regression significance tests exploring the influence of masculinity, femininity and sex on attitude toward Christianity, entered into the equation in that order, among thirteen- to fifteen-year-olds, are presented in full in table 2.4 in the appendices. These statistics confirm that femininity is the *key* predictor of attitude toward Christianity. Among this younger age group, however, masculinity is an additional predictor of attitude toward Christianity. Moreover, after controlling for masculinity and femininity, sex continued to contribute additional predictive power to explaining individual differences in attitude toward Christianity. In other words, these data among thirteen- to fifteen-year-olds do *not* replicate the findings of Thompson among undergraduates. Among this younger age group sex continues to be a significant predictor of religiosity, after taking gender orientation into account.

Comment

The basic differences between male and female levels of religiosity are confirmed by the Francis scale of attitude toward Christianity. Not only do females show a greater commitment to public and private Christian religious behaviour, but also they show a significantly more positive attitude toward Christianity. Findings from these studies also help us to adjudicate between the different explanations advanced to account for gender differences in religiosity and to explain why it is that females record a more favourable attitude toward Christianity than do males.

The crucial debate is between two very different kinds of theories. The first kind of theory concentrates on those experiences which are common to women because they are women. To this category belong the sex-role socialization location theory, the structural-location theories and the Freudian theory. The sex-role socialization theory argues that males and females are trained in very different ways from a young age, precisely because they are male or female. The structural location theories argue that males and females experience life very differently in terms of family roles, child-rearing roles and employment, precisely because they are male or female. The Freudian theory argues that males and females respond differently to the father figure, precisely because of the differential unfolding of their infant sexuality.

The second kind of theory concentrates on those psychological characteristics which are present to greater or lesser degree in both males and females, but which tend, in the population as a whole, to be more prominent among women than men. A number of major psychological theories demonstrate certain fundamental differences among men and women. For example, women are generally shown to record lower scores on the personality dimension of psychoticism[48] and higher scores on the personality dimension of neuroticism.[49] It is gender orientation theory, however, which most explicitly attempts to characterize the differences between male and female in terms of the psychological constructs of femininity and masculinity. The Bem Sex Role Inventory provides a widely accepted operationalization of these constructs.

If, using multiple regression, all the differences in religiosity between males and females can be accounted for by the gender orientation of femininity and masculinity, this provides clear support for the superiority of the second kind of theory over the first kind of theory. The problem is that the three studies by Thompson, Francis and Wilcox, and Francis, reported above, suggest that the gender-orientation theory is able to account for the differences in religiosity among older adolescents and among young adults, but not among younger adolescents.

To begin with, the findings presented by Francis among sixteen- to eighteen-year-olds, together with the findings of Thompson among undergraduate students in the USA and the findings of Francis and Wilcox among students in the UK, provide significant confirmation for the view that among late adolescents and young adults, observed gender differences in religiosity can be adequately accounted for in terms of gender-orientation theory. Individual differences in religiosity among these age groups are seen to be a function of psychological femininity, not of sex. Both males and females who are characterized by higher levels of femininity are more religious than males and females who are characterized by lower levels of femininity.

On the other hand, the data presented by Francis from the thirteen- to fifteen-year-olds suggest that gender-orientation theory may be less successful in explaining individual differences in religiosity among this younger age group. While gender orientation is a significant predictor of attitude toward Christianity among this younger age group, sex itself also remains a significant predictor. Sex-role socialization theory may help to account for the difference among the younger age group. Because religion and the churches appeal more to the feminine side of human personality, religion and churches have themselves become sex-typed. It may be easier, therefore, for adolescent girls who emphasize the feminine dimension of their character to remain in touch with the churches during the transition from childhood to adolescence than it may be for boys who equally emphasize the feminine dimension of their character. It is socially acceptable and socially normal for girls to lapse from church membership at a later age than is the case among boys.[50] By late adolescence, however, young people seem to have been liberated from the social constraints imposed on the expression of religiosity, and both males and females are freer to express their own personal disposition either positively toward or negatively against religion.

Further research is now clearly needed to explore the relationship between psychological theories of gender orientation and religiosity among different age groups and in different cultures. At the current state of knowledge we may offer one further explanation for this relationship. The Bem Sex Role Inventory, used by Thompson, Francis and Wilcox, and Francis, makes use of twenty adjectives designed to assess masculinity and twenty adjectives designed to assess femininity. Those which assess femininity include the following: 'gentle', 'tender', 'sympathetic', 'loves children', 'compassionate', 'affectionate', 'cheerful', 'childlike' and 'loyal'. All of these qualities are either found in the character of Christ as it is portrayed in the Gospels or are qualities commended by him. For example, Christ is described as being 'moved with compassion' (Matthew 9, 36), as rebuking the disciples for keeping children away from him (Matthew 19, 14), as speaking of his own joy (and therefore presumably cheerfulness) (John 15, 11), or commending love (and therefore presumably affection) (John 15, 12), of commending childlikeness (Mark 9, 36) and, implicitly, of condemning disloyalty (it were better for Judas that he had not been born) (Matthew 14, 21). Gentleness is attributed to Christ by Paul in 2 Corinthians 10, 1, tenderness is commended by Paul in Ephesians 4, 2, and sympathy is presumed by the injunction to weep with those who weep (Romans 12, 15). It is not difficult to understand how people who possess these feminine qualities are more likely to be attracted to Christianity. In fact they are not seen as feminine qualities but as Christian qualities.

In summary, we conclude that sex differences in attitude toward Christianity among young people may be best explained by gender-orientation theories and personality theories, though sex-role socialization theories need further exploration within an interdisciplinary framework. The drift from the churches may not be a phenomenon so much characteristic of men as a phenomenon characteristic of individuals who emphasize the personality characteristics of masculinity at the expense of the personality characteristics of femininity.

3

Age trends

Changes in attitude

It is clear that many human attributes change during the transition from childhood through adolescence and into adulthood. What is not always so clear or self-evident is the pace at which such changes take place or the phenomena associated with such changes. The value of making measurements related to children of different ages is that we are likely to begin to understand the processes of growth and socialization better. Some changes may be traceable to the effects of maturation, involving both physical and mental developments within the child, while others may be traceable to the effects of social and contextual factors.

There are two ways of demonstrating the extent to which attitudes are among those human attributes which change during the transition through childhood and adolescence. The *same* group of people can complete the same attitude scale at, say, yearly intervals so that their scores can be monitored over the age range through which the attitude scale is known to function reliably and validly. This is known as a *longitudinal* study. Alternatively, *similar* groups of people at different points within the age span through which the attitude scale is known to function reliably and validly can complete the attitude scale at the same time. This is known as a *cross-sectional* study. The first method has the advantage that it can really chart individual variations in attitude over several years. At the same time, however, it has significant disadvantages. It is impossible to organize if the questionnaire is completed anonymously, which is usually the case where school children are concerned. Familiarity with the questionnaire items may also eventually contaminate attitude scores. The second method has the advantage of being easier to organize and, provided that the cross-sectional samples have been properly constituted, generates a clear indication of the kind of changes occurring with ageing.

Over the last twenty years the second method of cross-sectional studies has been used extensively to build up a cumulative picture of the way in which attitude toward Christianity changes during childhood and adolescence. The Francis scale has been administered on its own and in conjunction with other scales to pupils of both sexes between the ages of eight and sixteen years in denominational and non-denominational schools in England, Wales, Scotland and Ireland, as well as in other parts of the world. A separate study, using a different kind of scale developed later, has been administered to pupils within the eight-to-sixteen age range to discover how their attitude toward lessons about religion compares with their attitude toward other lessons.[1]

The findings from these studies, summarized in this chapter, will be interpreted in the light of Jean Piaget's massive researches on child development and Ronald Goldman's subsequent attempt to apply aspects of these findings to religious thinking.

Piaget's researches took as their basis the interaction between the organism, in this case the human being, and the environment.[2] He accounted for mental development by suggesting that the child's physical actions upon the environment become mentally internalized in the form of intellectual constructs. These constructs enable the child eventually to predict how the environment will behave and how sets of similar objects can be classified. At about the age of seven, the child is able to think operationally in the sense that actions performed on the environment (for example pouring water into a glass from a jug) can be mentally reversed. At this stage the child's operations function in relation to the concrete world of visible and tangible entities.

A little after the age of twelve, the average child is able to think operationally about abstract entities like those found in mathematics. One of the defining characteristics of the theory is that it proposes distinct stages at which children can do and understand classes of activities. The earlier stage is that of concrete operational thinking, and the later stage is that of formal operational thinking. The essential point is that the theory does not propose gradual incremental changes in a child's mental life. The changes take place suddenly as a child moves from one stage to the next. Hence we should not, according to Piagetian theory, expect to find a record of linear development as we explore intellectually based outcomes among children spanning the age range between eight and sixteen, which is precisely the period when we should expect to detect the transition to formal operational thinking.

Goldman presented three bible stories and three pictures to a sample of 200 children aged between six and seventeen. The ability range was the same for each age group, apart from the fifteen-to-seventeen group which was considerably more able than the other groups. There were ten boys and ten girls at each age level (apart from the fifteen-to-seventeen band that was treated as one group). There were between three and five children from Free Church backgrounds and between eight and ten children from Anglican backgrounds in each age group. There was at least one child from a 'Gospel sect' in each age group and five or six children who had no religious affiliation. There were no Roman Catholics. Each child was interviewed and asked questions about his or her understanding of the bible passages. Of the total of twenty-two questions on these passages, answers on five were categorized according to the Piagetian stage developmental scheme.

Goldman published his findings in *Religious Thinking from Childhood to Adolescence* in 1964 and in a more popular form in *Readiness for Religion* in 1965. There is ambiguity in his presentation. For example he writes, 'Change there is from a concrete to a more abstract mode of thought, but it is a gradual change and the change-over appears in what may be identified as an intermediate state of thinking.'[3] Yet he also says, 'So about this time [adolescence] in school there is a real "break through" in most school subjects when childish modes of thought are left behind and a more adult intellectual quality is emerging.' And two pages later we are told, 'About the age of thirteen marks a change in religious thinking as in other school subjects.'[4] There is, apparently, a gradual change in religious thinking *and* a 'break through'. The gradual change is shown by the existence of intermediate states, but the break through applies to 'most school subjects'; it is a change that takes place within the intellect of the child. The ambiguity is compounded by Goldman's evident belief that his findings match the general Piagetian description of mental development. He suggests that an analysis of his results 'substantiates very clearly the view put forward by Piaget'.[5]

There is less ambiguity about the attitudes which Goldman believed accompanied these changes. He thought that some children who learnt to think in a concrete and childish way would come to reject their religious beliefs when formal operational thinking was attained. 'We have evidence', he writes, 'to support the view that at some period many adolescents jettison their theological framework as childish' and that this results in 'the loss of many pupils to the Christian faith'.[6] In speaking of pupils of secondary school age, he says, 'there is a tendency to see much previous teaching as "childish" and to reject it at that level.'[7] Yet he also thought that, 'by far the greatest proportion of our adolescent pupils who reject the Christian faith are those of lesser abilities. Many of them have not even achieved the level of full religious thought before negative attitudes have formed and a built-in rejection of belief has begun.'[8] Though his research did not deal with attitudes, his speculations led him to suppose that children rejected Christianity because they thought it was childish. Abler children, soon after the arrival of formal operational thinking, found their own earlier theology immature. Less able children rejected Christianity simply because it seemed childish, but without an intellectual critique.

Findings

From these studies nine main findings emerge. First and most fundamental, attitude toward Christianity declines during the years of compulsory schooling. Second, this decline applies to both sexes.[9]

The marked decline in scores of attitude toward Christianity which takes place among both male and female pupils between year three (seven- to eight-year-olds) in the primary school and year eleven (fifteen- to sixteen-year-olds) in the secondary school is clearly demonstrated by the mean scale scores for each age group presented in table 3.1 in the appendices. These figures are based on the responses of 200 boys and 200 girls, attending non-church-related state-maintained schools in England, from each of the nine year groups. In particular, this table demonstrates that between year three and year eleven, boys' scores fall by 32·2 points. The means for each year show a slight rise as pupils make the transition from junior to secondary school, but this gain is quickly lost, and the decline continues. The same pattern is found among girls. Overall, girls' attitude toward Christianity drops by 25·6 points between year three and year eleven, which is slightly less than that of boys.

The figures also show that the standard deviation, or dispersion, of the means is consistently greater for boys than for girls. This indicates there is greater variability of attitude scores among boys: there will be some boys who hold very positive attitudes and others who hold very negative attitudes. Girls will show a narrower range of positions.

Third, the decline in attitude toward Christianity takes place at such a steady rate during the nine years of compulsory schooling between year three and year eleven that, if a graph of attitude scores is plotted against age, the best-fitting line will usually be straight.[10] This indicates that there are no particular precipitators of decline or of accelerated decline in attitude toward Christianity during this age period. The drift is both consistent and persistent.

Fourth, this decline in attitude toward Christianity during childhood and adolescence found among young people attending non-denominational schools in England is also clearly found in other similar cultures. For example, the findings of a study by Gibson conducted among 4,405 pupils attending non-denominational state-maintained secondary schools in Scotland are presented in table 3.2 in the appendices.[11] Similarly the findings of a study by Francis and Greer conducted among 1,189 pupils attending Protestant state-maintained secondary schools in Northern Ireland are presented in table 3.3 in the appendices.[12] While the overall scores of pupils in Northern Ireland are considerably higher than is the case among pupils in England and Scotland, which is consistent with the higher levels of church attendance in Northern Ireland among the general population, the figures still show a consistent and persistent decline throughout the years of secondary education. This decline is also seen in the findings for a study of 619 secondary pupils in Eire attending a mixture of Roman Catholic and Protestant schools.[13] In general, although their attitude scores were higher than those found among pupils in England, the age-related linear decline was still observed.

Fifth, this decline in attitude toward Christianity takes place in single-sex secondary schools, just as much as in co-educational secondary schools, despite the quite distinct ethos each category of school generates. This point is clearly established by a study undertaken by Francis and Montgomery among 647 girls attending a Catholic single-sex secondary school.[14]

These five findings can be taken together. They indicate that there is a general deterioration in attitude toward Christianity during the years of childhood and adolescence. This decline occurs in schools of different types and in different geographical locations. The decline is well established and documented extensively. In essence children start with positive attitudes and end with less positive ones. Girls hold a more positive attitude toward Christianity than boys throughout the years of compulsory schooling, but the attitudes of the two sexes decline in step, at approximately the same rate; in statistical terminology there is no interaction between age and sex. The original study made by Francis in 1976, however, suggested a slightly more complex picture than that given by the basic trend. The linear decline occurred between the first year of the junior school (year three) and the fourth year of secondary education (year ten), but there was a sharper drop in attitudes in the fifth or final year of compulsory secondary education. In other words the main trend is not reversed but accentuated just before the majority of pupils leave school.

Sixth, this linear decline in attitude toward Christianity during childhood and adolescence is to be found in denominational as well as non-denominational schools. Although attitude levels are generally higher at denominational schools, the decline in attitude takes place between year seven and year eleven. Whatever is causing attitudes to decline affects boys and girls attending denominational and non-denominational schools equally. This point is clearly illustrated by table 3.4 in the appendices which displays the mean scores of attitude toward Christianity for males and females in Roman Catholic state-maintained secondary schools.[15] These figures are based on the responses of 2,892 pupils in England.

A comparison between the situations in non-denominational schools and Roman Catholic schools in England is clear-cut. In the non-church-related state-maintained schools in England, male pupils average an attitude score of 78·6, 71·5, 68·9, 62·2 and 55·7 in years seven to eleven respectively. The male pupils in the Roman Catholic state-maintained schools in England are roughly twenty points higher. The differences in the figures are most starkly brought home when the oldest and youngest pupils in both kinds of schools are compared. The difference between the youngest and oldest males in Roman Catholic schools is 17·1 points, but the difference between the youngest and oldest males in non-denominational schools 22·9; in other words *the decline in attitude toward Christianity is steeper in the state-maintained school.* The corresponding mean scores of attitude toward Christianity for girls at non-denominational state-maintained schools in England are 84·1, 83·7, 79·2, 74·3 and 70·4 in years seven to eleven respectively. Whereas the difference between the youngest and oldest girls in the non-denominational school is 13·7 points, it is only 11·2 points in the Roman Catholic school. The decline in the attitudes of girls is also steeper in the non-denominational state-maintained schools than it is in the Roman Catholic state-maintained schools.

The picture of declining scores of attitude toward Christianity among pupils attending Roman Catholic state-maintained schools in England is paralleled by studies conducted in Scotland and in Northern Ireland. For example, the findings of a survey conducted by Gibson and Francis among 1,431 pupils attending Roman Catholic state-maintained secondary schools in Scotland are presented in table 3.5 in the appendices.[16] The figures are very close to those reported in the study conducted in England. Similarly the findings of a survey conducted by Greer and Francis among 935 pupils attending Roman Catholic maintained secondary schools in Northern Ireland are presented in table 3.6 in the appendices.[17] While the overall scores are somewhat higher than those recorded by pupils attending Roman Catholic secondary schools in England, they clearly demonstrate the same decline in attitude toward Christianity during the years of secondary schooling.

Seventh, the decline in attitude toward Christianity is paralleled by a decline in attitude toward lessons about religion.[18] Using the Osgood semantic differential technique (see appendix 2) 800 pupils from the first year of junior school (year three) to the fourth year of secondary school (year ten) were asked to rate aspects of life at school on the same set of adjectival pairs: friendly–unfriendly, pleasant–unpleasant, bad–good, interesting–

boring, nasty–nice, sad–happy, important–unimportant. The aspects of school life chosen for investigation were: English lessons, maths lessons, school itself, lessons about religion, music lessons, lessons about history and games lessons. Since the adjectival pairs were presented for each aspect of school life in turn, it was possible to profile an exact comparison between pupil attitude toward each aspect.[19] When the adjectival pairs were averaged so that an overall favourability–unfavourability score could be calculated, Francis found that throughout the age range, games were consistently the most preferred subject. From the early years of junior school, however, two subjects declined in favourability while all the others, including attitude toward school itself, remained roughly constant. The two subjects which declined were lessons about music and lessons about religion. One explanation put forward to account for the particular decline in attitude toward lessons about religion, concerns the decreasing importance of this subject in the eyes of many pupils.[20] Such an explanation is deduced from the difference in the profiles of each aspect of school life which may be found when junior school pupils are compared with secondary school pupils. As pupils grow older the perceived importance of a subject rather than its enjoyment seems to determine their general evaluation of it.

Eighth, this decline in attitude toward Christianity during the years of childhood and adolescence is much less pronounced among pupils who are religiously active.[21] Francis divided religious activity into behaviour (dealing with attendance at church-related activities and personal prayer) and involvement (dealing with self-assessed level of religiosity). He found that attitude toward Christianity can be quite accurately predicted from religious behaviour and involvement throughout the eight-to-sixteen-year age range. For each point recorded on the religious-behaviour scale a pupil would score on average nearly five points more on the attitude-toward-Christianity scale. For each point on the religious-involvement scale a pupil would score on average nearly seven points more on the attitude-toward-Christianity scale. Since the involvement scale deals with self-image, it is more private. The behaviour scale, though, shows that weekly attendance at church and at a church-related youth group will tend to raise attitude toward Christianity by ten points, a highly significant amount.

Comment

The decline in attitude toward Christianity takes place in these studies over the period from eight to sixteen years of age. Much less is known, however, about the way in which attitude toward Christianity continues to change later in life after leaving school. The likelihood is that most people's attitude toward Christianity levels off after leaving school and remains more or less constant within the zone of indifference for a large part of their lives. Such an inference can be made by looking at opinion polls surveying basic religious beliefs and by deducing the likely level of attitudes from known statistics of church attendance. The remainder of the population, which attends church or rates itself as being religious in some other way, is likely to maintain a more positive attitude toward Christianity, similar to that which is held by religious pupils at the upper end of secondary schools. Unfortunately, hard research on attitude toward Christianity in the post-school period is still minimal and the area remains in need of serious exploration.

The parallel decline in pupils' favourability toward lessons about religion and attitude toward Christianity suggests a related cause. It suggests that it is not simply Christianity itself which is assessed at a declining rate, but religion in general. The more academic subjects like maths and English, and school itself, show a slight increase in favourability in the eyes of pupils in the last years of secondary education. By contrast, games lessons decline slightly. It appears that pupils are preparing themselves for the world of work and that they are ready to give their support to what they think will help them in the future. This explanation would also cover the drop in favourability which affects music. For most pupils music is a leisure activity and not the doorway to a career.

The crux of the matter, though, is what causes attitude toward Christianity and attitude toward religion to decline in such a linear fashion between the ages of eight and sixteen. Clearly, if under some circumstances attitudes decline with age more sharply than under other circumstances, there may be factors which can be brought into play by the churches to mitigate the general trend. To address this problem satisfactorily, we need to go back to the definition of the construct of attitude. Attitudes are unidimensional psychological constructs which reflect evaluations of basic beliefs. We may, therefore, expect changes in attitude to occur as a consequence of changes in evaluative abilities or as a consequence of changes in belief. In practice such changes are likely to occur most noticeably and regularly in the process of growing up from the middle of the junior school to the last compulsory year of secondary education. This theory may account, to some extent, for the relationship between attitude toward Christianity and age.

This theory cannot, however, account for the *linearity* of the relationship, because the kinds of changes which take place in the years from eight to sixteen are likely to occur suddenly. A pre-adolescent growth-spurt occurs in both sexes. In Piagetian theory, formal operational thinking can be expected to take place roughly at the same time as puberty. Thus the *physical* changes of puberty put social relationships with adults on a new footing while the *mental* changes in adolescence put relationships with the intellectual world on a new footing. We would expect attitudes to Christianity to reflect these sudden changes.

Why, then, do we observe a linear relationship between attitude to Christianity and age? We can offer two main explanations of this finding. The first relates to the cognitive aspect of religious development. Goldman thought his researches supported gradual cognitive changes. Thus, if this is correct, gradual cognitive changes would simply occur in parallel with gradual attitudinal changes. These gradual changes would also echo changes brought about by socialization.

We suspect that the clue to the effects of socialization may be found in the parallel decline in attitudes both toward lessons about music and lessons about religion (in general). If we are correct in assuming that it is the salience of the subject in the life of pupils which causes them to attribute importance to it, and therefore to assess it favourably, then the declining attitude toward Christianity (specifically) speaks of a general slide into religious indifference. In modern British society it is this, rather than hostility, which is thought to be the prevailing stance toward religion. Growing up means becoming indifferent to religion. Becoming indifferent is associated with a gradual induction to the values of the adult world, and this induction is related linearly to age.

There is a theory which supports the socialization explanation and is relevant to the association between church-related activities and positive attitudes. Attitudes are changed when 'membership groups' become 'reference groups'.[22] Statistics of church attendance show that there is a decline in the number of pupils who have a relationship with the church. As pupils become older, they increasingly become members of non-church-related groups, and it is these which then become their reference groups and determine their attitudes. Only pupils who retain membership of church-related groups will escape many of the effects of secular group membership.

There is certainly empirical evidence for the growing involvement of young people in pop and youth culture which takes place during the same years when attitudes to Christianity decline. An analysis by Francis and Gibson confirmed the finding that those social groups which spent more time watching television, and especially *Top of the Pops*, also spent less time attending church.[23] The drift from the churches takes place not only by patterns of attendance but also within the minds and hearts of many young people. The church must introduce itself to teenagers where they are only barely aware of its existence.

The second explanation for the linear decline in attitudes to Christianity derives from Goldman's reference to a 'break through' in religious thinking during the early phase of secondary education. The failure to find sudden changes in attitudes can be accounted for *either* by suggesting that Goldman's findings are unreliable *or* by suggesting that cognitive development and attitudes are unrelated (despite the cognitive element in the formation of attitudes) *or* by suggesting a more complicated interaction between the onset of formal operational thinking and the separate elements which underlie attitudes. This last suggestion depends on the postulation of contradictory effects on these underlying elements. Such effects would smooth out the peaks and troughs of attitude change and have an overall result of making attitudes to religion decline gradually.

In order to understand this idea of the contradictory effects of formal operational thinking, we need to recall that attitudes are emotionally toned evaluations of beliefs and to see that, for purposes of analysis, evaluation and emotion can be distinguished.

It may be that the evaluative capabilities accessible to formal operational thinking are nearly equally balanced in their detrimental and non-detrimental effect on attitude to Christianity. Formal operational thinking is destructive of faith in the sense that it allows for more scrupulous examination of what appear to be textual inconsistencies in canonical writings or theological absurdities within the church. Formal operational thinking is constructive of faith in the sense that faith contains its own logic, its own structures and relationships which are part of the mind-set of all those who believe. Since faith gives meaning, and meaning implies coherence, it is this which formal operational thinking grasps.

In the same way, formal operational thinking deals with imaginative possibilities that may affect faith in two ways. Negatively, imaginative possibilities suggest secular political programmes or artistic ideals which replace the vision given by religion. Positively, imaginative possibilities fasten on to the dimension of religion which finds its fullest expression in works of literature, music or art on religious themes.

With regard to the emotional aspect of attitudes, Piagetian theory has less of relevance to contribute. The theory is not at its strongest in accounting for emotional changes. The understanding which people bring to the emotions is derived from their general intellectual framework. Emotions are not easily symbolized, but it is the manipulation of symbols which is particularly facilitated by formal operational abilities. The emotional aspect of religion is therefore likely to be largely impervious to abstract thinking, and for this reason Piagetian theory may be unable to make any predictions about the effects on emotion of the movement from one intellectual stage to the next.[24]

This theory about the contradictory effects of formal operational thinking needs to be tested. The problem for researchers is that, since Goldman, it has been tacitly assumed that formal operational thinking tends to lead to negative attitudes to Christianity. His notion was that able children are either imprisoned within a childish theology or, by using their newly found powers of formal operational thinking, criticize and reject their earlier faith. Less able children reject their early beliefs as childish, though for less coherent and less intellectual reasons. What Francis's research has been able to show, however, is that Goldman's speculations about the connection between formal operational thinking and attitude do not add up. The decline in attitude to Christianity is not connected with Piagetian stage development. It is a decline which does not appear to have a single crisis point.

Of the explanations we have offered, the socialization theory seems the most plausible. This theory allows for gradual and linear change and, at the same time, makes allowance for different rates of socialization in different denominational contexts and in different cultures. Moreover, it is a theory which is compatible with a Piagetian theory of cognitive development and the implications of cognitive development for attitudes to Christianity.

4

Generation changes

Monitoring change over time

Society often changes too slowly for us to be completely aware of what is happening. The changes, too, are often so complex and varied that we fail to grasp the detail of what is taking place. Changes happen at different rates, and there are certain periods of time when many changes happen all at once. If you found a photograph of a market town outside London taken in 1935, you might compare it with one taken in 1995. The changes would be quite obvious and revealing. What the two photographs would not show, however, would be the rate at which the changes took place; nor would they give much clue about the causes of changes. There might have been particular damage in the 1939–45 war, or special expansion in the 1950s if the town had received overspill population from London. The trams might have given way to trolley buses, and the trolley buses to cars, and so on. The two photographs taken sixty years apart, however, would not give any of this detailed information.

A much more effective monitoring of change would occur if a photograph were taken from the same camera position at regular intervals, perhaps every four years. By this means, it would be possible to show whether the rate of change in 1939–45 was especially rapid or whether the decade of the 1950s was a period of greater change than the decade of the 1970s. Moreover, the photographs would begin to tell a story of causes and effects. Traffic congestion in one photograph might be replaced by a wider road in the next photograph. It would be possible to infer that the wider road had been made to cope with the volume of traffic in the earlier photograph. The wider road might also have an effect on the character of the High Street: small stores, suitable for light traffic, might be replaced by supermarkets fronted by car parks, and later supermarkets might be replaced by superstores on the edge of town. All these details would help to explain how and why the town had changed in the years during which the photographs had been taken.

We cannot photograph society in the same way that we can photograph a town. Instead we have to detect social change by census or survey statistics. Properly assembled and used, these statistics can provide a photograph of social or psychological factors. Statistics can show quite easily, for example, how the popularity of church weddings relative to registry office weddings compares over a period of time, or what shifts in percentages take place over the years in the number of babies who are christened. Similarly, it is easy to discover how burial customs shift or what percentage of the population takes on part-time work. In effect, the figures of this nature relating to public and social behaviour are relatively easy to collect. More problematic, however, is their *interpretation*. If registry office weddings increase and church weddings decrease, this probably says something about attitude toward church and religion in society, but there is a difficulty in working out exactly what this is without a reliable and valid measurement of the underlying attitude. What is required is an attitude scale and a measure of behaviour which work in tandem. Then, if attitudes and behaviour change together, it is possible to be much more confident about explaining and interpreting the behaviour figures.

Collection of figures relating to changes in attitude over a period of time is difficult. In this sort of study the interest is not in finding out how the attitudes of the *same* people change over the years, but in finding out how the attitudes of *exactly equivalent* people in each generation are different. A prolonged and patient research project must be mounted. Figures must be collected at regular intervals from a similarly constituted sample. If the sample is not constituted similarly, then the value of the whole project is undermined. There must also be continuity within the data-processing procedures. When the figures change, then, since everything else has remained the same, it is possible to interpret these changes as being caused by overall changes within schools and ultimately within society.

Very few studies have been systematically replicated in this way for the purpose of monitoring change over time. Three exceptions are provided by studies conducted by Derek Wright and Edwin Cox in England and by E. B. Turner and by John Greer in Northern Ireland. Wright and Cox[1] conducted a study of sixth-form religion and morality in 1963. This study was then replicated in 1970.[2] Unfortunately the study was never replicated further. Turner[3] conducted a study of religious understanding and attitudes among twelve- to fifteen-year-old boys in Belfast in 1969. The study was replicated ten years later in 1979.[4] Unfortunately the opportunity to replicate the study further in 1989 was lost and the subsequent attempt to do so in 1991 was only partly successful.[5] Better success, however, was achieved by Greer. Greer conducted his original study in 1968 concerned with the religious beliefs, opinions and practices, and moral judgements of sixth-form Protestant pupils in Northern Ireland.[6] Greer completed successful replications of this study in 1978[7] and again in 1988.[8] Although this is a fine piece of research, the study suffers from two weaknesses. First, the questionnaire employed in the study assesses behaviours and opinions. No attempt was made to assess or to scale the underlying attitudinal dimension. Second, there is a problem with basing research on sixth-formers. Unlike the groups lower down the school, the sixth form is a self-selecting group of young people. It is not, therefore, possible to generalize from findings of studies conducted among sixth-formers to the whole population of that age group. Nor is it possible to assume that the sixth forms were constituted in identical ways in 1968, 1978 and 1988.

Problems like these with other studies which have attempted to monitor changes in young people's attitudes toward religion over time make the particular findings reported in the present chapter so unusual and so valuable.

Francis started a project in 1974 in which he collected information from the first five years (year seven to year eleven) of two non-church-related state-maintained comprehensive schools in England. Four years later, in 1978, a replication study took place and the same questionnaire was administered to the next generation of pupils sitting at the same school desks. Nothing had changed apart from the pupils. Again four years later in 1982, exactly the same questionnaires were given out in exactly the same manner to the next generation of pupils in exactly the same schools. This was repeated in 1986, 1990 and 1994.[9] Thus, over the course of twenty years, the same questionnaire has been administered six times. On each occasion, before any conclusions were drawn, the statistical properties of the questionnaire were checked. The coefficient of reliability (alpha) was calculated and the scale was checked for unidimensionality and construct validity. The unidimensionality was checked by principal-components analysis, while the construct validity was checked by the scale's correlation with religious behaviour and religious involvement. On each occasion, the scale functioned in the same way. Its alpha coefficient remained at between 0·96 and 0·97 and the correlation with religious behaviour remained at 0·56 or more and the correlation with religious involvement at 0·69 or more.

Once the questionnaire had been administered, a random sample of fifty boys and fifty girls was taken from each year group so that, on each occasion when the age cohort was inspected, 500 pupils were involved. Over the years, therefore, the responses of 3,000 pupils have been processed in this project.

Francis has analysed the data from this twenty-year project in three different ways. First, the data were analysed to calculate the average attitude score for the 500 pupils participating on each occasion. This gives a figure for each year in the sample and the trend from 1974 to 1994 can be displayed. Second, the data were analysed by reference to the attitude scores of each of the five year groups between year seven and year eleven taken individually on each of the six occasions. Thus we can compare year seven in 1974 with year seven in 1978, and so on. Third, the data were analysed by reference to the pupils' changing responses on individual items making up the twenty-four-item scale. In this way we can, for instance, see how many pupils believe that God helps them, or how many believe that saying prayers helps them a lot on each of the four-yearly occasions.

Findings

The first and most fundamental step in data analysis indicated that the internal statistics of the scale remained consistent over the twenty-year period and on the six occasions it was administered. The alpha coefficients for the six separate adminis-trations are as follows: 1974, 0·97; 1978, 0·96; 1982, 0·97; 1986, 0·97; 1990, 0·96; 1994, 0·96. This shows that the basic evaluative structure identified by the scale in the early 1970s has not subsequently undergone any change. In other words, the concepts of God, the bible, Jesus, school religion, church and prayer related to each other in pupils' minds in the same way in

1994 as they did in 1974. This is an important discovery, because it provides clear confirmation that it is legitimate and sensible to make direct comparisons between the attitude scores recorded at different points over the twenty-year period.

As the second step in data analysis, the mean scale scores were calculated for each group of 500 pupils sampled between 1974 and 1994. These figures (displayed in the first column of table 4.1 in the appendices) make it clear that the average scores for the groups of 500 pupils in each of the years 1974, 1978, 1982 and 1986 showed a slow and steady decline. In 1974 the mean score of the 500 pupils on the twenty-four-item scale was 77·8. Four years later in 1978 the mean score had dropped by three points to 74·9. Four years later in 1982, it had dropped again by more than four points to 70·4. Four years later in 1986 there was a further drop to 68·4.

In twelve years, therefore, a drop of just over 9 points had taken place. Not surprisingly, given the correlational figures on religious behaviour and involvement, the standard deviation, or dispersion, of scores in each of these cohorts remained more or less the same (ranging from 21·6 to 19·8). The similarity of dispersion indicates that the drop in scores cannot be the result of a few particularly antagonistic pupils who arrived after 1974. The average score moves down each time, but the spread of scores hardly alters. The only interpretation of these figures which is possible is that there is a gradual and general erosion of favourability in attitude toward Christianity within the population as a whole.

In 1990, the average score *rose* for the first time. It went back up to 70·4, the level of the 1982 study. Four years later, however, it had fallen again to its 1986 level, to 68·5. In twenty years the drop is still just over nine points. This is a fall of 11·9 per cent.

In order to provide a more detailed interpretation of these findings, the mean attitude scores were calculated separately for churchgoers and the unchurched for each of the six surveys conducted between 1974 and 1994. These figures are also set out in table 4.1 in the appendices. The most striking result of this analysis is that the fall in scores of attitude toward Christianity among unchurched teenagers and among churchgoing teenagers, considered separately, is relatively small. We cannot say, on the basis of these figures, that there has been a sudden or dramatic rejection of Christianity within the unchurched proportion of the population. If we look at the figures in more detail, it is clear that the means for the unchurched young people drop between 1974 and 1994 by 3·0 points or 4·7 per cent and that the means for churchgoing young people drop in the same period by 3·5 points or 3·7 per cent. This shows that in absolute terms there has been a slightly greater fall in attitude toward Christianity among churchgoers than among their non-churchgoing contemporaries, though in percentage terms it is the non-churchgoers whose attitudes have been most eroded.

Yet, why should there be a fall of 11·9 per cent in the overall means in the period between 1974 and 1994? The answer lies in the shrinkage of church attendance. A smaller proportion of pupils in 1994 go to church than was the case in 1974. There is indeed a drift from the churches. As the proportion of church-goers decreases and the proportion of unchurched young people increases, the overall mean for scores of attitude toward Christianity in the population as a whole falls.

The third step in data analysis gives detailed attention to the way in which responses change to the individual items of the attitude scale. While the mean scale score is able to identify the underlying attitudinal predisposition, additional information can be gained by scrutinizing the responses to the individual opinions through which the underlying attitude is expressed. A detailed comparison between the responses to the twenty-four individual items of the attitude scale made by the six generations of pupils in 1974, 1978, 1982, 1986, 1990 and 1994 is presented in table 4.2 in the appendices.

Psychological theory regarding the nature of attitudes suggests that overt opinions of this nature are considerably less stable and more volatile than the covert attitudinal predisposition which they reflect and to which they point.[10] For this reason it is necessary to treat the fluctuations in the percentage responses to the individual opinion statements from year to year with some caution. What the figures presented in table 4.2 confirm, however, is a remarkably close similarity between the pupils' responses in 1986 and 1994, after a consistent period of decline between 1974 and 1986.

Regarding their attitude toward God, in 1994 25 per cent of the pupils agreed that they knew that God helps them. The figure for 1986 was also 25 per cent, compared with 42 per cent in 1974. In 1994 41 per cent of the pupils agreed that God helps people. The figure for 1986 was 42 per cent, compared with 59 per cent in 1974.

Regarding attitude toward Jesus, in 1994 22 per cent of the pupils agreed that they want to love Jesus. The figure for 1986 was 23 per cent, compared with 39 per cent in 1974. In 1994 18 per cent of pupils agreed that Jesus is very close to them. The figure for 1986 was 20 per cent, compared with 36 per cent in 1974.

Regarding attitude toward prayer, in 1994 19 per cent of the pupils agreed that saying their prayers helps them a lot. The figure for 1986 was 18 per cent, compared with 36 per cent in 1974. In 1994 31 per cent of the pupils believed that God listens to prayers. The figure for 1986 was 29 per cent, compared with 47 per cent in 1974.

Regarding attitude toward the bible, in 1994 51 per cent of the pupils said that it was boring to listen to the bible. The figure for 1986 was 49 per cent, compared with 33 per cent in 1974. In 1994 28 per cent of the pupils thought the bible was out of date. The figure for 1986 was 30 per cent, compared with 20 per cent in 1974.

Regarding attitude toward the church, in 1994 14 per cent of the pupils agreed that the church is very important to them. The figure for 1986 was 15 per cent, compared with 27 per cent in 1974. In 1994 56 per cent of the pupils described church services as boring. The figure for 1986 was also 56 per cent, compared with 39 per cent in 1974.

Regarding religious practice in school, in 1994 42 per cent agreed that saying prayers in school does no good. The figure for 1986 was 41 per cent, compared with 36 per cent in 1974. In 1994 18 per cent reported that they liked school lessons about God very much. The figure for 1986 was 21 per cent, compared with 32 per cent in 1974.

The fourth step in data analysis computed the mean scale of scores of attitude toward Christianity for each year group within each of the six samples. Since this time each mean score is based on the responses of only 100 pupils, the figures are much less reliable than those computed on all 500 pupils to calculate the mean score for the whole cohort. Nevertheless, the set of figures presented in table 4.3 in the appendices suggests some further important clues about the nature of the drift from the churches which has occurred among young people during this twenty-year period.

The overall movement during this twenty-year period is seen most clearly simply by comparing the figures for 1974 and 1994. Although over the years there has been some fluctuation among year-eleven pupils, the mean score recorded in 1994 is only three points lower than the mean score recorded in 1974. Overall, it seems that in 1994 sixteen-year-olds may be only slightly more alienated from the church than was the case in 1974. Again, although over the years there has been some fluctuation among year-seven pupils, the mean score recorded in 1994 is only five points lower than the mean score recorded in 1974. Overall, it seems that in 1994 twelve-year-olds may be only slightly more alienated from the church than was the case in 1974. The real and significant drift has taken place among pupils in years eight, nine and ten. Between 1974 and 1994, the mean score among year-eight pupils has dropped by twelve points; the mean score among year-nine pupils has also dropped by twelve points; the mean score among year-ten pupils has dropped by fourteen points.

Looked at from another perspective the mean attitude score of year-seven pupils in 1994 is as low as that of year-ten pupils in 1974, while the mean attitude score of year-nine pupils in 1994 is as low as that of year-eleven pupils in 1974. In other words, negative attitudes are creeping down the school, so that the sort of attitudes which were found only among those who were about to leave school in 1974 are by 1994 common in the middle of the secondary-school age range.

Comment

The internal behaviour of the attitude scale over the period of twenty years is consistent. The beliefs and evaluations which make up the scale reflect an underlying continuity. The camera which took photographs of the market town is still working properly and the things being photographed by the camera are still things of the same type. It is still a town. Young people still respond to questions about God, the bible, Jesus, school religion, church and prayer with comprehension, and this cluster of concepts is seen as belonging together. In other words, these concepts relate to one underlying attitudinal dimension, and not to many, because the world view of young people has not been completely fragmented in the twenty years monitored by these studies.

This study has completed a twenty-year survey which set out to monitor changes in attitudes toward Christianity among secondary-school pupils in England. By administering the same instrument to successive generations of pupils occupying the same school desks at four-yearly intervals, the study has been able to assess the nature of change between 1974 and 1994. The major conclusion of the study is that there was a significant and progressive deterioration in pupil attitude toward Christianity between 1974 and 1986. Pupil attitudes were less favourable in 1978 than in 1974. In 1982 they were less favourable than in 1978. In 1986 they were less favourable than in 1982. Since 1986, however, there has not been further deterioration in pupil attitude toward Christianity.

The analysis of the scores of attitude toward Christianity by year groups shows that the decline over the twenty-year period has taken place in the top three age groups, that is, among pupils aged fourteen to sixteen years. This is where the drift from the churches is most apparent.

The data are taken from only two schools in the whole of the British Isles, albeit schools which are typical of the vast majority of those in the state system. A caution must be entered about the generalizability of the findings drawn from their pupils. Ideally a much larger sample of schools would be linked into a series of replications of this nature. Yet, when this caution is accepted, it is clear that the data provided here give a unique picture of changing attitude toward Christianity in British secondary schools. No other comparable research project has collected so much data in such a precise manner over such a long period of time. The frustration remains that more resources were not available when the project was inaugurated in 1974 to facilitate the participation of a larger number of schools.

5
School influence

Measuring school effects

Research concerned with the effects, rather than the processes, of schooling usually follow a 'black-box' model. For the purposes of analysis, the school is regarded as a 'black box' and questions are not, at this stage, asked about what goes on inside it. What interests the researcher most is what goes into the 'black box' and what comes out of it. Differences between input and output can be attributed to the effects of the 'black box'. When the model is applied to the field of religion, it helps to show how a question about the religious effects of schools on pupils might be posed. It must be posed in terms of a valid and reliable index of religiosity which is known to function within the age range of pupils under examination; in 'black-box' terms, the index must operate correctly at the point when pupils go in and at the point when pupils come out. The Francis scale of attitude toward Christianity does this job very well. With this model and this tool in place, it makes sense to ask if schools influence pupil attitude toward Christianity and, if so, whether this influence is of a positive or a negative nature. At first sight it appears that we might answer this question simply by measuring pupils' attitudes before and after they attend school.

Mathematically there are several different ways of calculating the effect of the 'black box' on the pupils. An approach used frequently relies on two key concepts concerned with measurement. First, it is essential that the 'output' variable or variables with which the research is concerned can be measured with a large degree of precision. Second, it is essential that as many of the other factors as possible which may influence the individual pupil's scores on the outcome variable are also taken into account and assessed.

A simple example is able to illustrate this point. Assume that a new curriculum approach to teaching mathematics is claimed to enhance pupils' attitude toward mathematics. In order to test this claim it would be necessary to identify a set of schools which employ the new curriculum approach and a set of schools which have not adopted the new approach. It would also be necessary to be able to measure pupils' attitude toward mathematics in the two sets of schools. Suppose, then, that the pupils attending schools using the new approach recorded a higher mean score on the index of attitude toward mathematics than the pupils attending the other schools. It would not, however, as yet be possible to attribute the *cause* of the difference to the new curriculum itself, since there may be a number of factors outside the 'black box' affecting the difference in pupil attitudes. For example, boys generally hold a more positive attitude toward mathematics than girls, and there may be a disproportionately high proportion of boys in the schools which employ the new curriculum. Or again, pupils from higher socio-economic backgrounds generally hold a more positive attitude toward mathematics than pupils from a lower socio-economic background, and there may be a disproportionately high proportion of pupils from higher socio-economic backgrounds in the schools which employ the new curriculum. In other words, a mathematical model has to be able to take these other factors into account before it is possible to attribute differences in the pupils' scores of attitude toward mathematics to the effect of the schools themselves.

Or, to put this in terms of the 'black box' again, some of the variation in output is caused by things happening *outside* the box. By subtracting this variation (using path analysis and multiple regression), only the effects of what is going on inside, in the school itself, are left. In practice, then, the background variables of pupils are collected, particularly those which research has already shown to be connected with the output variable.

There is good precedent for the use of this research strategy. It has been used by international surveys for looking at the effects of schools in different countries and cultures. For example, the International Project for the Evaluation of Educational Achievement (IEA) began in 1959 and proceeded with a pilot study (five subjects, twelve countries and 9,918 students), a cross-national study in 1960 (one subject – mathematics – twelve countries, and around 11,643 pupils) and a cross-national study in 1966 (six subjects, twenty-two countries, and around 150,929 pupils).[1]

In cross-national studies the identification of background variables is made especially difficult because, for example, social class in one country or culture cannot easily be equated with social class in another. In the same way, it is not easy to find measures of outcome which are equally applicable to all the students passing through the educational systems in the countries under investigation. Nevertheless, the IEA study, which made use of path analysis and allied techniques, was able to produce findings of importance to public policy. Related studies using the same techniques within the vast and varied educational system of the United States proved to be equally important.[2]

Church schools

The question regarding the influence of schools on pupils' attitude toward Christianity is of particular interest in England and Wales in view of the high proportion of schools within the state-maintained sector which are still linked either with the Anglican or the Catholic churches.

The original initiative for building a network of schools in England and Wales came not from the state, but from voluntary bodies. The various Christian denominations had a high profile in establishing such voluntary initiatives through church-related societies like the National Society, The British and Foreign School Society and the Catholic Poor School Committee.[3] A large number of church-related schools had, therefore, been established long before the machinery was put in place by the 1870 Education Act to found non-denominational or board schools.[4]

At the time of the 1944 Education Act, the churches still continued to own such a large stake in the nation's educational system, that they were able to exert considerable influence over restructuring schools for the post-war period. Out of the 1944 Education Act was born the present system of *voluntary aided* and *voluntary controlled* schools. This choice enabled schools which could afford to retain a high level of independence to do so, while those that either could not afford or did not desire to retain such a high level of independence could nevertheless retain something of their church-related character.

Aided schools are aided by the local education authority, while the denomination concerned retains some ongoing financial liability. The managers or governors of an aided school are responsible for the capital expenditure on alterations required by the local education authority to keep the premises up to standard, for external repairs to the school buildings, improvements and extensions to existing school buildings. Government grant aid was made available to meet 50 per cent of these costs in 1944. This proportion has subsequently risen to 85 per cent. In return for their continued financial involvement, the churches retained the right to appoint a majority of the school managers or governors and to provide denominational religious instruction and denominational worship throughout the school.

Controlled schools are controlled by the local education authority. Here the churches had reduced rights, but controlled status involved them in no ongoing financial liability. In this case, the churches retained the right to appoint a minority of the school managers or governors. Religious instruction is given according to the agreed syllabus, established for use in non-denominational schools, although parents may ask for denominational teaching 'during not more than two periods each week'. Provided the teaching staff of the controlled school exceeds two, up to one fifth of the staff can be 'selected for their fitness and competence to give such religious instruction'. The daily act of worship can also be denominational in character.

In 1944 the Roman Catholic church rejected controlled status completely. Just two small Catholic schools became controlled. As far as Church of England schools were concerned, the choice between aided and controlled status was left in the hands of the governors or managers of each church school, although some dioceses gave clear guidelines. For example, London, Southwark and Blackburn opted heavily for aided status, while Bristol, York, Canterbury and Lichfield opted mainly for controlled status. Figures provided by the Department for Education and by the Welsh Office demonstrate that by the early 1990s Catholic schools provided about one in ten state-maintained school places at both primary and secondary level. At the same time, Anglican schools provided one in six state-maintained places at primary level, and one in twenty-three at secondary level.

In the Australian context, De Vaus argues that 'one of the main stated purposes of denominational schools is to add a religious dimension to education.'[5] In the English context, the situation is not quite so straightforward. Historically the Roman Catholic position was clearly to promote the aim for 'every Catholic child from a Catholic home to be taught by Catholic teachers in a Catholic school'.[6] More recent Catholic comment speaks in broader terms of possibly bringing to bear 'a richer and more mature view of educational theory and practice' on the national approach to education.[7] The Anglican position, on the other hand, has tended to stress a blend of denominational concern with a more general theology of service to the nation. For example, the *Durham Report* argued that:

> The church should for the present see its continued involvement in the dual system principally as a way of expressing its concern for the general education of all children and young people rather than as a means for giving 'denominational instruction'.[8]

Whether church voluntary schools set out to influence the religious development of their pupils or not, it is a matter of some interest to know what influence the substantial church involvement in the state-maintained sector of schools actually has on the pupils who attend church schools.

Findings

In order to explore the influence of church schools on the attitude toward Christianity of pupils who attend them, Francis has conducted a series of studies. Each study builds on the findings of the previous one. The first study was conducted in East Anglia in 1974 and examined voluntary aided primary schools. After controlling for background variables, it found that Catholic schools appear to exert a positive influence on pupils' attitude toward Christianity, while some Church of England aided schools exert a negative influence. Replications of this study were carried out in 1978 and in 1982, and the same conclusions were reached.

The second series of studies was carried out in Gloucestershire with a much larger sample of schools and with both controlled and aided Church of England primary schools. These results again showed that Roman Catholic schools were exerting a positive effect on their pupils' attitude toward Christianity. The Church of England aided schools exerted neither a positive nor a negative effect, but the Church of England controlled schools were found to exert a small but significant negative effect.

In the third series of studies, Anglican and Roman Catholic *secondary* schools were also investigated. This series of studies showed that Anglican secondary schools exerted neither a positive nor a negative effect on their pupils, whereas Catholic schools again exerted a positive effect.

Finally, a study which attempts to look inside the 'black box', to explore the interaction between teachers and pupils in the classroom, is presented. This study concluded that the content of the religious-education syllabus and the classroom climate in which it was delivered affected pupils. The teaching of world religions could be detrimental to attitude toward Christianity, and the suppression of discussion in lessons whose content was biblical could also have a negative effect.

Primary pupils in East Anglia

The first study was set up in a sample of East Anglian primary schools in 1974.[9] Thirty comparable primary schools participated in the study, including fifteen county schools, ten Church of England voluntary aided schools and five Roman Catholic voluntary aided schools. The number of schools from each sector reflected the sector's relative contribution to the state-maintained system.

The survey questionnaire took pupil background variables into account. Socio-economic background was assessed in terms of the scale proposed by the Office of Population, Censuses and Surveys (1980) used in association with information about parental employment.[10] Intelligence was assessed in terms of IQ ratings made available from school records and collapsed into a scale of five categories. Questions were included about parental church attendance.

The questionnaire was administered to all third- and fourth-year junior pupils (year five and year six) within the participating schools by the class teachers. Completed responses were received from 2,272 pupils.

The data were analysed by means of linear multiple regression and path analysis. This allowed the effects of age, sex, social class, parental church attendance, IQ and religious behaviour to be eliminated before testing for the influence of church schools on pupil attitude toward Christianity. Two key conclusions emerged from this path model: Catholic schools appear to be exerting a positive influence on the development of pupil attitudes, while some Church of England schools appear to be exerting a negative influence.

In view of the potentially controversial nature of these findings, the Social Science Research Council sponsored a replication of the study four years later in 1978.[11] The replication involved going to the next generation of pupils occupying the same school places.

A further replication was funded in 1982, after another period of four years, returning to the third generation of pupils occupying the same school desks.[12] For the third time path analysis identified the positive influence of Catholic schools and the negative influence of Anglican schools on pupil attitude toward Christianity.

The path model which results from merging all the data from the three studies conducted in 1974, 1978 and 1982 is presented in figure 5.1 in the appendices. This composite model confirms that, after controlling for the influences of age, sex, social class, IQ, parental church attendance, the child's own religious behaviour and the year of the survey, pupils in Roman Catholic aided schools recorded a more positive attitude toward Christianity than pupils in county schools, while pupils in Church of England aided schools recorded a less favourable attitude toward Christianity than pupils in county schools. Since the statistical model has carefully controlled for many of the other ways in which pupils in these different types of schools might differ, it is reasonable to attribute the final difference in pupil attitudes to the school systems themselves.

On the basis of these three studies, Francis concluded that voluntary aided church primary schools within the state-maintained sector do have an influence on at least one aspect of the religious development of their pupils, their attitude toward Christianity.

Pupils educated in Roman Catholic schools tend to record a more favourable attitude toward Christianity than pupils, of comparable sex, age, IQ and religious behaviour from comparable social-class homes with comparable levels of parental church attendance, educated in county schools. This means that they are more likely to hold a positive image of Jesus and God and to feel that they enjoy church, the bible, prayer and the religious education and worship in which they engage at school. The development of these attitudes seems highly consistent with the stated aims of Roman Catholic schools. At least at this level, Roman Catholic voluntary aided primary schools seem to be achieving something which the Roman Catholic church might find it less easy to achieve without its system of voluntary aided schools.

Pupils educated in Church of England schools tend to record a less favourable attitude toward Christianity than pupils, of comparable sex, age, IQ and religious behaviour from comparable social-class homes with comparable levels of parental church attendance, educated in county schools. This means that they are less likely to hold a positive image of Jesus and God and to feel that they enjoy church, the bible, prayer and the religious education and worship in which they engage at school. Since the stated aims of the Church of England's continued involvement in the state-maintained sector of education do not necessarily concentrate on emphasizing the religious distinctiveness of church schools, these findings are not necessarily a criticism of the success of Church of England voluntary aided schools. However, irrespective of the educational philosophy underlying the Church of England's involvement in church schools, we suspect that these findings might leave a theological problem for the Church of England to account for operating schools which actually lead to *less* favourable pupil attitude toward Christianity than county schools.

Primary pupils in Gloucestershire
Although the East Anglian study had been conducted among three generations of pupils, the generalizability of the findings remained limited in three serious ways. All the participating schools were located within the same part of England, each sector was represented by a small number of individual schools, and these particular schools might not necessarily have been representative of East Anglian schools in general.

The next study, therefore, was established to make an in-depth study of the situation throughout one entire local education authority, namely Gloucestershire.[13] The study, initiated with the support of the county, Anglican and Catholic education authorities, approached every primary and junior school within the county, inviting each school to administer the attitude survey to all year-six pupils. This invitation was issued to 111 county schools, forty-one Church of England voluntary aided schools, seventy-three Church of England voluntary controlled schools and eight Roman Catholic voluntary aided schools. Co-operation was given by 87 per cent of county schools, 83 per cent of Church of England voluntary aided schools, 78 per cent of Church of England voluntary controlled schools and 63 per cent of Roman Catholic voluntary aided schools. All told, 4,948 pupils completed questionnaires.

Once again path analysis was employed to control for sex, mother's social class, father's social class, mother's church attendance, father's church attendance, the pupils' personal church attendance, and differences between rural, urban and suburban environments, before testing for the influence of church schools on pupil attitude toward Christianity. Full details of the path model are presented in figure 5.2 in the appendices. These data reaffirm the positive influence of Roman Catholic voluntary aided schools on pupil attitudes, even after controlling for the effects of home and church. The Gloucestershire data, however, do not confirm the view that Church of England voluntary aided schools exert a negative influence on pupil attitudes. In Gloucestershire attendance at a Church of England aided school makes no difference in one direction or the other to pupils' attitude toward Christianity. Unlike the East Anglian study, however, the Gloucestershire study also included Church of England voluntary controlled schools in the sample. This time path analysis demonstrates that Church of England voluntary controlled schools exert a small but significant negative influence on pupil attitude toward Christianity.

The generalizability of findings from the Gloucestershire study is still limited by two factors. Only one local education authority was involved in the survey. In the case of Church of England voluntary aided schools some conflict has clearly emerged between the East Anglian and the Gloucestershire findings. Further research, therefore, is now needed to clarify these issues.

Anglican secondary schools

Considerably less is known about the impact of Anglican secondary schools on pupil religious development than is known about the impact of Anglican primary schools. Two comparatively small studies have explored aspects of this question.

The first study administered the Francis scale of attitude toward Christianity to a sample of 802 year-eleven secondary pupils within twenty-one Church of England, Catholic and county schools.[14] Path analysis indicated that Church of England secondary schools exerted neither a positive nor a negative influence on their pupils' attitude toward Christianity.

The second study examined the religious beliefs, practices and attitudes of 546 year-ten pupils attending the four county and one Church of England voluntary secondary school within the same town.[15] The data demonstrated that the Church of England school recruited a higher proportion of pupils from churchgoing homes and that churchgoing homes tend to represent the higher social classes. After taking into account the influence of sex, social class and parental religiosity, path analysis indicated that the Church of England school exerted neither a positive nor a negative influence on its pupils' religious practice, belief or attitude.

Catholic secondary schools

During the past decade a series of inter-related studies has explored different aspects of the relationship between Roman Catholic secondary schools and pupil attitude toward Christianity.

To begin with, surveys in England,[16] Scotland[17] and Northern Ireland[18] have employed the Francis scale of attitude toward Christianity to profile the attitudes of pupils in Catholic schools and to compare these profiles with comparable data collected in county schools in England,[19] non-denominational schools in Scotland[20] and Protestant schools in Northern Ireland.[21] Data from all three cultures confirm that there is a more positive pupil attitude toward Christianity among pupils in Catholic schools. The kind of analyses undertaken in these studies, however, is not able to attribute the *cause* for this difference to the effect of the schools themselves.

In Scotland the Catholic church both provides separate schools within the state-maintained system and offers separate religious education courses within some non-denominational schools. Rhymer employed the Francis scale of attitude toward Christianity to compare the attitudes of 1,113 Catholic pupils attending three different types of school: 882 pupils were drawn from Catholic schools, 121 were drawn from non-denominational schools receiving Catholic religious education, and 110 were drawn from non-denominational schools not receiving Catholic religious education.[22] Rhymer describes this as a stratified sample representing the distribution of Scottish Catholic pupils between Catholic and non-denominational secondary schools, and drawn from areas of Strathclyde Region typical of geographical and economic conditions in Scotland as a whole. In the re-analysis of these data, the path model presented in figure 5.3 in the appendices demonstrated that both the separate school system and the provision of Catholic religious education in non-denominational schools contributes to the development of positive pupil attitudes.[23]

In parts of England the development of middle schools involved the Catholic church in restructuring its educational system.[24] Boyle employed the Francis scale of attitude toward Christianity to assess the implications of such restructuring for pupil religiosity.[25] He administered the scale to 1,205 twelve- and thirteen-year-old pupils drawn from six Catholic schools within two Northern metropolitan districts, one of which had developed a three-tier system of schools and the other had not. In the re-analysis of these data, the path model demonstrated that there was no difference in attitude scores between comparable pupils attending middle and secondary schools.[26]

Demographic shifts in the Catholic population in England led during the 1980s to a growing proportion of non-Catholic pupils being admitted to Catholic schools, generally recruited from other-denominational churchgoing backgrounds. The Francis scale of attitude toward Christianity was employed in a study designed to examine the implications of this change in pupil recruitment both for the non-Catholic pupils admitted to Catholic schools and for the general religious ethos of the Catholic school.[27] All the pupils from year seven through year eleven in five Catholic comprehensive schools in two Midland conurbations were invited to take part in the survey in 1981. Completed questionnaires were received from 2,895 pupils, representing 88.9 per cent of the total school population. The data indicated a significant increase in the proportion of non-Catholic pupils admitted in the first year, 17 per cent compared with 7 per cent in the fifth year. The path model indicated that non-Catholic pupils, even from churchgoing backgrounds, in Catholic schools show a less positive attitude toward Christianity than Catholic pupils. On the basis of these findings the recommendation is made that, if Catholic schools recruit a higher proportion of non-Catholic pupils, the doctrinal, liturgical and catechetical assumptions of the school need to be modified in order to preserve the good will and enhance the religious development of the pupils from other denominational backgrounds.

These findings open to scrutiny the whole assumption that Catholic schools function as an extension of the faith community. This assumption was tested by Egan in a large-scale study of the year-eleven pupils attending fifteen of the sixteen Catholic state-maintained secondary schools in Wales during the academic year 1983–4.[28] Completed questionnaires were returned by 1,638 pupils. In the re-analysis of these data, the path model identified three clear groups of pupils: practising Catholics, non-practising Catholics and non-Catholics.[29] By looking in closer detail at possible aspects of pupil disaffection from the Catholic school, this study suggested that the real problem comes not only through the recruitment of non-Catholic pupils, but also through the recruitment of Catholic pupils from non-Catholic backgrounds. This is a much larger problem for the Catholic church in Wales. While less than 9 per cent of Egan's sample of pupils claimed themselves to be non-Catholics, less than half of the girls and only slightly more than two-fifths of the boys were weekly mass attenders themselves, while about two-fifths of both sexes were supported by weekly mass-attending mothers and only one-quarter by weekly mass-attending fathers.

Given the significance of these findings for the underlying philosophy regarding Catholic schools as an extension of the faith community, Egan replicated the Welsh study in both the USA[30] and Australia.[31] In both cases the basic conclusions of the Welsh study were reinforced.

Inside the schools

When we 'open the black box' to look at the sorts of things going on inside the school which may affect pupils' attitude toward Christianity, three studies throw light on what is happening. One shows that syllabuses do not make a difference to attitudes in primary schools and another that syllabuses can make a difference in secondary schools. The third shows that science or arts preference in secondary schools does not have a measurable effect on attitude toward Christianity.

In a study of the top two years of primary-school pupils, Francis found there was no difference in attitude toward Christianity between non-denominational schools which offered no religious education, non-denominational schools which followed a bible-based syllabus and non-denominational schools which followed a more experimental thematic syllabus.[32]

In a study of denominational and non-denominational secondary schools in England, Ulster and Eire, Kay tested not only the content of the religious-education syllabus but also the classroom climate in which it was taught.[33] Turning to the classroom climate first, he found, after removing the effects of age and sex by multiple regression, that if teachers forbade discussion (regardless of the content of lessons) there was a consistent tendency for pupils to form less positive attitude toward Christianity. Turning to the content of the syllabus, he found, after removing the effects of age and sex by multiple regression, that in English state-maintained schools and among Ulster Protestants, the teaching of world religions was detrimental to pupil attitude toward Christianity. When he examined the teaching of the bible in conjunction with classroom climate, he found, after removing the effects of age and sex by multiple regression, that bible teaching without discussion was associated with less positive attitude toward Christianity than bible teaching where discussion was allowed.

Kay also made a study on a sample of 1,431 pupils aged eleven to fifteen in fourteen schools chosen following a stratified random procedure of local-authority schools in England, Northern Ireland and Wales.[34] He was interested to find out if science-preferring pupils would register lower attitude toward Christianity than arts-preferring pupils. He hypothesized that the apparent conflict between science and religion might result in less favourable attitude toward religion being found among pupils who studied sciences. The age range of the pupils selected in his study was sufficiently wide to include both pupils who followed generalized science courses and those who had opted for specialized courses (for example, on physics or chemistry).

The results showed that there were no differences between the science and arts groups when the effects of sex differences had been removed. This was done both by comparing science-preferring girls and arts-preferring girls, and then making similar comparisons between boys. Then, on a separate set of tests, by using multiple regression to partial out sex differences, further comparisons were made separately for pupils in Church of England, Roman Catholic and state schools. Moreover, the arts- and science-preferring groups were drawn up in two different ways. Thus the first arts group were those pupils who preferred art, drama or English, and the science group were those pupils preferring chemistry, mathematics or physics. The second arts group was made up of art-, drama-, English-, history- and music-preferring pupils and compared with chemistry-, mathematics-, physics- and technical-studies-preferring pupils. In all cases the results were the same. Subject preference was not reflected in attitude toward religion.

Comment

As common sense would suggest, schools *do* make a difference to the pupils who pass through them. They make a difference to pupils' attitude toward Christianity, a matter of great importance to the likely future religious behaviour of school leavers. This difference is quantifiable and statistically significant. It is a difference which exists even after all those other factors which are known to influence attitude toward Christianity have been taken into account.

In addressing the drift of young people away from the churches, the most important conclusion from this study is that church schools *can* influence young people positively toward adopting a more positive attitude toward Christianity, in addition to any influence exerted by home and by church.

At the same time, the data from these studies indicate that the positive influence on the part of church schools is neither inevitable nor consistent. In particular, the data present two clear challenges which the churches may or may not wish to address.

The first challenge is directed most clearly to the Anglican church. Data from both the East Anglian and from the Gloucestershire study suggest that *some* Anglican schools may promote a less positive attitude toward Christianity than comparable county schools. To the outsider it may seem somewhat puzzling that a denomination should wish to finance an educational system which actively undermines its *raison d'être*.

The second challenge is directed most clearly at the Roman Catholic church. Data from a set of studies in the USA and Australia, as well as within the UK, suggest that there is now a radical discontinuity between the theory of the Catholic school as a faith community and the actual beliefs and attitudes of the pupils who constitute the school community. In practice today the Catholic school community comprises three distinct groups of pupils: practising Catholics, lapsed Catholics, and practising members of other Christian denominations. The discontinuity between theory and practice is leading to a growing alienation of some pupils. To an outsider it may seem somewhat puzzling that the religious and educational policy of some Catholic schools does not more accurately reflect the religious disposition and needs of the pupils.

6

Home influence

What counts as 'home'?

An influential book on the effects of schooling was entitled *Fifteen Thousand Hours* because this is the amount of time that most children spend at school between the ages of five and sixteen.[1] The rest of their lives up to the same age, 125,000 hours, is spent at or around or in the care of the home. The home is the place where the child first learns to speak and understand, and perhaps to read. If it is a religious home, the child will learn to pray there and from there be introduced to church or Sunday school.

By the time the child is eighteen years old he or she may be ready to leave home. At the end of this process of growing up, it is reasonable to ask whether the home or the school has been more powerful in forming the child's religious attitude and behaviour. Immediately this question is posed, it presents difficulties. The school may be treated as a 'black box' with input and output variables, but the home can hardly be treated in this way because it is practically impossible to collect data about the home relating to the child's infancy; memory of it is unreliable. Moreover, though the child starts to attend a school and then, when the time comes, leaves it, the child does not usually deal with the home in this way. Attendance at home continues in parallel with attendance at school for all but the tiny minority who are sent to boarding schools.

More problematic is the kind of home in which the child lives. In practice it is not usually possible to collect information on each child's home by interviewing parents or sending them a questionnaire. And, even if this approach were adopted, there is a sense in which it would be inadequate, because what is really of interest is the home *as it is perceived by the child*. It therefore makes sense to collect information about the home from the child. Some of this information is relatively objective, like the question, 'What sort of job does your father do?' Other information, however, is relatively subjective, like the question,

'Are your parents happily married?' Yet it is the subjectivity which is important because it is children's perception of their parents which is likely to affect emotional development. A very stable child may cope with tension in the home, and disregard tension in the home, much more easily than a very unstable child. If the child thinks his or her parents are unhappily married, this may affect the way he or she thinks about them, even if the parents consider themselves to be no more argumentative than any other couple.

Thus, the kind of information which can be collected about the home is that which the child may reasonably be expected to supply. For this reason, it is best to collect this sort of information from pupils of secondary-school age. Yet, when this has been decided, there is a further question which needs to be addressed in any consideration of the influence of the home. We need to ask how we should categorize church attendance. Clearly, parental church attendance could be classified on its own as a church-related variable and, in some studies, this has been done. But in an examination of the effects of the home, parental church attendance is a genuine home-effect variable. The parent or parents, if they attend church, carry out this behaviour, and it is a behaviour which, like shopping or going on holiday, affects the pattern of life in the home, a pattern which is especially relevant to the child if it involves being *taken to church*. Much church attendance by children is exactly of this kind. It is attendance which stems from the dynamics of the home. Only later do children learn that they have a choice in the matter, a choice which may be realized much more sharply if one parent attends church and the other does not. Consequently church attendance, whether it is attendance by the parents or the child's own attendance, may realistically be considered a variable descriptive of the home.

Once church attendance, or Sunday-school attendance, is seen as belonging to the child's home, further possibilities suggest themselves. Is there a stronger link between maternal church attendance and a daughter's attitude toward Christianity than there is between maternal church attendance and a son's attitude toward Christianity? Or, more simply, do mothers affect their daughters more than their sons, and fathers their sons more than their daughters? Further, does parental church attendance make more impact on the religious attitudes of young children than it does on those of older children? We may even ask if church attendance in a place where it is at a generally high level (like Eire) has quite the same influence at it does in places where congregations are less well supported.

In many sociological studies the main variable by which the home is described is social class or socio-economic status. The choice of this variable is partly dictated by the long-standing classification of employment by the Office of Population Censuses and Surveys, and partly because much sociological theory is designed to explain the distribution of power within society as a function of occupational and economic status. Yet, in terms of religion, the social class of the home has another relevance. Social class may be considered as a shorthand designation for the value system of the home, and this, clearly, has an affinity with the values implicit in religion. Both Weber and Tawney thought that the values of Protestantism were transferable into economic behaviour.[2] Historical studies certainly confirm the connection between a text-based religion like Christianity and the priority given to reading and study. Social class, then, is not simply a means of referring to private wealth. It goes much wider than this. Social class is a way of referring to the rhythm of life, the sense of autonomy enjoyed by those who act in a professional or managerial capacity, the use of language,[3] the 'social distance' between the home and the clergy and the balance between short-term and long-term personal and family objectives.

Findings

Francis and his collaborators have reported five main groups of findings concerning different aspects of the home on shaping attitude toward Christianity during childhood and adolescence. These findings concern the influence of social class, the importance of parental church attendance (giving particular attention to the comparative influence of mothers and fathers on sons and daughters), the influence of attending Sunday school, the influence of denominational identity, and the *comparative* influence of home and school.

Social class

A great deal of research shows that there is a clear relationship between religion and social attitudes.[4] Social attitudes are generally described as operating along two unrelated continua. The first continuum moves from tender-mindedness to tough-mindedness. The second continuum moves from liberal to conservative (in a non-political sense). Individuals from higher social classes tend to espouse more tender-minded and more liberal social attitudes. Individuals from lower social classes tend to espouse more tough-minded and more conservative social attitudes.

These general findings present a puzzle regarding the hypothesized relationship between social class and attitude toward religion, since religion is thought to belong both to the domain of tenderminded social attitudes and to the domain of conservative social attitudes. If the tenderminded aspect of religion predominates, then we would expect the higher social classes to report a more positive attitude toward Christianity. If the conservative aspect of religion predominates, then we would expect the lower social classes to report a more positive attitude toward Christianity.

At the same time, any straightforward relationship between attitude toward Christianity and social class is confounded by the relationships between social class and church attendance and between church attendance and attitude toward Christianity. A great deal of research shows that, within the UK, the higher social classes attend church more often than the lower social classes.[5] If we expect church attendance to go hand in hand with a positive attitude toward Christianity, then we should also expect the higher social classes, overall, to report a more positive attitude toward Christianity.

In the first study in this series, Francis, Pearson and Lankshear examined the relationship between social class and attitude toward Christianity among a sample of 5,288 ten- and eleven-year-old children attending state-maintained schools in England.[6] On first analysis, there appeared to be no correlation between attitude toward Christianity and social class among this sample. More sophisticated statistical analyses, however, demonstrated that the apparent lack of relationship between social class and attitude toward Christianity disguises two significant but contradictory influences. On the one hand, parents in higher-social-class occupations attend church more frequently and take their children with them. The data then confirm that church attendance promotes a more positive attitude toward Christianity. On the other hand, children from lower-social-class backgrounds appear to espouse more conservative social attitudes which tend to promote a more positive attitude toward Christianity. Thus, after controlling for differences in parental church attendance, children from lower-social-class backgrounds tend to hold a more positive attitude toward Christianity than children from higher-social-class backgrounds.

In the second study in this series, Gibson, Francis and Pearson replicated the analysis described in the previous study among a different age group and in a different cultural context.[7] This second analysis was based on information supplied by 2,717 fourteen- and fifteen-year-olds in Scotland. Once again, this study found that, although parents and adolescents from higher-social-class backgrounds attend church more frequently, and church attendance is associated with a more positive attitude toward Christianity, after controlling for differences in parental church attendance, adolescents from lower-social-class back-grounds record a more positive attitude toward Christianity.

In a third study in this series, Kay explored the effects of social class, as measured by the father's job, in the different cultures of Ulster, Eire and England.[8] He found that children in Eire from higher social classes, in both Roman Catholic and Protestant homes, recorded a more negative attitude toward Christianity than children from lower social classes. In England the figures were reversed: children from higher social classes in both Roman Catholic, Church of England and county schools showed a more positive attitude toward Christianity than children from lower social classes. The explanation of this finding is to be taken from the variation in church attendance between England and Eire and the contradictory mechanisms discussed above. In Eire, church attendance is one of the highest in Europe. At the time when the survey was made, 94 per cent of Roman Catholic fathers and 96 per cent of Roman Catholic mothers attended church weekly. The respective figures for Eire Protestants were 42 per cent and 50 per cent. In England, the figures were much lower: 40 per cent of Roman Catholic mothers and 34 per cent of Church of

England mothers attended weekly; 30 per cent of Roman Catholic fathers and 27 per cent of Church of England fathers attended weekly. Since church attendance is very high in all social classes in Eire, and in the case of Roman Catholics, *higher* among fathers in *un*skilled occupations than among those in professional occupations, the combination of conservative social attitudes and church attendance leads to strongly positive attitude toward Christianity being held by pupils from lower-social-class homes. These results, then, are in the predicted direction. Social class and church attendance appear to work in the same way in different cultural settings.

Parental church attendance
A number of studies point to the relationship between parental church attendance and child church attendance, and between parental church attendance and child attitude toward Christianity. The mechanism is thought to be clear. Parents who attend church take their children with them. Children who attend church adopt a more positive attitude toward Christianity than children who do not attend church. Beyond these general impressions, however, three important issues remain less clear. First, there is considerable debate regarding the comparative influence of mothers and fathers on the religious development of sons and daughters. Second, it is unclear whether parental influence becomes more or less important over the age range of secondary education. Third, it is unclear whether parental influence really has a stronger influence on adolescent religious practice or on underlying religious attitudes.

From a theoretical perspective, some clear and conflicting hypotheses exist regarding the nature of parental influence on adolescent behaviour, attitudes and values. Some strands in socialization theory suggest that fathers may be more influential than mothers in the transmission of certain political and social values.[9] On the other hand, exchange theory suggests that mothers may be more influential than fathers on the grounds that the mother typically has a higher frequency of interaction with the offspring.[10] At the same time, psychoanalytic theory suggests that the same-sex dyads (father–son and mother–daughter) will evince stronger association or similarity.[11] Youth-subculture theory suggests that peer-group influence replaces parental influence as the dominant force shaping adolescent attitudes, values and behaviours.[12]

In order to generate new insights into the influence of parental church attendance on both church attendance and attitude toward Christianity among adolescents, Francis and Gibson explored this relationship among two samples of young people in Scotland.[13] From a large data base only information from those pupils who reported belonging to complete family units, including both mothers and fathers, was analysed. Two age groups were selected from this data base in order to compare parental influence at different stages of adolescent development. The first sample comprised 1,747 eleven- to-twelve year olds; the second sample comprised 1,635 fifteen- to sixteen-year-olds.

In the analysis of these data two separate multiple-regression equations were computed for each of four subgroups of the sample: eleven- to twelve-year-old boys, fifteen- to sixteen-year-old boys, eleven- to twelve-year-old girls, and fifteen- to sixteen-year-old girls. The first equations in each set examined the influence of father's church attendance and mother's church attendance on child church attendance. The second equation in each set examined the influence of father's church attendance and mother's church attendance on child attitude toward Christianity, after controlling for the child's own church attendance. All eight regression equations are present in table 6.1 in the appendices.

The first question to be addressed by these figures concerns the comparative influence of mothers and fathers on sons and daughters. When the figures were examined, the answer to the question turned out to be unambiguous. The beta weights demonstrate that the mother's church attendance is the most powerful influence on sons' and daughters' church attendance both in the eleven- to twelve-year-old age range and in the fifteen-to-sixteen age range. Having said this, though, there is a distinction between the influence of the mother and the father on sons' and daughters' church attendance. While the mother has an almost equally strong effect on both sons and daughters, the influence of the father, at both age levels, is noticeably stronger on sons than on daughters. The influence of the father is particularly crucial with regard to eleven- to twelve-year-old boys. Only in this age group does paternal church attendance yield additional predictive information about the son's attitude toward Christianity over and above that given by the son's own church attendance. On the brink of the teenage years the support of the father within the churchgoing home is important if the son's religious socialization is to go smoothly.

If we ask whether parents have more influence on a child's church attendance than his or her attitude toward Christianity, the answer is once again clear. The strength of the beta weights indicates that parents may, by their example, influence the child's church attendance much more directly than they affect the child's attitude toward Christianity. The outward and public manifestations of Christianity are susceptible to parental influence; private and covert effects are much less susceptible to parental influence.

Sunday school
Some have seen the Sunday school as a helpful extension of the home, adding positively to the religious nurture of the young. Some recent church reports, however, have been much more sceptical about the positive contribution of Sunday schools in today's society.

In order to check the validity of these two conflicting views, Francis, Gibson and Lankshear report on the influence of Sunday-school attendance on attitude toward Christianity among a sample of 4,079 eleven- to fifteen-year-olds, attending state-maintained schools in Scotland and who identified themselves as belonging to either no religious group or to non-Roman Catholic denominations.[14] Roman Catholics were excluded from this sample in view of the different catechetical strategy of this denomination. The data from this study demonstrate that, after controlling for the influence of personal and parental church attendance, age and sex, attendance at Sunday school between the ages of four and twelve makes a small significant contribution to the promotion of a positive attitude toward Christianity. Moreover, the data also demonstrate that this effect is incremental, in the sense that the more years during which Sunday school attendance took place, the greater is the effect of the attendance.

Denominational identity

There is clear evidence to suggest that a much higher proportion of the adult population in England continues to identify with one of the Christian denominations than actually attends church on a Sunday.[15] Similarly, although the proportion of babies baptized in church has declined considerably over the past three decades, many more parents still seek baptism for their infant than are themselves regular churchgoers.[16] There is a sense in which infant baptism continues to signify denominational membership for the young person so baptized. What is not so clear, however, is what denominational membership actually means to adults, or to children, who do not express that membership in terms of active participation in the life of a local church.

In order to illuminate this precise issue, Francis explored the relationship between denominational identity, church attendance and attitude toward Christianity among a sample of 4,948 eleven-year-olds.[17] The key finding from this study is that denominational identity is associated with a more positive attitude toward Christianity among young people who never attend church. In other words, even nominal membership of a church carries with it a more positive attitude toward Christianity than that held by children who have no denominational identity. In this sense, homes which convey even nominal church membership to their children contribute toward enhancing their attitude toward Christianity.

Family stability

A study by Kay examined the effects of bereavement, separation, marital discord and divorce on attitude toward Christianity in a sample of 1,431 pupils aged between eleven and sixteen years old.[18] No difference was found between the attitude toward Christianity of children who had both parents alive and those who had lost one parent through death. Death itself, then, did not have a measurable effect on attitude toward Christianity, despite the possibility that children might have been inclined to blame God for the loss of a parent. When a comparison was made between children who came from homes where they thought their parents' marriage was happy and other children from homes where a divorce had taken place, children from broken homes were found to have a significantly lower attitude toward

Christianity. When the same comparison was run between children of happily married parents and children who thought their parents were not often happy together, there were no significant differences in attitude toward Christianity. This implies that it is the fact of divorce, with all the trauma that this creates, which has an impact on children's attitudes. This conclusion is strengthened by a comparison made between children who came from homes where parents are happily married and where they are separated. In this instance the children from separated homes show *higher* attitude toward Christianity than those from happily married homes.

The divorce rate within different social classes and in different denominational groups is known to be different, and Kay used multiple regression on the findings to rule out spurious associations. These checks did nothing to overturn the conclusions. Despite variations between the sexes in their perception of their parents' marital happiness and variations in the divorce rate among parents of children attending Church of England, Roman Catholic and county schools, divorce still proved to be an experience negatively related to the child's attitude toward Christianity.

Home and school

Kay undertook a series of analyses dealing with pupils from England, Eire and Ulster who attended Church of England (or in Ulster Protestant), Roman Catholic and non-denominational state-maintained schools, in order to explore the comparative influence of home and school on shaping attitude toward Christianity during adolescence. In these analyses, the home was shown, in all instances but one, to be more influential than the school on shaping children's attitude toward Christianity.[19] This is partly a consequence of the greater variability of homes than schools. Yet it is also an indication of the power of parental church attendance, even in the midst of a cluster of other background variables related to the school, to make a decisive mark on attitude toward Christianity during the years of secondary education.

The analysis which establishes this finding is made on three groups of variables. There are variables associated with the *individual* (age, sex, personality scores, verbal ability, religious behaviour, lie-scale scores and personal prayer), variables associated with the *home* (parental church attendance, marital happiness and social class) and variables associated with the *school* (its type, location, religious-education syllabus and the classroom climate of its religious education). The analysis is made complicated because the individual, home and school blocks of variables correlate with each other.

One way to disentangle these correlations is to use blockwise multiple regression to measure the contribution to attitude toward Christianity of the individual, the home and the school, separately and jointly. The total contribution of the school is then calculated by adding the specific contribution of the school to that contribution which is common to the school and the individual and that which is common to the school and the home. The two other variables can be treated in the same way and the overall contributions of individual, home and school can then be compared. What emerged in Kay's study was the tendency of the home in England and Ulster to account for between 16 and 26 per cent of the variance in attitude toward Christianity scores. Typically, the school accounted for between 6 and 11 per cent of the variance in attitude toward Christianity scores. This analysis must be caveated by the slightly higher proportion of variance accounted for by the school than the home among Eire Protestants and the much higher proportion of variance accounted for by the homes of Ulster Catholics.

Nevertheless, the IEA (International Project for the Evaluation of Educational Achievement) study involving more than twelve countries used exactly the same techniques as those described here and found the effect of the home on the academic performance of pupils outperformed that of the school by a ratio of about two or three to one, a finding not dissimilar to the ratio between the different percentages found between home and school contributions here.[20] The 125,000 hours of the home, perhaps not unexpectedly, have a greater impact that the 15,000 hours of the school.

Yet, there is a twist to this finding. Kay's analysis was able to show that the effect of denominational schools on boys or girls whose mothers never attended church was significant. If, for some reason, non-religious parents make use of the services of a denominational school, rather than a non-denominational school, the effect on the child's attitude toward Christianity is measurable, significant and positive. On this small subsection of the total population the school may therefore be more important in determining the child's attitude toward religion than the home.

Comment

The home is a rich and varied environment, and educational research has not been able to explore it as thoroughly as it has explored the school. There are issues of privacy and sensitivity about the propriety of detailed enquiries into the child's home. Yet, the statistics of social class, parental church attendance, divorce, bereavement and marital happiness have enabled a sketch to be drawn of the *kind* of home which will be conducive to the development of a positive attitude toward Christianity during childhood and adolescence.

Clearly the formation of attitudes within the life of the child is an internal and unobservable process. Nevertheless, these findings have shown that church attendance, whether by the child or the parents, helps positive attitude toward Christianity to be formed. Within the community of the church, and by means of its worship and its creeds, children must begin to take hold of the beliefs and evaluations which result in a positive attitude toward Christianity. Somehow, by mechanisms that are not well understood, the beliefs about God and Jesus and the bible which are fundamental to a positive attitude toward Christianity begin to be articulated and accepted by the child. Moreover, these mechanisms seem to apply equally well within various denominational groups and in various cultures.

That the home can underline and supplement the beliefs of the child seems obvious. That the father has a greater influence upon the son than the daughter, but that the mother has a greater influence on either child than the father, suggests that the processes of socialization are, if one may put it this way, *maternal*. They are nourishing, protective, caring – all those things which are associated with the relationship between the mother and the child. At the same time, the correlation between father and son suggests that there is an element of identification with the same-sex parent. The process of religious socialization has at least these two aspects.

The study of the effects of bereavement, separation and divorce on children's attitude toward Christianity resonates with a Freudian possibility. Children from separated homes show significantly higher attitude toward Christianity than those from happily married homes. What psychological account can be given for this? One possibility is that children fantasize about their missing parent in the hope that he or she will return to the home (always a possibility in the case of separation) but where divorce takes place, and reconciliation has been finally and legally ruled out, children either blame God for the destruction of their parents' marriage or postulate a defective model of deity based on the absence of one parent, usually the father.

Both the IEA study and the studies reported here suggest that homes vary more than schools. This should not be taken to mean that schools do not vary; they vary immensely, but homes vary more. A consequence of this greater variation is that the home can explain a greater amount of the variation of outcome variables with which both school and home are associated. This is a statistical truth which cannot be avoided.

When theories of attitude change are examined, it is the theory of reference groups (discussed in chapter 3) that may throw light on the identification of son with father. If attitudes change when membership groups become reference groups, as the theory suggests, then identification with a parent may be seen as a special case of the adoption of a reference group; the father becomes a 'reference person' for the son. We may posit a series of transformations using a theory derived from Émile Durkheim.[21] The Durkheimian notion is that it is from membership of a group that members develop not only a sense of obligation but also a sense of the divine. The group, which transcends the existence of any individuals which comprise it, is personified in the reality of a divine being, who also transcends individuals in the same way as the group. By this account, the father becomes a representative of the group and therefore of the divine.

7
Personality and religion

Introduction

There is a sense in which each person is like every other person, like some other people and like no other person. There is also a sense in which no two people see the same situation identically. These reasons alone are sufficient to explain divergent approaches to the scientific description of personality. Some theorists have stressed the uniqueness of individuals and others have stressed the similarities between people. Some theorists have stressed the importance of situations in determining behaviour, others have given more weight to personality factors; yet others have seen the best predictions of behaviour as arising from an interaction between the person and the situation.

There are also other, more fundamental, reasons why scientific descriptions of personality have not reached consensus. These reasons relate partly to the underlying model of personality each theory presupposes and partly to the nature of the evidence used to support the various models. This chapter begins by providing a brief introduction to two very different kinds of personality theory. The first kind of theory has its roots in a form of depth psychology and employs the tools of psychoanalysis or analytical psychology. The major concern of this kind of theory is to be able to account for psychological disorders. The theories of Sigmund Freud and Carl Jung illustrate this approach. The second kind of theory has its roots in a form of social psychology and employs the tools of measurement and factor analysis. The theory of Hans Eysenck illustrates this approach. The second half of the chapter demonstrates how the Francis scale of attitude toward Christianity has been set to work to test hypotheses derived from Eysenck's theory and from Freud's theory about the relationship between personality and religion.

Freud
Over the period of his life Sigmund Freud used several methods

to collect information from his patients. He was interested in the detailed recall of memories under hypnosis, though he later came to prefer a method of 'free association' by which patients allowed their minds to wander freely, often ranging over childhood experiences and dreams. Eventually his case studies led him to propose a personality composed of three parts: the ego, which was in touch with reality; the id, which was the seedbed of primitive and instinctual desires; and the superego, which was the seat of ideals or conscience implanted by early parental authority. The mind itself contained both a conscious and an unconscious part, and both the id and the superego were largely confined to the unconscious. This was not because they were unimportant, but rather because they were so important that they threatened to overwhelm the ego and were suppressed by it.

The course of normal development begins with the new-born child whose behaviour is dictated entirely by the id. Quite quickly the child comes into contact with external reality and part of the id is separated off to become the ego and, at a still later stage, the superego is formed. The ego moderates the pleasure-seeking demands of the id and develops strategies for dealing with illicit desires which, in the case of those diagnosed as being in need of psychoanalytic treatment, must be uncovered so that the symptoms of illness can be removed.

According to Freudian theory, the child passes quite rapidly up to the third year through three stages of development defined by that part of the body where pleasure is to be found. An infantile sexual attachment to the mother soon occurs, but this has to be repressed because of the father's exclusive claim on her love and attention. It is the fear of castration at the hand of an angry father that leads to the eventual formation of the superego, a mechanism which must operate differently in girls and which, according to Freudians, explains the comparative weakness of the female superego. Both sexes develop through a genital stage before adulthood, but the eventual personality of the adult must be understood in terms of the struggle between the id, ego and superego, whose relative strength was determined by the process of their formation in childhood.

Jung

Carl Jung's theory, which was worked out partly as a reaction against Freud's emphasis on sexuality, drew on a wide variety of written sources as well as clinical experience. He believed that the ego is the centre of human consciousness and inseparable from it. Beneath the conscious mind is the *personal* unconscious, but beneath or within this are layers of the *collective* unconscious, the origins of which are traceable to the beginning of the human species. It is in the context of the collective unconscious that *archetypes* are manifested. Archetypes are structures, or structural elements, which account for the recurrence of themes found universally in myths and folk tales. Archetypes can also be thought of as 'forms without content' that are inherent in the human being at birth. In many respects they may be thought of as being analogous to those philosophical, or *a priori*, concepts which are indispensable to thinking and common to all. During the course of life, and through experience, the archetypes take on individualized expressions. In normal daily life, the ego projects a *persona*, or mask, which is a socially acceptable expression of the individual's self.

But the persona is not the true self; it is only an outward construct. The true self is much more difficult to find and it cannot simply be equated with the ego. This is because the true self contains the totality of the personality, including the unconscious aspects. Since Jungian psychology makes the unconscious both individual and collective, the true self is rarely uncovered or fully expressed.

Progress to maturity may be made by exploring all the undesirable qualities which the persona conceals. These qualities are thought of as a *shadow* initially dissociated from the conscious life. In the interests of mental health the persona and the shadow must be harmoniously related and eventually integrated so that the energy of the shadow may be creatively expressed by the ego.

Once the relationship between persona and shadow has been resolved, the person has to face the inner world of the *animus* or *anima*. This is the archetype that represents the soul (or inner attitude), and its complementarity is evident in the fact that it is the opposite gender to the persona. The soul of women is masculine, while the soul of men is feminine. Persona and soul must be reconciled and, only after this, may the true self begin to be understood and complete individuation take place.

The normal life cycle involves three main stages. The first stage occurs between birth and puberty. The second stage takes place up to about the age of forty. In the long period between middle age and old age an attempt is made to bring the separate parts of the personality together. The whole Jungian scheme is based on the presupposition that the various opposites, conscious and unconscious, persona and shadow, soul and self may be united in ever more fruitful integrations.

The various internal entities described by Jung are distinct from the four main psychological *functions* by which energy is dispensed round the personality system. These four functions operate in all mature people regardless of the degree of integration they have attained. The functions are in two pairs: feeling and thinking, and sensing and intuition.

Feeling is a process that takes place between the ego and a 'given content' (anything about which feelings are possible) such that a definite value is placed on the content in terms of acceptance or rejection. Thinking connects concepts together and enables rational judgements to be formed. Sensing is identical with perception, though it is related to internal as well as to external stimuli. Sensing is effectively sense-perception and is the first information-gathering means open to children. Its counterpart is intuition that transmits perceptions in an unconscious way. Through intuition any one content is grasped as a complete whole and, like sensing, the process is irrational in that it cannot be controlled by reason. During the course of a child's growth, thinking and feeling are developed from sensing and intuition.

These four functions operate in the service of two main orientations. Extraversion is the orientation of the personality outwards to the objects of the external world, whether people or things; introversion is the orientation inwards to the world of thoughts and ideas. The combination of the extràvert and introvert orientations together with a preference for one of the four functions leads to the formation of certain *types*.[1] For instance, Jung proposes not only a basic introverted or extraverted type, but an introverted thinking type, an introverted feeling type, an introverted sensing type and an introverted intuitive type. The four same types are also found among extraverts.

The Freudian and Jungian descriptions of personality have revolutionized understandings of childhood and of the religious impulse. Yet they have also introduced entities and terms which are difficult to pin down and to test empirically. According to the standpoint which seeks to base science on observation and measurement, and to test theories which are translatable into measurable and observable variables, Freudian and Jungian systems cannot be accepted, without considerable refinement, as they were first presented.

Eysenck

An alternative tradition in psychology began work on the description of personality from the 1920s onwards. This tradition was certainly influenced by behaviourism, the notion that since only behaviour is observable, it is the only legitimate study for a science of people (see appendix 1). In England this tradition was most vigorously pursued by Hans Eysenck in a series of experiments and publications that resulted in the compilation of a questionnaire designed to measure personality.

The behaviouristic tradition to which Eysenck belongs emphasizes the stimulus-response unit as a basis for human behaviour: each stimulus is met by a corresponding behavioural response. Some responses are voluntary and others involuntary. Each stimulus which elicits a voluntary response is capable of being classified by the mind of the respondent. There is a flexibility, then, of response to the stimulus according to the mind's classification but, at the same time, the possibility that responses of a more generalized nature might be established. Habitual responses may then be clustered into traits, and a series of traits can be put together to form a personality type. Thus, in this model of personality, the scientific insistence on specific observable behaviours is applied at the lowest end of the descriptive hierarchy, while the presence of traits can be deduced from the self-reported behaviours addressed by the questionnaire items, which also must count as a form of observation. By this means personality types, that are not directly observable, are nevertheless testable. For example, we should expect to find differences in the social behaviour of introverts and extraverts. Traits and types are therefore conceptually similar, and the main difference between them is that types are more inclusive in scope. In Eysenck's scheme, however, types are understood dimension-ally so that a person can be scored as more extravert or less extravert, and not simply assigned to one type or another without further quantification.

The beauty of the Eysenckian position is that it allows personality to be explored objectively through other-observation of specific behaviour or through self-observation generated by questionnaires. In addition it allows the insights of less objective personality systems to be adapted and adopted. The Jungian notion of personality type finds expression in the Eysenckian notion of personality dimension. In this way subjective and objective approaches to personality may help each other.

In working through the detail of his model, Eysenck drew on experimental work (for example that of Pavlov and his salivating dogs) showing how a stimulus and a response might become paired and so lead to the building up of habitual responses. But it also led him to critique the Freudian components of personality and their associated mechanisms on the grounds that behaviourism can account for the same phenomena more simply.[2] Eysenck, instead of making use of id, ego and superego, considers that he can account for data on personality development without recourse to anything other than the constitution of the body's nervous and endocrinal systems.[3]

It is Eysenck's questionnaire for the measurement of personality that has been used in most of the studies reported later. For this reason it is necessary to consider not only its development but also criticisms of its rationale.

In the late 1940s Eysenck looked at thirty-nine items of personal information given by 700 soldiers who were regarded as neurotic, but who had not suffered brain damage or physical illness. He factor-analysed these items and extracted two uncorrelated factors. One of these factors referred to extraversion–introversion, while the other factor referred to neuroticism–stability. The extravert was characterized as being sociable, risk-taking, talkative, easy-going, optimistic and without a tight control of his or her feelings. The introvert was characterized as being quiet, reserved, careful, bookish, unaggressive and reliable. The neurotic tends to worry, be moody, depressed, to sleep badly and be excessively emotional and have difficulty in returning to calmness after emotional stimuli; the stable person shows the opposite of these tendencies. These results were published in 1947, and in 1952 Eysenck proposed another factor uncorrelated with the other two. Psychoticism was found after study of psychiatric patients, though the dimension was present more moderately in the normal population. The high scorer on the psychoticism scale may be thought of as being solitary, not caring for people, troublesome, perhaps cruel and inhumane, lacking in feelings and empathy, insensitive, hostile to others, aggressive and with a liking for unusual things and a disregard for danger. An alternative term for the high psychoticism scorer is 'tough-minded'.

Because the scales were uncorrelated, scores on one dimension could not be used to predict scores on either of the other two. Although scores on the dimensions were more or less normally distributed, that is, distributed with most people in the middle and a gradually diminishing number at either end, it would be possible for someone to score at any point on any of the scales. A highly extravert person might also be highly stable or highly neurotic and be very strongly psychotic or not psychotic at all. When tests were done on different subgroups of the population as a whole, it was found that extraverts with high psychoticism and neuroticism scores were numerous in the prison population and that successful business men and women tended to be stable extraverts. Successful academics were stable introverts. The scales were further refined and tested on literally thousands of subjects. The manual for the adult version of the questionnaire lists age and sex norms and reliability coefficients for each of the three dimensions.[4]

In order to check whether people were responding honestly to the questionnaire, a lie scale was incorporated. This scale was made up of statements to which, like the rest of the question-naire, respondents had to answer simply 'yes' or 'no'. The lie-scale items were written so as to imply almost impossible standards of honesty and probity. 'Have you ever taken anything (even a pin or a button) that belonged to someone else?' is an example. If a person replies negatively to this question, the original assumption behind the scale is that a lie is being told. However, contrary to expectations, the lie scale showed an internal reliability independent of any motivation to dissimulate. To explain these results, four main interpretations were put forward. First, that the lie scale was, as designed, a measure of dissimulation, of lying, despite the pointlessness of so doing;

second, that it measured a tendency to social conformity; third, that it was a genuine index of honesty and, fourth, that it measured lack of self-insight, or immaturity.

A children's version of the adult personality scales was constructed by rewording some of the items to make them applicable to children and by adding new items. The same factors were found, namely the three uncorrelated dimensions of neuroticism–stability, extraversion–introversion, tender-mindedness–tough-mindedness (psychoticism), and an internally reliable lie scale. Age and sex norms were published for children between seven and sixteen years of age. Reliabilities were also calculated for the same age range and these increased steadily as children grew older.[5]

Along with the construction of the questionnaires used to measure the three dimensions, Eysenck worked out a strong theoretical framework to account for his results. The human body has two nervous systems, the central nervous system which mainly controls voluntary behaviour, and the autonomic nervous system which controls involuntary behaviour like breathing and digestion. He suggested that an individual's position on the extravert–introvert dimension was determined by part of the central nervous system, the reticular activating system at the base of the brain. In a state of high excitation connections are formed between the neurons that make up the cerebral cortex but, after a while, an inhibitory process makes connections less easy to form and a stimulus ceases to have its first effect. At first the smell of a flower or of fresh coffee seems strong, but after a while we stop noticing it. The extravert is distinguished by a normally low level of arousal. In him or her inhibition builds up quickly and dissipates slowly, and this has the effect of reducing the impact of sensory stimulation. The extravert's behaviour is therefore marked by a search for arousal from strong stimuli, for example by loud music, excitement, social interaction and adventure. The excitation–inhibition balance within the brain of the introvert is the other way round. He or she is aroused by much weaker stimuli and is therefore capable of concentrating for long periods because inhibition dissipates quickly. The orientation of the extravert to the outer world is explained by the attraction of its constant and varied stimuli; the orientation of the introvert to the inner world is explained by the sufficiency of the stimuli to be found through the emotional and ideational life within.

The neuroticism–stability dimension was related to the autonomic nervous system. Strongly neurotic individuals react powerfully and quickly to stressful situations. Their pulse, blood pressure, sweating and adrenaline flow all rise in response to the promptings of the autonomic system; they feel anxiety. Neuroticism levels remain fairly steady for boys as they move through their teens, but girls experience a rise in neuroticism levels at the onset of puberty.

Although the biological basis of the psychoticism scale is less well explored, Eysenck suggests that it may be related to the average level of the male hormone, androgen, within the blood stream.

There has been one main modification to Eysenck's original conceptualization of the three dimensions of personality.[6] The trait of impulsivity, which was detected by a subset of items within the original questionnaire, was at first placed within the extraversion dimension. After considerable analysis, Eysenck moved this trait to the psychoticism dimension where it fitted better. The consequence of this shift is that studies using the earlier version of the extraversion scale need to be interpreted with care. The later versions of the extraversion scale are composed mainly of sociability items.

Criticisms of trait-type theories

The description of personality based on the measurement of dimensions derived from questionnaire data has been subjected to criticisms of two different kinds. First, questionnaires as a data-gathering method have been critiqued.[7] Second, the description of traits, as building blocks for a personality model, has been contested; in effect, the usefulness of the trait-type model of personality as a whole has been called into question.

Questionnaires rely on self-reported responses of a simple kind. These responses may be given dishonestly or inaccurately or they may refer to behaviours inappropriate to the person concerned. More fundamentally, questionnaires exclude reports on behaviour by a neutral observer or the ratings of someone, like a teacher, who knows the respondent well.

These criticisms, however, may be answered by pointing to the systematic elimination of weaknesses which takes place in the testing and developing of a good questionnaire. Responses to each item are compared with responses to all the other items and those items which give equivocal or unusual response patterns can be discarded. Trials of the questionnaire in prototype are made on the sorts of populations on which it will eventually be used. Age ranges are carefully delimited and, in the case of Eysenck's scale, for example, a modified version was produced for use with the prison population. In the same way variants can be produced for use with children.

The use of teacher ratings in preference to self-reported data generated by questionnaires is unnecessary since information from both these sources may be compared with each other. Teachers' ratings of pupils correspond quite closely with pupils' questionnaire responses. And the same sort of comparisons can be made when one person is asked to fill in a questionnaire on behalf of another person whom they know well.

The personality models derived from questionnaires almost always deal with traits.[8] Traits have been seen as resting on circular arguments. The trait of, for example, laziness is discovered because a person reports himself or herself to be lazy in several situations and then the person's subsequent lackadaisical behaviour is attributed to the existence of the laziness trait. Such a criticism may be answered by pointing to the explanatory power which accrues from the joining together of several traits into the three main personality dimensions.

Additionally, the usefulness of traits has been criticized. Although the trait of talkativeness or sociability may be very strong in some situations (for example, at parties or with small groups of friends), it may quite fail to be of any use in predicting behaviour in other situations (for example, in the library or on a train). The consequence of this is that traits are, at best, only applicable to small, highly specific situations and that the more dissimilar two situations in which the trait is to be manifested are, the less similar will be the respondents' behaviour. Moreover, the various situations in which people find themselves are differently perceived so that what, to one, is a threatening situation is, to another, a stimulating situation. People's reactions and behaviour will depend on how they interpret each situation, and this in turn will depend on a whole range of factors associated with past experience.

Both these criticisms have been rebutted in some detail.[9] The rebuttal revolves around the psychological meaning of consistency and the relationship between the consistency and reliability of tests. It also depends on the extent to which tests of cross-situational consistency are performed by younger or older people. It would be unreasonable to expect children, who are undergoing all the changes associated with maturation, to be as consistent as older people. In the same way, it is important to decide exactly how similar and how different situations are when tests of cross-situational consistency are made. It is important, in other words, to classify situations according to rational criteria rather than to assume that situations which are superficially similar are seen in that way by everyone.

Moreover, when attempts are made to predict behaviour on the basis of personality variables it is important to assess the validity of the theoretical position on the basis of which the predictions are being made. It is unsatisfactory to lump together successful and unsuccessful predictions made on the basis of different personality theories, which are only similar in that in some way or another they use traits.

There is a more technical criticism of traits that relates to their being 'moderator' variables. A moderator variable is one which exists between two others. In this context the moderator variable intervenes between the stimulus and the behaviour in the situation. In the light of a threat, the trait of aggression intervenes between the threat and the subject's violent response. Traits have therefore been dismissed as being redundant. The threat and the response can be measured. Why bother with an intermediate variable? And, if no intermediate variable is necessary, how can a theory of personality types built up from traits survive?

Again this criticism has been answered by the analytic benefits implicit in trait theory. If there are more than two independent variables and two dependent variables (in this instance, two situations and two responses), then the intervening or moderator variable produces an increased efficiency in prediction by reducing the number of functional relationships which have to be calculated. Thus if there were, for example, three similar situations and three dependent variables, nine functional relationships would need to be calculated, one between each of the situations and each of the responses. But if a moderator variable is used, each situation can be correlated with it and then the moderator can be correlated with the response, which makes only six functional relationships. Certainly, it can be shown that, in measurements of correlation between situation and response, if personality is omitted, the amount of variance attributed to error rises disproportionately. Or, to put this another way, by making use of personality variables, whether at the level of trait or at the level of dimension, correlations between situation and behaviour are significantly improved. This last consideration goes toward answering the criticism about the utility of personality models derived from questionnaires.

This raises the matter of interaction between personality and situation. On the one hand, if the situation is inflated in importance, personality disappears; all behaviour is situationally dependent. On the other hand, if personality is treated as Eysenck has treated it, as a biologically based phenomenon, then it is to be understood as a product of genetic factors working in conjunction with the environment. Personality may then be anchored in a wider biological understanding of the human species, and some human behaviour may be brought about by conditioning. This leads to testable predictions about religious behaviour because, according to the Eysenckian theory, not all personality dimensions condition equally easily.

Whether correlational techniques or clinical observations are to be preferred is essentially a matter of philosophical debate about scientific methods. Clinical observation may bring out a personality theory as rich as Jung's, but it is also true that some of Jung's insights are untestable and those which are, like the proposal of the two orientations, extraversion and introversion, are included by Eysenck's theory and validated by it. In this respect the imaginative hypotheses of Jung are raw material for testing by empirical means. The two methods of data collection, whatever the status of the information they give on their own, may enhance each other.

Theoretical expectations

Predictions can be made from each of the personality dimensions in turn. To understand how this may be done, it is necessary to consider the concept of conditioning. Although there are various types of conditioning depending on whether the conditioned behaviour is voluntary or involuntary, the idea is similar. The basic idea is that a particular behaviour becomes attached to a particular stimulus. In the case of Pavlov's dogs, the giving of the food was paired with the ringing of a bell. Salivation normally belongs with the arrival of food, but after a short time the dogs salivated when the bell was rung and when no food was presented; they had been conditioned to salivate at the sound of the bell rather than the sight of food. Similarly, Skinner's pigeons learnt to release food by pecking switches of certain shapes in their cages. They were conditioned to peck certain shapes and, although this was a *learnt* response, it was also a conditioned response because it was performed in answer to the need for food.

Extraversion

Extraverts, according to the Eysenckian theory, customarily have lower levels of arousal than introverts, and inhibition which builds up in them is slower to dissipate. If society is thought of as imposing customs and conventions on the growing individual, then those individuals who are most aware of these customs and conventions, most of which carry penalties of different strengths for their breach, will condition most quickly. Introverts on this basis will conform to society's expectations more readily than extraverts. If religion is seen as being part of the value system of society, the ultimate sanction against anti-social behaviour and the encourager of restrained and law-abiding behaviour, then introverts will be more religious than extraverts.

This scenario, of course, presumes that religion has a place in society similar to that which it carries in much of the western world. Certainly, where religion, and especially Christianity, is taught in schools, reinforced by school worship, underlined by religious holidays like Christmas and Easter, affirmed by oaths on the bible in law courts and upheld by marriage and funeral services, it is reasonable to suppose that most children will learn to locate the source of moral restraint in religious life. Moreover, there is a sense in which, since religion in modern British society has become a private matter, and is held to be so by young people, it makes sense for introverts to be more likely than extraverts to find meaning in this way, in religion.[10] In atheistic and totalitarian states, the opposite set of conditioning forces may be expected to operate and conditioning may make introverts fervently atheistic.

Previous research by Eysenck has explored the association between personality and social attitudes.[11] He concluded that social attitudes are either tough-minded or tender-minded. The tough-minded person supports the use of coercive measures to achieve social ends. For example, he or she tends to support the death penalty, long prison sentences for criminals, stringent economic policies and less liberal policies for disadvantaged groups. The tender-minded person is more inclined to liberal attitudes, to 'good causes' and to less punitive measures against social misfits. Extraverts tend to be tough-minded and introverts tend to be tender-minded. Religion has an ambivalent relationship with social attitudes. In one respect a positive attitude toward Christianity is typical of the tender-minded constellation of sympathies; sympathy for Christianity may be accompanied by sympathy for poorer and weaker members of the community. In other respects, however, attitude toward Christianity is typical of tough-minded attitudes in the sense that religion is linked with conservatism, with authoritarian social structures and strict morality.

Arising from these conclusions, predictions about the correlation between attitude toward Christianity and extraversion may be made either way: if tender-mindedness predominates, the correlation will be negative; if tough-mindedness predominates, the correlation will be positive.

Neuroticism
Neuroticism is expressed by anxiety and is connected with apparently irrational behaviour. Such behaviour is often thought of as maladaptive because it is not suited to bring about any improvement in the circumstances which it is intended to alleviate. In its severest form panic causes repeated and pointless actions without averting danger. Freud thought that religious rituals were a form of neurotic behaviour and, though he did not comment specifically on attitude toward Christianity, his entire stance toward religion is hostile and depends on the presumption that religious people are immature. God is no more than the exalted father of childhood and has no metaphysical reality.

On the other side of the debate, it is arguable that religion, particularly as an inner disposition, may be a form of self-knowledge and may foster stability, which is the opposite of neuroticism. Gordon Allport, for example, drew an important distinction between intrinsic religious orientation (which is concerned with inner thoughts and feelings) and extrinsic religious orientation (which is concerned with outward observances and communitarian norms).[12] Empirical findings based on this distinction show that an intrinsic religious orientation is negatively correlated with depression, and therefore presumably with neuroticism.[13] The intrinsic orientation is by definition less concerned with religious practices and ceremonies than the extrinsic orientation, and to this extent is in line with Freud's speculations. In Jung, symbols, and especially religious symbols, are an important means by which the conscious and unconscious aspects of the mind are reconciled, and it is this which gives symbols their power.[14] The person who discovers the value of religious symbols (and Christ himself is seen to have a symbolic role) will experience a beneficial impact on his or her personality resolving intra-psychic tensions. These considerations lead to the conclusion that neuroticism and attitude toward Christianity will either be uncorrelated or be negatively correlated.

There is a further facet of neuroticism which is relevant to prediction. Although the three personality dimensions are uncorrelated, neuroticism may act as an incentive to learning, especially when taken in connection with other personality dimensions. The introvert may be expected to be religious, but the neurotic introvert more so. Neuroticism may act as a psychological drive. Low levels of anxiety promote conscientiousness, and therefore conscious learning; they may also increase conditionability. Yet in other circumstances, when levels of anxiety are high, anxiety may act as an inhibitor to learning; panic prevents rational thought. We should therefore expect moderate levels of neuroticism to have the optimum effect on conditionability and to increase the effects of extraversion or of psychoticism.

Psychoticism

Psychoticism is characterized by a lack of care for people, perhaps even cruelty and inhumanity, insensitivity, aggression and a lack of empathy. Given the role of religion, and particularly of Christianity, as being concerned, especially in the context of the school, with respect for other people, forgiveness, concern for Third World problems and other tender-minded attitudes, psychoticism will be negatively correlated with attitude toward Christianity.

The impulsivity component of the psychoticism scale may be expected to reduce the high psychoticism scorer's liability to social conditioning. Impulsivity is, in many respects, the reverse of patterned behaviour marked by stimuli and fixed responses.[15] By definition the impulsive person may or may not follow a previous behaviour. The fixed sequence of (same) stimulus followed by (same) response has little chance to become established in impulsive people, and so conditioning will not easily take place. When impulsivity is added to the uncaring traits which are a major part of the psychotic type, it is clear that an antipathy to Christianity is the likely result.

The lie scale

The lie scale lends itself to several predictions because of its interpretative complexity. One option is to interpret lie scores as an index of truthfulness. Highly religious populations might simply be more honest than non-religious populations, in which case low lie-scale scores should be found among those with a very positive attitude toward Christianity.

But it is also reasonable to suggest that social pressures may form both religious attitudes and deter people from taking anti-social action. In this case, the lie scale measures social conformity: those who score low on the lie scale are those who conform to social norms. Alternatively, the lie scale may be understood as an index of immaturity or lack of self-insight. The reasoning here is that immaturity and lack of self-insight deny unpleasant truths. Those who score low on the lie scale do so because they deny doing wrong. They are unable to judge themselves by the standards they apply to others and so unwittingly tell lies about their own conduct.

Eysenck gives two suggestions about the way to decide between variant interpretations of the lie scale. If there is a correlation between lie-scale scores and neuroticism, it is possible that the lie scale, in this instance, is measuring dissimulation. This interpretation is reached because, under circumstances in which there is an incentive to lie, for instance in an employment selection test, lie-scale scores have been observed to increase and neuroticism scores to decrease. If, however, a correlation between the lie scale and extraversion is found, this points towards the lie scale's detecting social acquiescence or conformity. This is because introverts are more observant than extraverts of ethical and social norms; they are more conformist.

Findings

In all the explorations of personality and attitude toward Christianity, it is important to remember sex differences. Girls are more inclined than boys to hold a positive attitude toward Christianity. Girls are also less extravert, less tough-minded (low-scoring on psychoticism), more neurotic and more inclined to score high on the lie scale than boys. Consequently, any correlations calculated in big samples of boys and girls taken together will reflect these sex differences. The figures will show a negative correlation between attitude toward Christianity and extraversion and a positive correlation between attitude toward Christianity and neuroticism. To find the true relationship between the personality dimensions and attitude toward Christianity, it is necessary either to calculate results for boys and girls separately or to make statistical adjustments to remove the effects of sex differences.

There are similar pitfalls with regard to age. Attitude toward Christianity declines with age among the majority of the population, and especially among non-churchgoers. Extraversion scores tend to rise slightly for both sexes between the ages of seven and thirteen, while neuroticism scores rise for girls but not for boys. Lie-scale scores drop quite noticeably in the seven-to-sixteen age range.

Extraversion

A series of three early studies set out to explore the theory that introverts would be more religious. In the first of these studies,[16] the relationship between the extraversion scale of the Junior Eysenck Personality Inventory and the Francis scale of attitude toward Christianity was analysed among a sample of 1,088 year-ten and year-eleven pupils. These data demonstrated a significant negative correlation between extraversion and attitude toward Christianity, and no significant interaction between extraversion and sex. In other words, the more extraverted the pupil, whether male or female, the less sympathetic his or her attitude toward Christianity.

The second study in this series set out to check the findings of the first study, but with two important changes in the research design. This time the age range was extended to comprise 1,715 young people between the ages of eleven and seventeen. This time a more recent form of the extraversion scale was employed from the Junior Eysenck Personality Questionnaire.[17] In the meantime, Eysenck had begun to refine his concept of extraversion by removing part of the impulsivity component. In this second study, after the removal of the influence of age and sex by multiple regression, extraversion continued to correlate negatively and significantly with attitude toward Christianity, although the correlation was less strong than in the original study. In other words, these findings suggested that the relationship between introversion and religiosity was weakened by removal of some of the impulsivity items.

The third study in the series set out to solve this puzzle by inviting a sample of 191 young people between the ages of fourteen and sixteen to complete the Francis scale of attitude toward Christianity alongside *three* different versions of the extraversion scale, each containing a different level of impulsivity items.[18] The three scales were taken from the Junior Eysenck Personality Inventory, the Junior Eysenck Personality Questionnaire and the Eysenck Personality Questionnaire. The findings from this study demonstrated the strongest negative correlation between extraversion and religion in the Junior Eysenck Personality Inventory (where the impulsivity component was highest), no correlation in the Eysenck Personality Questionnaire (where the impulsivity component was thoroughly removed) and a significant but smaller correlation in the case of the Junior Eysenck Personality Questionnaire (where the impulsivity component had been partly removed). These findings, therefore, confirmed the view that the sociability component of extraversion is irrelevant to individual differences in religiosity, while the impulsivity component of extraversion was an important predictor of individual differences in religiosity.

Neuroticism

Another series of three studies set out to explore the truth of two conflicting theories regarding the relationship between neuroticism and attitude toward Christianity. The first theory suggested that neurotic individuals were attracted to religion, or indeed that religion was an expression of neuroticism. The second theory suggested that religion promotes individual stability and reduces neurotic instability. In the first study in this series,[19] the relationship between attitude toward Christianity and the Junior Eysenck Personality Inventory neuroticism scale was explored among the sample of 1,088 year-ten and year-eleven pupils. At first there appeared to be a significant positive correlation between neuroticism and religion. Multiple regression analysis, however, demonstrated that this finding was entirely the by-product of the fact that females in the sample recorded higher scores on both the scale of attitude toward Christianity and the neuroticism scale. Once these sex differences had been taken into account, there was no significant correlation between neuroticism and religion.

The second study in this series set out to check this conclusion among the sample of 1,715 eleven- to seventeen-year-olds who completed the Junior Eysenck Personality Questionnaire.[20] Again, after controlling for sex differences, no significant correlation emerged between neuroticism and religiosity. The third study in this series employed *six* different measures of neuroticism among the same group of 177 fifteen- to sixteen-year-olds.[21] Again no significant correlation emerged between neuroticism and religion in relationship to any of the six indices. The findings from this series of studies is, therefore, clear-cut. Neuroticism and attitude toward Christianity are unrelated factors in general population studies.

However, in studies conducted among samples not representative of the general population, some rather different findings have emerged. One group of studies has explored the relationship between neuroticism and attitude toward Christianity among people who may be assumed to be particularly religious, both among clergy and among adult churchgoers.[22] In both cases a more positive attitude toward Christianity is related to lower neuroticism scores. In other words, it may be the case that, among practising Christians, mental stability promotes a greater surety of faith, or surety of faith promotes greater mental stability.

Another study has explored the relationship between neuroticism and attitude toward Christianity among a sample of 290 low-ability children in a residential home operated by a church-based organization.[23] In this sample, after controlling for sex, age and differences in intelligence, a significant positive correlation emerged between neuroticism and attitude toward Christianity. The authors of this study explain this finding in the following terms. They argue that, in this population, high neuroticism scores can be regarded as an indication of anxiety. On this account, anxiety would predispose the subjects to conform more to the prevailing social norms of the environment, which in a church-based residential school would mean accepting a higher level of religiosity.

Personality quadrants

Having examined the relationship between neuroticism and religion and between extraversion and religion separately, it is also necessary to check whether there is any interaction between these two personality dimensions. Some theories, for example, might suggest that high neuroticism could both accentuate the formation of a positive attitude toward Christianity among introverts and accentuate the inhibition of the formation of a positive attitude toward Christianity among extraverts. The analysis undertaken by Francis, Pearson and Kay among the sample of 1,088 year-ten and year-eleven pupils provided support for neither of these perspectives and confirmed that neuroticism was not implicated in shaping individual differences in attitude toward Christianity.[24]

Psychoticism

Another series of three studies set out to explore the theory that, within Eysenck's dimensional model of personality, it is psychoticism which is the dimension of personality fundamental to religiosity, in accordance with Eysenck's theory regarding conditioning and social attitudes. The first study in this series was conducted by Kay among 1,431 pupils in years seven, eight, nine and ten. These pupils completed the Francis scale of attitude toward Christianity together with the psychoticism scale of the Junior Eysenck Personality Questionnaire.[25] From these data, Kay found a significant negative correlation for boys in each of the four year groups, but no significant correlation for girls in any of the four groups. Since the theory does not predict a different pattern of relationships between religion and psychoticism among males and females, this finding was puzzling.

In the second study in this series, Francis and Pearson set out to test the view that the major problem with Kay's original study concerned his choice to use the Junior Eysenck Personality Questionnaire. Several commentators had already drawn attention to the poor psychometric properties of this scale, especially among girls, and in comparison with the adult scale. Consequently they asked a sample of 132 fifteen-year-olds to complete the Francis scale of attitude toward Christianity together with *both* the junior and adult forms of the psychoticism scale.[26] After taking into account sex differences by means of multiple regression, this study found the predicted negative correlation between attitude toward Christianity and the adult psychoticism scale, but no relationship between attitude toward Christianity and the junior psychoticism scale. These findings clearly suggest that Kay's earlier findings are more likely to imply criticism of the scale than criticism of the theory.

In the third study in this series, Francis administered both the adult and the junior forms of the psychoticism scale, together with the scale of attitude toward Christianity, to a much larger sample of 1,347 year-nine and year-ten pupils.[27] Among a sample of this size a significant negative correlation emerged between religion and both forms of the psychoticism scale. The inverse relationship between psychoticism and attitude toward Christianity is, therefore, now well established.

A final confirmation was given to the part played by impulsivity in shaping the negative correlation between psychoticism and attitude toward Christianity by a study conducted by Pearson, Francis and Lightbown.[28] This study gave close attention to the way in which different aspects of impulsivity related to attitude toward Christianity among a sample of 569 eleven- to seventeen-year-olds.

Lie scale

The relationship between attitude toward Christianity and lie-scale scores has also been explored by a series of three studies. The first study, conducted among 1,088 year-ten and year-eleven pupils, established the finding that there is a significant positive correlation between attitude toward Christianity and lie-scale scores.[29] The problem, then, is that of interpreting such a finding. In view of the different interpretations of lie scale scores by different groups of psychologists, this finding could imply that religious people are bigger liars, that they are more socially conformist, or that they lack insight into their true behaviour. The pattern of correlations between all the personality variables in this first study led to the conclusion that religious children tended to lack self-insight.

In view of the problematic nature of this conclusion, a second study replicated the analyses among a sample of 3,228 eleven- to sixteen-year-olds.[30] Once again the same conclusion emerged.

The third study took the conclusion much further by administering three forms of the lie scale, together with the Francis scale of attitude toward Christianity, to a sample of 191 fifteen- to sixteen-year-olds.[31] Since there were many more lie-scale items in their study, the analysis was able to distinguish between two different sets of lie-scale items. Only one of these two sets of items correlated significantly and positively with attitude toward Christianity, while the other set of items was uncorrelated with attitude toward Christianity. The conclusion drawn from this study is that religious adolescents are generally better behaved and that their higher score on the lie scales used in other studies is a result of their truthful reporting of their better behaviour. Paradoxically, the higher scores recorded by religious people on the lie scale may indicate that they are being more truthful.

Replications

Following these series of focused studies, other studies have generally confirmed the overall findings among different samples, including a study among fifteen- to sixteen-year-olds,[32] among eleven-year-olds,[33] among eleven- to sixteen-year-old girls in a single-sex school,[34] among female drug misusers[35] and among students in the UK.[36]

The most recent attempt to confirm the pattern of relationships between the Eysenckian dimensions of personality and attitude toward Christianity is a study conducted among four samples of undergraduate students: 378 students in the UK, 212 students in the USA, 255 students in Australia, and 231 students in Canada.[37] The correlation coefficients between the personality variables (extraversion, neuroticism, psychoticism and the lie scale) and attitude toward Christianity for the four samples separately are presented in table 7.1 in the appendices. In all four samples there is a significant negative correlation between psychoticism and attitude toward Christianity, while no relationship emerges between attitude toward Christianity and either neuroticism or extraversion.

Freudian theory

A short series of studies has explored the relationship between one aspect of the Freudian theory of personality and attitude toward Christianity and church attendance. Freudian theory explains religious ritual as a form of neurotic, obsessive behaviour. The studies reported here have concentrated on the distinction between obsessional traits and obsessional symptoms. The 'obsessional personality' is characterized by obsessional *traits* such as orderliness, rigidity, and overemphasis on hygiene and self-control, but the 'obsessional neurotic' is characterized by obsessional *symptoms* such as compulsive thoughts and impulses, indecision, guilt and ritualistic behaviour.[38] Findings based on a study of 108 female and forty-two male undergraduates recorded no significant association between church attendance and either obsessional traits or obsessional symptoms among women. Among men, by contrast, there was a significant association between church attendance and obsessional symptoms.[39]

When attention was shifted from behaviour to attitudes and, in a sample of 106 female and thirty-three male undergraduates, attitude toward Christianity was correlated with measures of obsessionality, significant positive associations were found between obsessional traits and attitude toward Christianity among both sexes, but not between attitude toward Christianity and obsessional symptoms.

Lewis regarded these findings as offering no empirical support for Freud's postulation of a genuine similarity between obsessional actions and religious practices or obsessional symptoms and religious attitudes.[40] Nevertheless the linkage between obsessional traits and attitude toward Christianity needs further exploration. One way of doing so would be to locate obsessionality within the broader Eysenckian framework of psychoticism, since impulsivity and obsessionality correlate negatively. The impulsive person does not exercise the rigid self-control so characteristic of the obsessive.[41]

Comment

This chapter has introduced two major psychological approaches to the description of personality. Concentrating specifically on theories advanced by Sigmund Freud and Hans Eysenck, we have then set out to test systematically hypotheses generated by these theories regarding the relationship between personality and religion. The studies designed to test these hypotheses have generated more confidence in the validity of Eysenck's approach than in the validity of Freud's approach.

Using Eysenck's theory, and the instruments developed to operationalize this theory, we have shown that the linkage between personality and attitude toward Christianity is well established and, although the levels of correlation are not high, they are significant both statistically and substantively. According to this theory, it is the personality dimension of psychoticism which is fundamental to individual differences in religiosity. At the same time, it is clear that according to the earlier definition of extraversion, which included a component of impulsivity, introverts may also emerge as more religious than extraverts.

In all this exploration, it is important to recall that personality dimensions *dispose* people to act in certain ways without forcing them to do so. Introverts are more likely to behave quietly, but they can act out of character. High psychoticism scorers are unlikely to do good deeds, but they may occasionally and impulsively do so. Neuroticism may tend to produce erratic behaviour, but does not always do so. The measurement of personality dimensions does not produce a deterministic model of human behaviour. The analogy is with certain abilities. Individuals with perfect pitch and good auditory memories may gravitate towards the music business, but there is no guarantee that they will do so. Their musical abilities may be used to detect birdsong or in mimicry.

It is usual to think of the personality dimensions as given and the attitude toward Christianity as less fundamental. Throughout this chapter the causal link has been assumed to be in the direction that starts from personality and leads to attitude toward Christianity. This assumption is justified on the grounds that individual differences in personality can be explained biologically and genetically and are consequently prior to individual differences in religiosity. Less extravert and less psychotic individuals will more probably find Christianity conducive to their way of thinking and feeling than those with personality profiles of a different sort. Yet, the causal pathway may be in the opposite direction. Theologically it makes sense to consider that Christianity has the potential for cultivating caring attitudes, removing or suppressing psychotic tendencies and changing individual lives. In this conceptualization personality may be dependent on attitude toward Christianity.

At the moment what is clear from the research data is that the drift from the churches during childhood and adolescence is more pronounced among the tough-minded than among the tender-minded, and may be more pronounced among the extraverts than among the introverts.

8
Science and religion

Introduction

One way to view science and religion is to see them as two ways of knowing. Religion has been characterized as the sort of knowing which emanates from revelation, from fixed unchanging truths, from a source outside the universe, from holy people and from sacred texts. Science has been characterized as the sort of knowing which emanates from observation and measurement, from experiment and testing, and from men and women trained in particular methods who read the universe like a book.

This comparison has led to a stereotypical contrast between the priest and the scientist. The priest, in vestments and standing at the altar steps holding a chalice, speaks to society with unquestioned authority on behalf of God. The priest, assisted by the serving church, promises society the blessing of God if it will obey the divine voice. The scientist, in a white coat and standing at the laboratory steps holding a test tube, speaks to society with unquestioned authority on behalf of the universe whose secrets have been wrested into the daylight. The scientist, assisted by the handmaiden of technology, promises society the blessings of nature if it will obey the voice of reason. The priest belongs to the superstitious past, while the scientist belongs to the liberated future.

This stereotypical contrast, of course, rests upon huge oversimplifications of the nature of both science and religion. Nevertheless, it is precisely this kind of stereotype which lies at the back of the very real conflict between *scientism* and *creationism*, and which may undermine the young person's ability to maintain a positive attitude toward Christianity alongside a positive attitude toward science.

Scientism is the view that absolute truth is obtainable through science and science alone.[1] The person who embraces scientism thinks that science will eventually gain complete control over the world and that nothing should be believed unless it can be proved scientifically. Scientific laws are founded on scientific facts and these are unalterable and absolutely proved. All the questions of human life should be approached scientifically, and whatever answer science gives to these questions must be correct. Human origins must be understood scientifically and without reference to any form of divine activity. What science cannot discover cannot be known.

Creationism is equally certain of its position.[2] Creationism is founded on a literal interpretation of the opening chapters of Genesis. This literalism leads to the view that the world was made by God in six twenty-four-hour days and that human beings were made on the last of these days and had no ancestry among other living beings. The world itself, by using calculations from the genealogies in Genesis, is roughly 6,000 years old, and Noah's flood affected the whole world with catastrophic effects that help to explain the extinction of dinosaurs. Creationism takes this literal interpretation and applies it to the data of modern science so that any presumption that the world is older than six thousand years, that the process of creation took longer than a week, that Noah's flood might have been local, or that human beings might have a common ancestor with other primates is fiercely rejected. Moreover, in its extreme form creationism argues that it, and it alone, offers the explanation of the origin of the world and of life which is compatible with true Christianity.

Scientism and creationism are both marked by their certainty. Scientism is a broader perspective and may be applied to any contentious issue. Creationism is narrower and stems from Genesis. In its dispute with scientism, creationism gives rise to 'creation science' which makes use of scientific methods to support the interpretation of Genesis which it holds to be correct. There can be no divergence between 'creation science' and creationism since, if there were, 'creation science' would become ordinary science.

The clash between scientism and creationism is inevitable since the former excludes the possibility of God's existence and the latter is predicated on God's existence. Since neither admits of probabilistic premises or conclusions, with the uncertainty inherent in probabilism, there is no room for co-existence.[3] If scientism is correct, creationism is incorrect, and *vice versa*.

Both scientism and creationism must be sharply distinguished from their counterparts: an interest in science and a belief that God is the creator.

A scale to measure *interest in science* may simply ask pupils if they find the subject interesting, but it may also ask whether they find studying science pleasurable or whether they think the world would benefit from more scientists. The commitment to science does not presuppose any particular *kind* of science. There may well be differences in the kinds of sciences preferred by boys and girls. Studies have shown that boys tend to prefer technological or mathematically based kinds of science and that girls prefer life sciences. But the point is that there is a genuine interest in and curiosity about one of the sciences.

The ensuing commitment to science, however, does not presuppose any special approach to science. There *may* be elements of scientism in a young person's approach, but this does not follow from the interest the individual feels. Interest in science does not presuppose that science is the only road to absolute truth. Scientism and interest in science are two conceptually independent variables.

A belief that God is the creator of the world and of human life need have no implications for the course of the creative process. This can be shown by the way different theistic religions give somewhat different accounts of the origins of the world and of human life. God may create the world in one day, or in six, or six epochs, or in thousands of years. Genesis may be read literally or metaphorically, or metaphorically in some places and literally in others. For example the six days of creation in Genesis 1 may be seen as a stylistic account where the first day matches the fourth and the second matches the fifth. The absence of the sun from the created order till the fourth day suggests that the first three days, at any rate, are not to be taken as periods of twenty-four hours, and the repetition of the creation of Adam and Eve in chapters 1 and 2 of Genesis suggests that the opening chapter may be an abbreviated summary of what is given in detail later.[4] These are matters of interpretation and dispute. Creationism depends on reading the text in a particular way, whereas a belief in God as creator holds constant this one article of faith but remains undogmatic on others.

So, just as an interest in science may or may not lead to scientism, so an acceptance of Christianity may or may not lead to creationism. Just as scientism tends to consider its approach to science is exclusively correct, so creationism tends to consider its approach to Christianity is exclusively correct. But how strong these tendencies are remains to be found out.

Reich's model

One way of thinking about the potential interaction between scientism and creationism in detail is by a stage-related or level-related model. One such model is advanced by Helmut Reich, who examined young people's understanding of a problem for which competing explanatory theories were offered.[5] At the first level, young people stated that either the one theory or the other theory was correct. At the second level, there was some examination of the possibility that both theories might be correct. At the third level, both theories are regarded as necessary for an adequate description. At the fourth level, the two theories are immediately understood as complementary and the mutuality of their relationship is discussed. At the fifth level, the problem is considered afresh from basic principles and a sophisticated synopsis of logically possible relationships is considered and presented.

In the small samples used to test these levels, about 33 per cent of eleven- to fourteen-year-olds functioned at the second level. A further 33 per cent of eleven- to fourteen-year-olds were at the third level. The fourth level is found among about 80 per cent of twenty-one- to twenty-five-year-olds. What this suggests is that the ability to regard apparently contradictory theories as compatible explanations grows with age. It suggests that most young people aged below eleven years of age are *intellectually unable* to regard two apparently contradictory theories as both being true. But by the time young people reach about fourteen years of age, about a third would be able to take the view that both theories are *necessary* for an adequate decision.

The shift between levels two and three is greater than any of the other shifts in level. Reich suggests that at first young people dismiss one theory because they feel it is incompatible with the other, but not because the theory they dismiss is full of intrinsic weaknesses. That this must be the case is shown by their acceptance of the validity of the theory they previously dismissed at the next level. The third level, therefore, allows for both theories to be held in the mind at once without dissonance. All the other shifts from level three upwards explore the relationships between the theories.

Scientism and creationism appear to function at the first level. Each rules out the opposing theory. When Reich re-interviewed his young people in a follow-up study he was interested to discover that most of the sample had moved to a different level, but one young person, who had remained at the same level, had the view that there exists only one kind of truth, and this is factual truth. The only question this young man was interested in asking about the Book of Job, for example, was, 'Did this really happen?' He was not interested in any questions about the suffering of the innocent. A failure to move beyond the first level in the model will occur if people retain an essentially simple world view, one in which only one type of variable is allowed.

Implications for attitude toward Christianity

Attitude toward Christianity exists as a variable quite distinct from creationism and scientism. A positive attitude toward Christianity indicates a generally favourable attitude toward Christianity as a whole, but not to any particular aspect, doctrine or historical feature of Christianity. A positive attitude toward Christianity can exist with creationism or without creationism, since doctrines of creation are only one aspect of the sum total of Christian doctrines. A positive attitude toward Christianity also exists as a variable quite distinct from interest in science. Young people may have a positive or negative attitude toward both science and Christianity, or a negative attitude toward one and a positive attitude toward the other. This is especially so for pupils who appreciate the complementarity of theories from different intellectual domains.

A series of studies was mounted to explore the relationship between the variables under discussion and two key hypotheses were generated.

The first hypothesis argues that the strength of creationism is that it offers a certain and authoritative answer to the question of origins. If this hypothesis is correct, young people who perceive Christianity as necessarily involving creationism are likely to hold a more positive attitude toward Christianity than those who do not perceive Christianity in this way.

The second hypothesis argues that creationism serves to bring science and religion into closer and clearer conflict in the adolescent mind. On this analysis, the weakness of creationism is that it offers a controversial view of origins which can be called into question alongside fresh scientific data. If this hypothesis is correct, young people who perceive Christianity as necessarily involving creationism are likely to hold a less positive attitude toward Christianity than those who do not perceive Christianity in this way.

Findings

In the first study in this series, a questionnaire was completed by 624 form-six students aged between sixteen and twenty-four years in Kenya.[6] The mean age of these students was 18·9 years. The students described themselves as belonging to the Christian religion and they attended ten secondary schools.

The questionnaire included four main instruments. The first instrument was the Francis scale of attitude toward Christianity. The second instrument was a five-item Likert scale designed to measure scientism. Its items were: 'science will eventually give us complete control over the world', 'theories in science can be proved to be definitely true', 'the laws of science will never change', 'theories in science are proved with absolute certainty' and 'nothing should be believed unless it can be proved scientifically.'

The third instrument was a four-item Likert scale designed to measure the extent to which Christianity was thought to involve creationism. The four items were, 'Christians believe the whole bible is historically accurate', 'true Christians do not believe Darwin's theory of evolution', 'all church leaders teach there are no errors in the bible' and 'true Christians believe the universe was made in six days of twenty-four hours each.'

The fourth instrument was a four-item scale of religious behaviour, combining items concerned with attending Christian meetings in school, church attendance during school holidays, personal prayer and personal bible reading. The questionnaire also included background variables dealing with the students' level of academic achievement, subjects studied at school, religious behaviour, parental church attendance, parental socio-economic status, education and sex.

All four instruments achieved satisfactory alpha coefficients. For scientism the alpha coefficient was 0·62; for perception of Christianity as necessarily involving creationism the alpha coefficient was 0·61; for religious behaviour the alpha coefficient was 0·70; and for attitude toward Christianity the alpha coefficient was 0·94.

The path model constructed to explore the interrelationships between the variables in this study shows three things relevant to the current discussion. First, after controlling for sex, parental education, parental church attendance, academic achievement, study of religion and study of science in forms five and six, the path model shows that the perception that Christianity necessarily involves creationism has no impact either on religious behaviour or on attitude toward Christianity. Second, after controlling for the same background variables, the path model shows that scientism makes a negative impact both on religious behaviour and on attitude toward Christianity. Third, after controlling for background variables, the path model shows that academic achievement, as measured by the Kenya Certificate of Education, is negatively related to scientism. Less able pupils, therefore, adopt scientism and hold less positive attitude toward Christianity.

In the second study in this series, a partial replication of the Kenyan study was carried out in Scotland.[7] A questionnaire was completed by 729 secondary-school pupils aged sixteen years and over in twelve schools in Scotland. There were 314 males and 415 females in the sample.

The questionnaire employed in Scotland included the scales and many of the background variables used in the Kenyan study. In addition, this study included two additional instruments. The first instrument was a four-item scale exploring the pupils' personal interest in science. The items here were, 'I do not have much interest in science', 'more scientists are urgently needed', 'studying science gives me great pleasure' and 'science has done a lot of harm.' The second instrument was a five-item scale exploring parental encouragement to go to church, to say prayers, to say grace before meals, to believe in God and to follow Jesus. Again all the scales showed satisfactory alpha coefficients. For scientism the alpha coefficient was 0·56; for perception of Christianity as necessarily involving creationism the alpha coefficient was 0·63; for interest in science the alpha coefficient was 0·70; for parental encouragement the alpha coefficient was 0·86; and for attitude toward Christianity the alpha coefficient was 0·97.

The correlation matrix of all the variables used in the path model is presented in table 8.1 in the appendices. The whole matrix is not discussed here, but the correlation between the perception that Christianity necessarily involves creationism and attitude toward Christianity was negative and significant at the 0·001 level.

The relationship between parental social status and parental church attendance was in line with that found in other studies. In other words more frequent church attendance was found among parents of higher social status. Parents who attended church tended to encourage their children to do so, and this led to the child's church attendance. All this is clearly demonstrated by the path model in figure 8.1 in the appendices.

Scientism was the first attitudinal variable to be entered into the model, after taking into account sex, father's occupation, mother's occupation, father's church attendance, mother's church attendance, parental encouragement and personal church attendance. The model shows that pupils' personal church attendance and parental encouragement to attend church are the most important predictors of scores on the index of scientism. Pupils who never attend church and receive no parental encouragement to do so are those most likely to adopt the perspective of scientism. Or, putting this the other way, pupils who attend church, and who are encouraged to do so, are those least likely to adopt the perspective of scientism.

Perception of Christianity as necessarily involving creationism was entered into the model next. The model shows that pupils who adopt the perspective of scientism are those most likely to think of Christianity as involving creationism. The model also shows that, after taking scientism into account, neither personal nor parental church attendance convey any further predictive information about the perception that Christianity involves creationism. Scientism is, therefore, a powerful predictive variable in its own right.

Interest in science was the third attitudinal variable to be entered into the model. The model shows that pupils' interest in science is unrelated to their own church attendance or the encouragement and example of their parents. Churchgoing young people may or may not be interested in science. Their churchgoing does not predispose them one way or the other toward science. But the significant negative path leading from creationism to interest in science indicates that pupils who believe that Christianity necessarily involves creationism tend to show less interest in science. The young creationist is unlikely to be a budding scientist.

Attitude toward Christianity was placed in the model last. The model shows that there is no direct influence on attitude toward Christianity from either the perception that Christianity involves creationism or from interest in science. According to this study among sixteen- to eighteen-year-olds, young people who are creationist and other young people who are not creationist may have equally favourable attitude toward Christianity. Likewise young people who are interested in science or who are uninterested in science may have equally favourable attitude toward Christianity.

The variable which *does* influence attitude toward Christianity in this model is scientism. Here pupils who adopt the perspective of scientism are less likely to adopt a favourable attitude toward Christianity. This finding is supported by the results of the Kenyan study.

A further stage of analysis required a separate regression calculation to explore the interactive effect on attitude toward Christianity of creationism and interest in science after controlling for sex, church attendance and parental encouragement. The purpose of this step was to discover whether pupils who hold the view that Christianity necessarily involves creationism are likely to experience greater difficulty in combining a positive attitude toward science and a positive attitude toward Christianity. The figures confirmed that creationist pupils find it difficult to be interested in science *and* to take a favourable view of Christianity. Or putting this another way, a creationist view of Christianity, combined with a positive attitude toward Christianity, is detrimental to an interest in science.

A second interactive analysis explored the effects of creationism and interest in science as before but also after taking into account the interactive effect of scientism and interest in science on attitude toward Christianity. The purpose of this step was to discover if pupils with an orientation toward scientism who felt a high interest in science might also hold a positive attitude toward Christianity. What the regression equation showed was that it was difficult for pupils with an orientation toward scientism and a high interest in science to hold a positive attitude toward Christianity. The second interactive term was statistically significant and more significant than the first one.

The third study in this series, also conducted in Scotland, focused on attitude toward Christianity and the perception that Christianity necessarily involves creationism.[8] This study made use of a much larger sample of pupils and a wider age range than the two previous studies. The questionnaire was completed by 5,917 pupils attending Roman Catholic and non-denominational state-maintained secondary schools in Dundee. The sample comprised 3,058 young people between the ages of eleven and thirteen, 2,371 young people between the ages of fourteen and fifteen, and 488 young people between the ages of sixteen and seventeen.

The Francis scale of attitude toward Christianity was used together with other scales. The same index of perception of Christianity as necessarily involving creationism was provided by the four-item Likert scale used in previous studies. This scale functioned reliably and validly among secondary-school pupils in Scotland throughout the age range included in the study.

In this study separate analyses were conducted among the three separate groups of eleven- to thirteen-year-olds, fourteen- to fifteen-year-olds and sixteen- to seventeen-year-olds, in order to test whether the same pattern of relationships between creationism and attitude toward Christianity held true among the different age groups, or whether a change took place in this pattern with age. The correlation coefficients between attitude toward Christianity, the view that Christianity necessarily involves creationism, and sex, for the three age groups separately are presented in table 8.2 in the appendices.

The figures presented in this table demonstrate that, throughout the age range, there is a consistent positive correlation between sex and attitude toward Christianity, confirming the general finding that females record a more positive attitude toward Christianity than males during childhood and adolescence as well as adulthood. Among the youngest age group there is a very small significant negative correlation between sex and the view that Christianity necessarily involves creationism, but no significant relationship among the older age groups. This lack of relationship between sex and the view that Christianity necessarily involves creationism is consistent with the findings of Fulljames and Francis among sixth-form students in Kenya. The key finding of this table, however, concerns the relationship between attitude toward Christianity and the view that Christianity necessarily involves creationism. While this view is associated with a positive attitude toward Christianity among eleven- to thirteen-year-olds, it is associated with a negative attitude toward Christianity among sixteen- to seventeen-year-olds. This latter coefficient is consistent with the earlier Scottish study.

Comment

The large third study resolves a puzzle set by the earlier two studies. Both of the two conflicting hypotheses regarding the nature of the relationship between the view that Christianity necessarily involves creationism and adolescent attitude toward Christianity are supported by the data, but among different age groups. Among eleven- to thirteen-year-olds, pupils who perceive Christianity as offering clear and unambiguous teaching on issues like creation hold a more positive attitude toward Christianity than those who do not perceive Christianity in this way. At this stage certainty appears to be attractive. Among sixteen- to seventeen-year-olds, however, pupils who perceive Christianity as necessarily involving creationism hold a less positive attitude toward Christianity than pupils who do not perceive Christianity as necessarily involving creationism. At this stage controversial views of origins appear to be called into question alongside fresh scientific data.

This changing relationship between the view that Christianity necessarily involves creationism and attitude toward Christianity during the age span from eleven to seventeen years is consistent with Reich's theory regarding the development of complementarity in the religious thinking of young people. It is reasonable to suppose that eleven- to thirteen-year-olds are unable to separate creationist Christianity from conventional Christianity. Creationist Christianity and conventional Christianity operate as two theories, one of which must be true. Those who take a positive attitude toward Christianity are inclined to take a positive attitude toward creationism. Pupils above sixteen years of age, however, can see that creationist Christianity and conventional Christianity are distinct, but that both may be true in some sense. A positive attitude toward Christianity may co-exist with creationism as easily as with conventional Christianity. Because creationism runs contrary to the consensus of mainstream science, however, it is less easy for young people to hold it. Those who are favourable to Christianity therefore opt for the conventional, non-creationist position.

The implication of this finding for the church or for the teaching of Christianity within schools is complex. If Christianity were deliberately presented as being inevitably creationist to young children who, when they were older, were taught that what they had previously been told was untrue, it is difficult to believe that positive attitude toward Christianity would survive intact. The only real option is to present the elements that creationism and conventional Christianity have in common so that, when they are older, pupils can make a painless choice between them or hold both theories in tension as true in their own way. What creationism and conventional Christianity have in common is their belief in God as the creator and in the special position of human beings in the universe.

One of the recommendations drawn from the Kenyan study was that there is a need in churches and in school curricula for attention to be given to the nature of science. This cuts both ways. In the Kenyan situation pupils who have studied science at the upper end of secondary education are less likely to embrace scientism. But it is also the case that pupils whose mothers attend church regularly are less likely to study science. If the churches were to take a more favourable stance toward science, more churchgoing young people would be inclined to pursue science options in school.

Following on from this recommendation was the recognition that the Kenyan churches weighted their own teaching in a creationist direction. Consequently their young people were being presented with a difficult dilemma. Those who chose science were likely to endanger their faith. If the Kenyan churches make their own teaching more synoptic on the matter of origins, they are likely to serve their young people better.

In Scotland alternative views of origins are already prominent in Christian education and in public debate. The problem arises from the tunnel vision caused by scientism. Scientism excludes all other truth possibilities and consequently depresses or prevents the development of a positive attitude toward Christianity. The Scottish data show that schools need to broaden their pupils' understanding of the scientific enterprise, to show them the sorts of problems scientific methods are best able to handle and those which lie outside science's reach. Part of the problem rests with the misapprehension scientism generates about the nature of Christian belief concerning origins. Scientism presumes Christianity is creationist, and therefore dismisses it. Scientism is unable to see how Christians hold variant positions on origins and that not all of these are incompatible with the pursuit of science.

The Scottish data show that those pupils least likely to take a scientistic stance are those who attend church. The mechanism by which scientism is averted by church attendance is not clear. Clearly scientism's stress on scientific proof as the only valid kind of proof and its simplistic belief that science will give human beings complete control over the world are not going to commend themselves to thoughtful churchgoers. Churchgoers will see other forms of proof, like the sort that is demanded in a court of law and which is not strictly scientific, as appropriate to their beliefs. They will also find completely unrealistic the notion that human beings, through science, will subdue the world. They will be aware of the terrible effects of science, in terms of weapons of mass destruction and industrial waste, that appear to verify the traditional religious doctrines of human sinfulness and fallibility.

We may also have a clue to the nature of scientism because it is a fundamentally male phenomenon (as evidenced by its significant negative correlation with sex in both the Scottish and Kenyan samples). In a large-scale study of English and Welsh school children aged between thirteen and fifteen Francis and Kay found girls held religious positions more inclusively than boys.[9] Other writers exploring sex differences comment on a form of *subjective knowledge* that attracts young women in their teens because it is intuitive and not dependent on external authorities.[10] Boys, then, are often non-intuitive and exclusive in their epistemological stance, and so find scientism psychologically comfortable.

Scientism and interest in science are unconnected in the path model presented in figure 10.1. This also gives a clue about the nature of scientism. If it were correlated with an interest in science, it would be reasonable to suppose that it was linked with intellectual curiosity. But the independence of an interest in science from scientism points to the ideological nature of scientism. It is closed, rather than open-ended, not enlivened or enlarged by further scientific information and not a stimulus to scientific achievement or quest.

On the religious side, interest in science is unconnected with church attendance. Interest in science is also unconnected with attitude toward Christianity, after taking into account background variables. Interest in science is neither suppressed by religiosity nor encouraged by it. Nor does interest in science suppress or encourage a favourable attitude toward Christianity. We are left with the conclusion that interest in science and attitude toward Christianity are not seen by teenagers as competing or contradictory theories that can only be held together once complementary thinking is possible.

But the situation is quite different where a creationist position is adopted. In such circumstances a positive attitude toward Christianity will work against an interest in science. In essence, then, scientism is detrimental to attitude toward Christianity and creationism is detrimental to an interest in science. The two closed positions, scientism and creationism, have implications for the open variables with which they may be associated. What is alarming about this finding is that both the path models on which it is based recruit their data from samples where, in Reich's terms, young people are capable of complementary thinking. If Reich's theory is generally correct, this finding can only be explained by supposing that complementarity is unattainable where two theories define themselves against each other. Creationism and scientism cannot be complementary, even at level three, because they are founded on contradictory predicates.

We have seen that a switch-over takes place between attitude toward Christianity and creationism as pupils move through their teens. The certainties of creationism sit with a positive attitude toward Christianity for pupils in their low teens, but not for pupils in their high teens. If interest in science operates in a way analogous to an attitude scale, it may be that a similar switch-over takes place. Scientism would then be attractive to younger pupils but less attractive to older pupils. This is a matter for further research. Nevertheless, there are some pupils who *do* combine a high interest in science with scientism, and these pupils show a very negative attitude toward Christianity (as the second interactive equation mentioned above shows). We may speculate that, for those relatively few pupils who combine scientism and an interest in science (and this must be a small number since the overall correlation between scientism and interest in science is not significant),[11] interest in science is used by scientism to fuel a greater rejection of Christianity. The reason for this rejection must be the same as before: scientism is predisposed to assume that Christianity involves creationism.

Finally, the information generated by these three studies gives an insight into the psychological factors that help to shape young people's changing ideas about science and religion. These studies do not, and are not intended to, adjudicate on questions of whether scientism or creationism are true, or can both be true, or are both false. Such questions belong to an altogether different area of discourse.

9

Religious experience

Introduction

This chapter discusses studies concerned with two understandings of religious experience. The first understanding of religious experience is very broad and builds on the young person's own interpretation of what counts as religious experience. The second understanding of religious experience is much narrower and more focused. This understanding is specifically concerned with what is generally known as religious conversion.

The psychological study of religious experience in general or religious conversion in particular faces the danger of reductionism, the danger that what is being described will be turned into something less than itself. The religious conversion becomes 'nothing but' an emotional decision and the religious experience becomes 'nothing but' a heightened sense of awareness caused by adrenaline or other stimulants. The danger is that an objective examination of religious conversion or religious experience will fail to match the subjective nature of the data necessarily implicated in the study. But even if we grant that subjective experience remains elusive, objective measures can still provide its correlates. By this we mean that objective methods may provide measures of variables *associated* with religious conversion and religious experience.

We have made use of the Francis scale of attitude toward Christianity and tested the attitude of young people who have undergone a religious conversion or who have claimed a religious experience. Our concern, then, has not been with understanding or interpreting religious conversions or religious experiences directly, but with the attitudes that might be generated by them.

Religious experience

At one level the study of religious experience has proved enormously difficult. To begin with, the idea of experience itself is so large and vague. Where does experience end? What part of human consciousness is not in some way open to experience? Then if we turn to the notion of 'religion', the same problems also arise. What part of life is not potentially capable of religious interpretation? Anything which happens may be seen as an answer to prayer or a source of religious insight. For these reasons, it is usual for research projects concerned with religious experience to avoid attempts at definitions of religion and experience.[1] Instead, the respondents are invited to respond in their own way to the broad terms used in the questionnaire. The crucial issue concerns the way in which the question is phrased.

Research projects which ask people if they have had a religious experience normally find that sensible and meaningful answers can be given. There is evidence that questionnaires addressed to non-specialist populations will function quite satisfactorily and elicit meaningful data; the consistency of survey results points in this direction. The same questionnaires addressed to more academic or philosophically trained populations may be returned with puzzlement and requests for greater clarity.[2] The studies reported here were directed entirely at general populations.

The classic question now used in surveys concerned with religious experience was developed by Alasdair Hardy, founder of the Religious Experience Research Unit in Oxford. Hardy asked, 'Have you ever been aware of or influenced by a presence or power, whether you call it God or not, which is different from your everyday self?'[3] Hardy's early training was as a biologist and he viewed religious experience as a rare species of animal. The first step in the process was to find it, study its dimensions, observe its geographical distribution and then to try to relate it to other entities of the same kind. Hardy's question elicited over 3,000 reports of religious experiences that were sent to him in response to an advertisement. These replies were classified into higher or lower levels, but they affirmed the presence of transcendent reality and a sense of personal relationship with this. Many of the experiences had taken place unexpectedly, and in the case of many respondents, many years before, and their results had been almost entirely beneficial. They conveyed a sense of completeness, peace, security, love, happiness, and often had directly religious connotations, sometimes growing out of memories of childhood. People who had had such experiences were glad to recall them because they had often been turning points in their inner life. Many of the experiences collected by Hardy have been incorporated into the reports written by Edward Robinson.[4]

Subsequently Hardy's question was employed by David Hay in a series of studies. On the basis of answers to Hardy's question, Hay was able to show how often people admitted to an experience which was literally extraordinary.[5]

Hay made use of Gallup Poll in 1985 to survey opinion in Britain systematically and found that 33 per cent of respondents answered 'yes' to Hardy's question. As many as 6 per cent said that they were aware of the presence or power 'all the time', and 10 per cent said they had been aware 'several times'. When responses in Britain and the United States were compared, using the slightly different question, 'Have you ever felt as though you were very close to a powerful spiritual force that seemed to lift you out of yourself?' the percentages were very similar: 31 per cent said 'yes' in Britain and 35 per cent said 'yes' in the United States.

A representative sample of 1,000 people living near San Francisco showed that 39 per cent affirmed an experience of feeling 'in harmony with the universe'.[6] In another survey about half of those who claimed mystical experiences felt great peace. In a different study, about half claimed that their experience was sacred. In a smaller study of a different kind those who claimed mystical experiences were asked for a description and, when these open-ended replies were analysed, only a small number were found to be mystical according to strict criteria of being associated with timelessness and a distorted spatial awareness. Indeed 12 per cent wrote about psychic experiences and another 12 per cent wrote about feelings of empathy and faith.[7] What these analyses show is that mystical experiences are, by their nature, hard to pin down and that what one person may call mystical another person may call by another name.

Further analysis of Hay's figures showed that women were more likely than men to report general religious experiences: 41 per cent of women in Britain, compared with 31 per cent of men, replied affirmatively to Hardy's question. When the incidence of reported experiences was broken down by age, there were generally more frequent positive responses among older people.

As many as 43 per cent in the fifty-five to sixty-four age group and 47 per cent in the sixty-five-plus age group replied 'yes' to Hardy's question. Only 29 per cent of those aged in the sixteen to twenty-four age group could agree with them. Such a difference, of course, may mean that the young are less religious than older people, or it may imply that many of the experiences reported occur sometime after the age of twenty-four.

When Hay's figures were analysed by reference to class, middle-class and upper-middle-class respondents were more likely than skilled and unskilled working-class respondents to say 'yes' to Hardy's question. Whereas 32 per cent of unskilled labourers reported religious experience, the figure for middle-class respondents was 49 per cent and for upper-middle-class respondents 47 per cent. The compatibility between the profiles of church attendance and the reporting of religious experience is clear-cut. In both instances, the sex bias is towards women and the class bias is toward the upper end of the scale.

This generalization may be caveated by Hood's studies, which indicate that non-religious mystical experiences may be found among non-church attenders and religious mystical experiences among church attenders. The effect of this distribution is to make occasional church attenders those least likely to claim mystical experience.[8] Nevertheless, the line between a purely mystical experience and generally religious experience must be difficult to draw. Many religious experiences may have mystical elements, and many mystical experiences may have religious meaning. And, in any event, how should an experience of answered prayer be classified? Is glossolalia mystical or not? What sort of attribution should be given to a sense of divine guidance? Particularly within the context of ordinary church services it is reasonable to expect that the line between mysticism and religion might be blurred and that the only thing respondents might be able to say about their experience was that it was in some way religious. In other words, the *context* of the experience would help define its *meaning*.

Conversion experiences

Conversion has been the target of psychological research at least since the end of the nineteenth century. Religious revivals were led both by Dwight Moody and by Charles Finney and were important among American Protestants. They made a considerable impact on American national life and, in the 1930s, supported the legislation of the Prohibition era, when drinking alcohol was banned. The kind of conversion most studied was that by which a man or woman spoke about being 'born again' and becoming a 'real' Christian.

The investigation of conversion was made by reference to personal documents, interviews and questionnaire-based surveys. Although there were theological objections to the scrutiny of what was held to be a divine work of grace, most of those who investigated religion made a point of arguing that their questions did not invalidate conversion or cast aspersions on its reality or divine origin. They saw their work as uncovering the natural accompaniments of a process which could be interpreted as being more than natural. Even so, more recent writers have felt compelled to argue for the independence of religious experience and the truth of the doctrine it is sometimes used to validate.[9] Thus for those who are converted, the experience validates the doctrine; for the empirical investigator the doctrine and the experience do not bear on each other's truth claims; and for some philosophers the experience cannot validate the truth claims of its doctrines.

Data collected by Starbuck at the end of the nineteenth century and subsequently confirmed in other surveys had shown that conversion tended to occur most frequently in adolescence[10] and was often preceded by intense feelings of guilt. Hall connected conversion with the onset of sexual maturity.[11] The role of guilt, indeed, in the process of conversion was highlighted by James in *The Varieties of Religious Experience*. He distinguished between the sick soul and the healthy-minded soul.

According to James, the sick soul was prone to morbidity, to a magnification of its own wickedness and the divided mind produced by constant unease. When the sick soul was converted the result was instantaneous and could be timed precisely. James gave several examples from the writings of men who had felt wretched and prayed, sometimes on their own and sometimes in the company of others, and immediately renounced their past lives and felt a sense of joy and peace which never left them. Their conversion was an experience which underlined the truth of evangelical theology. The healthy-minded soul, by contrast, was 'once born' and his or her religious life often stemmed from childhood without any serious interruption or questioning. In the healthy-minded soul, conversion was slow and undramatic, if it took place at all. In many instances the healthy-minded could remember no time when they did not believe. They went through no doubts or self-hatred or miserable guilt. They were constantly assured of God's love. Their theology was predominantly more liberal and their salvation was not, as in the case of their sick-souled contemporaries, by the surrender of their old selves but by relaxation into the truths they had always believed.

In essence, then, James related two kinds of conversion to two kinds of personality. His explanation of the more sudden and dramatic conversion depended on the work of the subconscious or subliminal mind, and the conversion's benefit to the individual resulted from an integration of personality. The divided life was psychologically united. Inner energies which had, till that moment, been locked against each other, were released. The healthy-minded conversion took place more slowly. It resulted from an active search for meaning and purpose rather than a perpetual sense of condemnation. It is illustrated by the Lutheran idea of accepting justification from sin or the Wesleyan idea of free grace.[12] It released the self from the constant effort of self-justification and might identify the self with Christ. There was usually no great emotional crisis, because the thrust of the search had been cognitive and the gradualness of the process resulted in a deepening of faith rather than a discovery of it.

In terms of frequency, timing and nature, studies disagree about whether sudden conversions are more or less common than gradual conversions. If sudden conversions are subdivided into those which are precipitated by a *definite crisis* and those which were triggered by an *emotional stimulus*, then the disagreement centres round the crisis conversions. Figures agree that the emotional-stimulus kind of conversion takes place in about a third of cases. Some findings, however, suggest that crisis experiences occur only in about 6 per cent of cases, but others suggest that they also account for about a third of conversions. The gradual conversions are estimated as taking place in between 30 per cent and 66 per cent of cases.[13] Because of the disagreement in these figures the other generalizations about conversions must be taken with caution. Briefly, however, sudden conversions tend to be found in middle or late adolescence while gradual conversions were found in late adolescence or early adulthood. Sudden conversions are often emotional, gradual conversions tend to be intellectual; sudden conversions result from stern theologies and gradual conversions from compassionate theologies.[14]

Conversions as changes in attitude

The model of conversion suggested by James and accepted, with modifications, by many other psychologists has centred on changes in the self. In some instances the divided self is united and in others the self takes on new aims and values. Coe speaks of 'self realization within a social medium', a new expression of the self in a new social setting, a religious setting.[15] Grensted speaks of 'the impulse to wholeness', a resolution of conflicts between the conscious and the subconscious that would fit either Freudian or Jungian approaches to transformations of the self.[16]

Yet the psychology of the self may be related to the psychology of attitude measurement. This is for two reasons. First, attitudes by definition express an emotionally toned evaluation of beliefs. The process of evaluation makes use of information, and this implies that people may hold an attitude about almost anything they have information on and can evaluate. Yet the process of evaluation, even if it is emotionally toned, allows both an almost infinite regress and an almost infinite set of referents. The regress is caused by the possibility of evaluating evaluations while the size of the set of referents must be coterminous with the universe of meaning. In practical terms, then, the evaluation process which contributes to forming attitudes is likely to prevent the holding of *contradictory* attitudes. Anyone who holds contradictory attitudes may be viewed as having a divided self.

This drive toward consistency has been explored in detail and with ingenuity by Leon Festinger in his theory of cognitive dissonance.[17] The theory states that individuals function to reduce the incompatibility between elements in their thinking. But the theory also suggests that, if someone were asked to do something contrary to his or her beliefs, the person would tend to move more in the direction of those contrary beliefs or attitudes if the reward for doing so were small. The person would be unable to justify the dissonant act to himself or herself without a measure of acceptance of the hitherto rejected belief or attitude. But, if the reward were large, the effect would be the reverse because the size of the reward would justify the behaviour. The large reward would of itself reduce the sense of dissonance.

The theory does not explain conversion, but it does show how a switch-over between consonance and dissonance may take place. For example, family church attendance would be less dissonant to a teenager if he or she adopted a positive attitude toward Christianity.

Second, attitudes need not refer to the external world, they may also refer to the inner world, to the world of thoughts and emotions about which beliefs may be held and evaluations may be made. This being so, beliefs about the self will lead to attitudes about the self. The sense of self-condemnation or guilt which is often a precursor to sudden conversion may be understood as an attitude toward the self. The sense of well-being following conversion may be understood as another attitude toward the self.

When studies are made to discover which attitudes are most resistant to change, it is found that those attitudes that relate most to the self are most fixed. One conceptual scheme envisages the division of beliefs into central and peripheral ones (the central ones deeply involve the self or ego). Brainwashing techniques attack the self and focus on the repudiation of the old self and the embracing of the new self.[18] Clearly, once the self changes, the evaluations carried out by the self will also change. Once the self changes, all attitudes will be revised.

In summary, we may expect that changes to the concept of the self will also change many attitudes. We may also expect that changes in attitudes only indirectly related to the self may also, in some circumstances, have the effect of changing the self. Changes to the self are bound to result in dramatic changes throughout the whole personality system, and may be related to sudden conversions. Changes to attitudes on the periphery of the personality system may be related to gradual conversions. The net results of both sorts of change, however, are in the long run likely to be similar.

The relationship between religious experience and moral judgements is problematic. If we take a Piagetian view of moral judgements, there is little reason to suppose that religious experiences, in the short term, will affect either the mental maturation or the social relationships on which morality depends. In the long term we may expect that religious experiences, particularly conversion experiences, may lead to church attendance, or increased church attendance, and that this may make an impact on the way moral judgements are made. The problem of predicting what influence experiences will have on moral judgements is made more acute by the width of experiences which might be relevant. The death of a friend might be counted as, in some sense, a religious experience, and such an experience might affect moral opinions. If, for instance, the friend died of AIDS, this might have an effect on one's view of drug-taking or sexual promiscuity. If, on the other hand, an individual had a religious experience of the love of God or of harmony with nature, this might make him or her more willing to accept all kinds of human behaviour, even those which are traditionally culpable. The experience, depending on its nature, could therefore reinforce or loosen moral strictures.

Findings

The first study concerned with the relationship between religious experience and attitude toward Christianity was conducted among a sample of 1,177 pupils in years ten, eleven and twelve (aged fifteen to seventeen years old), from ten Protestant and ten Catholic schools in Northern Ireland. These pupils completed a detailed questionnaire containing the Francis scale of attitude toward Christianity and a ten-item Likert scale of Christian moral values.[19] This scale included items referring to gambling, drinking alcohol, drunkenness, stealing, drug-taking, sexual intercourse before marriage, abortion, artificial birth control, suicide and divorce. In addition the questionnaire included background variables and a question about religious experience. This question asked pupils whether they had 'ever had an experience of God, for example, his presence or his help or anything else'. Responses to this question indicated that such experiences were claimed by 26 per cent of the Protestant boys, 38 per cent of the Protestant girls, 34 per cent of the Catholic boys and 56 per cent of the Catholic girls.

The correlation matrix, showing the relationships between religious experience, belief in God, personal prayer, church attendance, Christian moral values and attitude toward Christianity, is presented in table 9.1 of the appendices. The figures in this table demonstrate that every correlation within the matrix is statistically significant at the 0·001 level. The figures also show that religious experience correlates positively with sex, indicating that girls more than boys are likely to report having had a religious experience, that those who report a religious experience are more likely to record a positive attitude toward Christianity, that there is a significant correlation between religious experience and the holding of traditional Christian moral values, and that church attendance, personal prayer and belief in God are all also significantly related to religious experience.

When multiple regression analysis was performed, and the effects of sex, church attendance, personal prayer and belief in God were taken into account by inserting them as a block into the equation first, religious experience still showed a significant and positive correlation with attitude toward Christianity. Religious experience contributed a significant and positive amount of variance over and above that contributed by the other variables. This finding is consistent with the view that the recognition and acknowledgement of a religious experience promotes the development of a more favourable attitude toward Christianity.

When the scale of traditional moral values was examined in the same way, it was found that, after sex, church attendance, personal prayer and belief in God had been taken into account, religious experience added no further predictive power to the multiple regression equation. Religious experience neither increased nor decreased an individual's likelihood of supporting traditional Christian moral values.

This study also gave room for pupils to report their experience of God.[20] Content analysis suggested that their descriptions could be summarized in nine main categories. These were: help and guidance, exams, sickness, death, answered prayer, God's presence, conversion, good experiences, and miscellaneous. In general, divine help and answered prayer were the categories most likely to be cited by pupils attending both Catholic and Protestant schools. Conversion experiences were only described by pupils in Protestant schools.

The second study concerned with the relationship between religious experience and attitude toward Christianity replicated the first study across a wider age range and among a larger sample.[21] This time a total of 940 pupils attending Catholic schools and 1,193 pupils attending Protestant schools in Northern Ireland, between the ages of twelve and seventeen years, participated in the study.

Of the pupils attending Protestant schools, 31 per cent of the boys and 39 per cent of the girls reported having had a religious experience. Of the pupils attending Catholic schools, 35 per cent of the boys and 64 per cent of the girls reported having had a religious experience. Path analysis, conducted among the Protestant and Catholic pupils separately, confirmed the finding of the previous study that the acknowledgement and naming of personal religious experience is associated with the formation of a more positive attitude toward Christianity and suggested that the conclusion held true over a wider age range among Protestant and Catholic pupils equally.

In a separate study Kay investigated religious conversion.[22] Data were collected from 1,431 pupils between eleven and fifteen years of age in fourteen schools, of which three were Roman Catholic, three were Church of England, one was jointly operated by the Church of England and the Roman Catholic Church, and the other seven were non-denominational state-maintained schools.

Two methods were chosen to try to identify the young people within the sample who had undergone conversion experiences. The first method made use of a list contained in the questionnaire. Pupils were asked to write down from the list the main influence on their attitude toward religion. The list comprised: parents, teachers, church, reasoning, emotional crisis, other personal experience, bible, general boredom. Parents were the most common first choice. Nearly 27 per cent of pupils acknowledged parents to be the most important influence on their attitude toward religion. Only about 3 per cent registered personal experience as the most important influence and nearly the same number gave this place to emotional crisis.

The group of young people who had named personal experience were compared using t-tests with the group of young people who had named parents on their attitude toward

Christianity and on their personality measures of extraversion, neuroticism and psychoticism. The two groups were only found to be significantly different in their attitude toward Christianity. The group of pupils who recorded personal experience averaged a score of 90·4 on the scale of attitude toward Christianity, compared with a score of 79·1 averaged by the group who pointed to the influence of parents. The group who pointed to emotional crisis were also compared with the group who pointed to the influence of parents, but no differences were found either on their attitude toward Christianity or on any dimension of personality.

The young people who had identified personal experience as the main influence on their attitude toward religion were therefore identified as converts to Christianity, though there was still a question to be raised about whether or not this conversion had taken place gradually or suddenly. Two additional questions, 'In the past year have your feelings about religion become *much more* interested?' and 'In the past year have your feelings about religion become a *little more* interested?' (original italics in both cases), had both been used in the questionnaire. Pupils identified as converts were inspected for their responses on these two items, and 53 per cent were found to have answered 'yes' to them. This implied that about half the personal-experience group were made up of recent and sudden converts. They were sudden converts in the sense that their interest in religion had become 'much more' pronounced within only the previous twelve months. The rest of this group had recalled experiences that reached further back into childhood.

When the age of the converts was inspected, they were found to cluster in the middle years of secondary schooling, around years eight and nine, in the twelve-to-thirteen age range. The parental church attendance of converts was found to be no different from the parental church attendance of non-converts. This showed that, by this method of identification, long-term church attendance was not the crucial factor in bringing about the personal experience which converts had acknowledged as the main determinant of their attitude toward Christianity. The church attendance of converts themselves was slightly higher than that of non-converts, but only on a monthly basis. Converts did, however, read their bibles and pray more than non-converts, and a substantial proportion of them attended an Anglican boarding school.

There was one further test which needed to be done. It was possible that some of the pupils who had marked 'emotional crisis' and 'personal experience' as the main determinants of their attitude toward Christianity were pupils who had been turned against Christianity. A careful examination of the young people who named emotional crisis showed that only two pupils (much less than 1 per cent of the total) scored less than fifty-three on the attitude scale, significantly lower than the vast majority of the group and more than twenty points below the young people who had named the influence of parents. None of the young people who had named personal experience scored so low on the scale.

The second method of identifying the young people who had undergone conversion experiences used the questions, 'Would you say that you were very religious?' and 'In the past year have your feelings about religion become *much more* interested?' (original italics). Pupils who answered 'yes' to both questions were compared with pupils who answered 'no' to them. The converts identified by this method were found to have significantly more positive attitude toward Christianity than the non-converts and to have significantly lower scores on the psychoticism scale.

There was surprisingly little overlap between the two methods of identifying converts. They appeared to tap different parts of the sample. Only two pupils were common to both groups. The second method identified 2·3 per cent of the sample. What is evident, however, is that pupils who show an intensification of interest in religion in the middle years of secondary education and who also show high scores on the attitude-toward-religion scale need not necessarily attribute their interest or their attitude to personal experience or emotional crisis. The intensification may result from a mixture of factors. There was, for instance, a small group of pupils (1 per cent of the total) who placed 'reasoning' as the main determinant of their attitude toward Christianity. Most of these pupils registered a negative attitude toward Christianity, but a small minority registered very positive attitudes. If these pupils had become interested in religion within a year of their answers to the questionnaire, they would have been counted as converts by the second method of identification.

Comment

This chapter has placed religious experience and religious conversion together. This is because by the first method of identification pupils identified as converts combined a favourable attitude toward Christianity with personal experience as the main determinant of this attitude. We must assume that this personal experience is religious experience since it is, by the respondent's admission, directly linked with his or her attitude toward Christianity. What we have not been able to show is whether those who acknowledged the role of personal experience in their acceptance of Christianity also acknowledged a continuing religious experience. The figures showing that none of the Roman Catholic pupils recognized their experience of God as being a conversion experience suggests that, among Roman Catholic pupils, the two sorts of experience, conversion and continuing, should not necessarily be connected.

The very high percentage of Roman Catholic girls (64 per cent) who acknowledged an experience of God is correlated with the very positive attitude toward Christianity found among these girls. Similarly, the high percentage of Roman Catholic boys (35 per cent) who acknowledged an experience of God is correlated with their favourable attitude toward Christianity. Since we know that most of the Roman Catholics who attend Roman Catholic schools in Northern Ireland have been brought up as Catholics, we are likely to be correct in assuming that their attitude toward Christianity *preceded* the religious experience. Young people brought up in a Catholic home, and attending a Catholic school, are, even without religious experience, likely to manifest favourable attitude toward Christianity. The religious experience slightly increases the favourability of an already favourable attitude. This is evident from the multiple regression analysis mentioned earlier.

The role of religious experience in the Protestant tradition is likely to be slightly different from that found in the Roman Catholic tradition. Reports of conversions were found among the Protestants and not among the Catholics. The lack of reports of religious conversions among Roman Catholic young people suggests that religious experience is coloured by theological context. The similarities between Roman Catholic and Protestant petitionary prayer are sufficiently great to allow for the answered prayer experience to be the most prevalent kind of reported experience. But the Protestant stress on conversion and 'new birth' does not easily fit with a traditional Catholic theology. Experience is interpreted within the respondent's theological and conceptual frameworks.

Conversion has not, so far as we know, been quantified on a large scale in British schools. The most common type of study to date has made use of figures relating to evangelistic campaigns and presented figures showing the ratio between attendance and overt commitment.[23] The study reported here was based on the idea that conversion would lead to a suddenly increased interest in religion and, in the case of Christian conversion, a higher-than-usual score on the scale of attitude toward Christianity.

Furthermore the combination of personal experience and high attitude toward Christianity suggests that the dismissal of conversion as 'nothing but' personal experience is misplaced. Personal experience, in this instance, has the objective correlate of a favourable attitude toward Christianity. The experience issues in a measurable result.

Overall these findings suggest that personal experience may be an important inhibitor of adolescent drift from the churches. The churches might be wise, therefore, to encourage and to enable their young members to welcome and to name the experiential dimension of their faith.

10
Religion and life

Introduction

The previous set of chapters has concentrated mainly on exploring the antecedents of individual differences in attitude toward Christianity. They have drawn attention to the relative influence of such factors as school, home and personality. They have discussed the role of religious experience, conversion and understanding of science in shaping attitude toward Christianity. The present chapter turns the question in another and different direction. This chapter asks if there are any practical consequences which flow from a positive attitude toward Christianity. In particular, attention is drawn to three sets of studies employing the Francis scale of attitude toward Christianity which have explored some of the consequences of religion in the lives of young people. These three sets of studies are concerned with the way in which young people view others; the way in which young people view themselves; and the views young people hold on morality. Put crudely, then, is there any evidence to suggest that religion presents a more positive attitude toward others? Is there any evidence to suggest that religion presents a more positive attitude toward the self? Is there any evidence to suggest that religious young people hold different moral values?

Attitude toward others
A key psychological factor in shaping attitude toward other people is that of empathy. *Empathy* is an ability to feel what other people are feeling. It is an intuitive rather than analytical ability to identify with the emotions of others and to share their joy or pain.[1] Sympathy often triggers off action to relieve suffering, but empathy is more general because it embraces a wider range of situations. The empathic person is able to act appropriately with regard to other people whatever their state, and this has been considered a prerequisite of moral behaviour.[2] The first

appearance of empathy is thought to occur by means of the
young child's ability to register the facial expressions of the
mother. As the mother pretends to cry when the child is unhappy
and laughs when the child is glad, the child begins to appreciate
the mother's capacity to reflect feelings. The child then laughs
when the mother smiles and a reciprocal communication is
established. The feedback emotional response is similar to that
which takes place as the child learns to speak, though it is not
necessarily prolonged beyond the first year or so of life. Empathy
is developed in any normal upbringing in this way and, where
adults become psychopathic, this may be often traced to failures
in relationships very early in life.[3]

Empathy requires imagination and the capacity to put oneself
in the shoes of other people. For this reason it would be sensible
to expect that empathy should increase through the years of
childhood and make great gains with the arrival of formal
operational thinking. Formal operational thinking allows the
teenager to become more fully aware of the personal identities of
other people by using reasoning like 'Jane's relation to her
feelings must be like John's relation to his feelings; and this must
be the same as my relation to my feelings.' In other words,
abstract relationships between a person and attributes belonging
to that person can be transferred by means of a logical deduction
through a recognition that John, Jane and I belong to the same
class, to the class of human beings. In the same way the scope of
formal operational thinking allows individuals to shift their own
viewpoints and so escape the confines of egocentricity. 'I see the
situation this way, but Jane must see it that way; I see myself as
owing Jane money, but Jane must see me as being in debt to her.'
Once egocentricity is broken down, it is possible for individuals
to feel the sympathy for others which they reserve for themselves.
And, as we shall see, the maintenance of egocentricity prevents
the development of reciprocity and mutual obligation which, in
Piagetian theory, is the starting point for adult morality.

Empathy may be measured on appropriate scales and, when
this is done, it is found that empathy rises between the ages of
nine and eleven years but then, contrary to expectations, it
decreases or remains static in the teenage years.[4] These findings
apply to both sexes.

When personality variables are explored in relation to empathy, previous research has begun with the tough and tender-minded social attitudes that correlate respectively with extraversion and introversion. Extraversion, and therefore tough-mindedness, shows no correlation with empathy.[5] We should anticipate that, by contrast, psychoticism would correlate negatively with empathy. The very nature of psychoticism is contrary to empathy and it is hard to see how an ability to feel what other people feel could co-exist with the glacial, solitary, quirky and sometimes cruel characteristics of the high psychoticism scorer.

When attitude toward Christianity is added to the analysis, there are two opposite consequences that might be expected. On the one hand, we should expect, since attitude toward Christianity is negatively correlated with psychoticism, and since we should expect psychoticism to be negatively correlated with empathy, that a positive attitude toward Christianity would be associated with a tendency to greater empathy. In other words, whether personality was envisaged as causing a positive attitude toward Christianity, or Christianity was seen as producing a low psychoticism personality, the outcome would be the same: an ability to feel for other people, to be empathic. Moreover, in terms of Christianity specifically, rather than religiosity generally, there are theological grounds for regarding concern for others to be engendered by such examples as the Good Samaritan or the long tradition of ecclesiastical charitable work stemming from the ideal of service.

On the other hand, the bulk of the empirical evidence shows that religiosity and pro-social behaviour are rarely found together.[6]

Empirical evidence also shows empathy does not, as we might expect on the basis of mental development theory, increase with age. Other findings show that a positive attitude toward Christianity declines as children grow older (see chapter 3). One of the key questions this chapter asks is whether empathy will increase with age if attitude toward Christianity is maintained at a steady level.

Attitude toward self

Key psychological constructs for assessing attitude toward self are the assessment of self-concept and self-esteem. Both constructs are open to assessment by a range of measures and provide an index of the young person's estimate of his or her own self-worth.

It is reasonable to suppose that self-worth is initially assessed by the child through the parents' opinions. If the parents value the child, the child will accept this and adopt the parents' valuation as his or her own. Later, with the onset of formal operational thinking, it will be possible for the child to gain a sense of self-worth through institutional opinions (how does the school rate me?) and through a self-generated value system. Such a value system may depend on abstract principles or, more simply, on an evaluation of particular social roles. It may put footballers at the top and politicians at the bottom. It may be much more diffuse and value living things more than commercial transactions. Whatever the system, however, individuals must locate themselves within it.[7] Without a value system, decisions are almost impossible to make.

Furthermore, self-worth requires an understanding of the self, an ability to differentiate the self from other selves, and a rudimentary notion of the way the self may be represented in more than one social role. The child may be esteemed by the mother, devalued by the school and disregarded by the father. The child may be valued for one characteristic and devalued for another. Self-worth is therefore complicated by competing valuations that may be more or less forcibly conveyed to the child by external agents.

Yet, clearly, self-worth is distinct from a sense of purpose in life or the recurrence of depression. At some point self-worth is likely to be turned into a sense of purpose, but this need not necessarily occur in childhood or adolescence. Similarly, self-worth is not necessarily linked with a resistance to depression, particularly if self-worth is perpetually contradicted by the evaluations of others. Empirical findings show that girls have a greater sense of purpose than boys, but also that girls are more likely to feel depressed.[8]

Prevalence of depression is also linked with the frequency of suicidal thoughts, though the links are not the same in each sex. Boys tend to think about suicide less, but to commit it more. For boys, then, it is a sudden and violent act turned on themselves. For girls, it is more often the result of brooding on the matter.[9] Paradoxically, however, suicide may be linked with high self-worth in the sense that the greater the worth which an individual attributes to him or herself, the more devastating will be the presumed impact of the suicide on others.

Research shows that religious beliefs militate against suicidal thoughts. This research draws on the tradition initiated by Durkheim who found a higher incidence of suicide in Protestant countries than in Roman Catholic countries, a finding he explained partly by reference to the Protestant emphasis on individuality, on faith and conscience, on personal decision-making, rather than on the external authority of the church. Durkheim also noticed that suicide rates dropped in wartime, and he attributed this to the general level of violence in society which, through war, is directed outward to a common enemy.

The religious variable in studies of suicide has been regarded as having continuing importance, and current sociological literature has stressed the support system offered by religious beliefs and the means by which membership of a congregation creates a protective network of relationships. Psychological variables have shown that there is a significant correlation between religion and well-being which is mediated by a 'meaning-in-life' variable. For instance, setbacks and personal difficulties can be explained religiously as being ultimately beneficial to the individual who suffers them. This religious meaning to life militates against suicide and enhances well-being.[10] Such findings are not without interpretative difficulties because, as we have said, it is possible to construe situations in which suicide is a meaningful act. The best conclusion, therefore, is that religion nurtures a cluster of variables all of which together point away from suicide and toward well-being.

Morality

Morality is a much larger concept than the other two so far considered. In its Piagetian formulation it arises out of interactions between the individual and the group, and the capacity, as operational and then formal operational thinking develop, to manipulate and understand rules that relate to the group and stipulate its functioning. Early studies by Piaget showed how children understood the rules of a game of marbles; the rules were given and fixed and incapable of alteration.[11] These studies were integrated into the conception of the world held by the child where crude and unrealistic ideas of causation were thought to govern natural phenomena, and it was not difficult to see parallels between causation in the natural world and causation in the social world. At this stage children took the view that those who suffered accidents did so because they had offended against moral rules. The world itself acts morally by punishing them. At a later stage children learnt to distinguish between actions and motives, and motives and consequences. Morality began to develop through social relationships. The rules of the game could be altered if the whole social group decided so. This is partly because each person in the group has, by then, internalized the rules and made them his or her own. Facilitated by the capacity to see things from other people's points of view, egocentrism may diminish and reciprocal relationships, or the morality of co-operation, can replace the morality of authoritarianism. A conception of justice emerges from this reciprocity, and justice has meaning as something above authority.

The general direction of moral development could be explained as a movement from heteronomy, where others made rules, through socionomy, where society made rules, to autonomy, where rules were freely made by the mature young adult. But the interest of Piaget, and those who were later influenced by him, was not in the rules themselves which children or young adults thought were right or wrong. Rather it was in the sort of reasoning children employed to make their moral decisions. What sort of arguments counted as good moral arguments? What sort of considerations needed to be taken into account when moral judgements were to be made? How did young people cope with conflicting duties or contradictory rules?

Lawrence Kohlberg took this work forward by presenting children of a wide variety of ages with moral dilemmas and asking questions to find out how they reasoned. He concluded that there were several stages in moral development, related to the classic Piagetian stages of mental development, and that younger children function at a level of conventional role-conformity by placing moral values in the expectations of others. Right actions are defined by the general approval of others, and motives for actions are based on a respect for authority. Subsequently, children move to the stage of self-accepted moral principles when they take responsibility for their actions and fulfil their social duties because they assent to them intellectually. The institution to which children belong, or society as a whole, must be maintained so that, at this stage, the basis for morality rests less on interpersonal relationships, as it did with the previous stage, and more on a societal orientation. This stage gives way to one in which the individual is aware that people hold a multiplicity of values and opinions and that, while most rules are upheld for the benefit of particular subgroups within society, others, like life or liberty, have a more universal application.

There are other stages in the Kohlbergian scheme and there are various versions of the scheme, which makes discussion of it complicated, but those stages described here are applicable to the age group on which we have empirical data.[12] This is because moral development does not seem to be as age-related as other forms of development and many adults function at a level similar to that of young people.

For our purposes, the importance of this discussion is twofold. First, the acceptance of larger, more absolute or more overarching moral principles has a place in all of the three stages we have described. Young children see nearly all rules as being set in stone, as coming from higher authority. Older people see many rules as being fixed for the good of society. More sophisticated people see some rules as being socially based and others as being related to non-relative factors like reason.

Second, the basis of absolute rules may certainly be such as to include empathy. If absolute rules, that is rules which admit of no exceptions, are fixed for the good of society, the rules at least are not arbitrary or wicked. They are intended to benefit society. And, in the case of more sophisticated young people, at a more advanced Kohlbergian stage, autonomously generated rules take into account empathic factors. It is, in short, reasonable to take account of the emotions of other moral agents as well as their rationality.

Furthermore morality addresses the relationship between the individual and the group. Whether individuals act according to rules that they had a part in shaping, and whether individuals internalize rules or simply obey them out of fear of punishment, the rules are constantly seen as being relevant to the larger or smaller group to which an individual belongs. This shows how well-being and morality may be theoretically connected. Well-being depends partly on self-worth, and self-worth may initially be inferred from the appraisal of others. Relationships with others fall within the realm of morality. For this reason moral behaviour should lead to self-worth, and via self-worth to well-being. The negative perspective illustrates this more strongly: the immoral person is likely to lack the approval of others and therefore to suffer from reduced self-worth and a consequent diminution of well-being.

In summary, this connection between well-being and morality is made through self-worth, whether morality is considered as a set of rules or a set of values. This linkage is possible because rules and values are themselves connected. Rules express values; rules are ways of deciding between competing values.

Findings

Attitude toward others

In the first study in this series, a sample of 279 boys and 290 girls, aged between eleven and seventeen years, in a Roman Catholic voluntary aided school completed a measure of empathy together with the Francis scale of attitude toward Christianity.[13] The correlations between age, attitude toward Christianity, empathy and sex for this sample are presented in table 10.1 in the appendices. Age correlated negatively with attitude toward Christianity (see also chapter 3), and was non-significantly associated with empathy. Sex was positively correlated with attitude toward Christianity (see also chapter 2) and with empathy. Attitude toward Christianity was correlated positively with empathy.

The general findings support other research showing that girls are more religious and more empathic than boys and that older pupils are generally less religious and less empathic than younger ones. The large and significant positive correlation between attitude toward Christianity and empathy confirms the theological view that empathy should go hand in hand with religion. Those pupils who are more favourable to Christianity are also more inclined to empathy. Those pupils less favourable to Christianity are less inclined to empathy.

In order to explore the interrelationships between these variables in greater detail, a path model was constructed which is presented in figure 10.1 in the appendices. According to this model, the effect of age and sex were shown to be significant predictors of attitude toward Christianity. Moreover, age is *positively* related to empathy once different levels of attitude toward Christianity have been partialled out. Religion emerges as the 'missing link' in the psychology of empathy. If attitude toward Christianity remains constant, empathy rises with age, as theoretical considerations suggest it should. We may put this another way and say that a positive attitude toward Christianity counteracts the age-related erosion of empathy which is found in many studies.

In a rather different kind of study John Greer set out to assess the relationship between attitude toward Christianity and the attitude of Protestant and Catholic young people in Northern Ireland to members of the other religious group.[14] In this study 940 Catholic pupils and 1,193 Protestant pupils, aged between twelve and sixteen years, completed the Francis scale of attitude toward Christianity, together with a specially designed measure of 'openness'. The data from this study demonstrated that openness scores increased significantly with increasing age, while attitude-toward-Christianity scores decreased significantly with age. As a consequence, in the sample as a whole, there appeared to be an inverse relationship between attitude toward Christianity and openness. At the same time, Roman Catholic pupils were more open than Protestant pupils, and girls were more open than boys. As a consequence of this complex pattern of interrelationships between the variables, it was necessary to undertake a more sophisticated form of analysis. Once sex, age and religious affiliation were controlled for, there was found to be a positive relationship between attitude toward Christianity and openness. In other words, young people most favourably disposed toward Christianity were also the most open to the other religious traditions.

Both of these studies, therefore, provide some evidence for the view that a positive attitude toward Christianity promotes a more positive attitude toward other people.

Attitude toward self
In the first study in this series,[15] a sample of 802 sixteen-year-old pupils in England completed the Francis scale of attitude toward Christianity, together with the self-concept scale designed by Lipsitt.[16] The correlation matrix demonstrated that the girls recorded a more positive attitude toward Christianity than the boys, and also that the girls recorded a more positive self-concept

than the boys. In view of these clear gender differences, sex was partialled out before exploring the relationship between self-concept and religion. The result was a significant positive correlation indicating that a positive attitude toward Christianity goes hand in hand with a more positive attitude toward the self.

The second study in the series[17] set out to test the findings of the earlier study using a different measure of self-concept and a different age range of pupils. This time a sample of 166 children between the ages of nine and eleven completed the Francis scale of attitude toward Christianity together with the Coopersmith self-esteem inventory.[18] In this study girls recorded a more positive attitude toward Christianity than boys, while boys recorded a more positive self-esteem than girls. Again, however, after controlling for sex difference, a significant positive correlation was found between attitude toward Christianity and self-esteem.

In a rather different kind of study Carolyn Wilcox set out to assess the relationship between attitude toward Christianity and happiness among young people.[19] In this study a sample of 997 fifteen- and sixteen-year-olds completed the Francis scale of attitude toward Christianity, together with the Oxford happiness inventory.[20] In this study the data demonstrated that the girls recorded a higher score of attitude toward Christianity than the boys, while the boys recorded a higher score of happiness than the girls. The correlation between attitude toward Christianity and happiness was significant and positive, indicating that a positive attitude toward Christianity and greater happiness go hand in hand.

All three of these studies, therefore, provide some evidence for the view that a positive attitude toward Christianity promotes a more positive attitude toward the self.

Morality

In order to explore one aspect of the moral views of young people Francis and Greer developed a scale of Christian moral values, employing ten items in a Likert format.[21] Pupils were presented with items referring to gambling, drinking alcohol, drunkenness, stealing, drug-taking, sexual intercourse before marriage, abortion, artificial birth control, suicide and divorce, and asked whether they thought them always wrong, usually wrong, usually excusable or never wrong. There was also a mid-point where pupils could register indecision. This scale was developed and tested on a sample of 1,177 secondary pupils in Protestant and Roman Catholic schools. It showed that Roman Catholic pupils had a significantly greater tendency to agree with traditional Christian moral values, and that girls were significantly more likely than boys to be traditional in their moral outlook. The traditional position regarded the activities referred to by the items in the scale as being always or usually wrong.

In a subsequent study, Francis and Greer explored the relationship between scores on this scale of moral values and scores on the Francis scale of attitude toward Christianity, by surveying 571 pupils of secondary age attending Roman Catholic schools in Northern Ireland.[22] The analysis showed that girls were more likely than boys to accept traditional moral values, and that moral values were positive and significantly correlated, in ascending order of importance, with church attendance, personal prayer, belief in God and attitude toward Christianity.

As the next step in data analysis a path model was constructed to test the comparative importance of attitude toward Christianity in shaping moral values. This model is presented in figure 10.2 in the appendices. In this model belief, prayer and church attendance were first employed to predict attitude toward Christianity, after controlling for sex differences. Then attitude toward Christianity, belief, prayer and church attendance were employed to predict moral values. Though church attendance, prayer, belief in God and gender all correlated with the moral-values scale, the strongest and most significant path in the model was between attitude toward Christianity and moral values. Thus the effect of the other variables was largely mediated through attitude toward Christianity. To put this another way, a favourable attitude toward Christianity was the most decisive cause of an acceptance of traditional Christian moral attitudes, although it did not completely eclipse the effects of other factors.

This study, therefore, provides some evidence for the view that a positive attitude toward Christianity also promotes a more positive attitude toward traditional Christian moral values.

Comment

In the case of each of the three main areas which we have explored, attitude toward Christianity is important. A positive attitude toward Christianity seems to promote a more positive attitude toward others, a more positive attitude toward self and a more positive attitude toward traditional Christian moral values.

As far as attitude toward others is concerned, studies of responses to questionnaire items about Third World poverty confirm the empathy of churchgoers. Teenage churchgoers are much more likely to record concern than non-churchgoers of the same age.[23] Yet, if we ask what it is about attitude toward Christianity which leads to empathy, we enter the realm of speculation. A positive attitude toward Christianity implies a favourable and emotionally-toned valuation of the components of Christianity, of church, ideas of God, Jesus, the bible and prayers. None of these components of themselves require empathy, though each may do so. For example, prayer is often prayer *for others*, the bible speaks of loving one's neighbour, Jesus was moved with compassion, God is everyone's God, church teaches about concern for others, and so on. But further work is needed to explain why and how empathic attitudes are built up.

As far as attitude toward self is concerned, the relationship between this and attitude toward Christianity is slightly easier to explain. Positive attitudes are linked with churchgoing, and with certain doctrines, which address personal well-being very directly. To be baptized is to be accepted into a community, to believe in God is to assume that there is a purpose to the totality of human existence and the particularity of individual existence, to take holy communion is to accept the love of Christ, and to pray is to consider that the individual can make a difference to the world. In its traditional form conversion speaks of the forgiveness of sin, and therefore of guilt, and acceptance by God into the benefits of a new life. All these ideas are powerful and well established. They are arguably more coherent than humanistic ideas of well-being that depend on such concepts as self-actualization or self-expression.[24] It should be no surprise that a positive attitude toward Christianity is correlated with well-being.

The situation with moral values is more complex. The largest corpus of the psychological study of morality has not concerned itself with the *content* of morality but rather with the rationale for it. All the moral values presented within the scale may be held for reasons suggesting heteronomy, socionomy or autonomy. It would be possible to believe that abortion was always wrong simply because this was the official teaching of the Catholic church, and not to have thought any further on this topic. Such a reason for holding this anti-abortionist stance would suggest a lower Kohlbergian stage of moral functioning, a heteronomous stage. Yet, equally it would be possible to believe that abortion was wrong because it was ultimately detrimental to society. This is a socionomous stage. Yet again, it is possible to hold that abortion is wrong for reasons related to universal values. Human life is special, even sacred, and its preservation underlies other values. Without life there are no values. Such reasoning, if arrived at without coercion, is autonomous. A young person who argued in this way could be said to operate at one of the higher Kohlbergian stages.

Consequently, it is not clear that a positive attitude toward Christianity suppresses moral thinking or discourages moral development. Moreover, if, as we have shown, empathy and a positive attitude toward Christianity go hand in hand, then we would be correct to interpret the moral values of young people with a positive attitude toward Christianity in an empathic context. In each case the prohibition belonging to the traditional Christian moral position is one which may be seen as being put in place to prevent pain and not to spoil pleasure.

Moreover, and in keeping with this view, the correlation between attitude toward Christianity and moral values, and between attitude toward Christianity and openness, implies that moral values and openness are correlated. Those who adopt traditional moral values should not, therefore, be viewed as a prejudiced group. Their morality is expressed within the context of empathy. It appears to be a morality which transcends their sharply defined social or religious group and have a wider application. To this extent, then, it is a morality which belongs to the higher rather than to the lower Kohlbergian stages.

If the drift from the churches results in a decline in empathy, self-esteem, happiness, openness and traditional morality, we may reasonably ask what steps the church should take to reverse this process. The analysis may turn on the nature of these four outcomes. Openness and empathy are, in essence, risk-taking strategies. They invite rebuff and pain. High self-esteem or well-being is a state rather than a strategy, and provides the security which makes risk-taking possible. Traditional morality may be viewed as a way of maintaining the security provided by well-being. The appeal of the church, therefore, can be angled toward the needs of young people so that those who want risk may be offered risk and those who want security may be offered security. At the traditional door to the church stands Christ who offers both risk and security in equal measure.

11
Conclusion

This book has drawn together a range of studies concerned with attitude toward Christianity during childhood and adolescence, conducted over a period of nearly twenty-five years. The synthesis of these studies is considerably easier to achieve than the synthesis of the research in related areas conducted during the previous twenty-five years, for one main reason. All of these studies, conducted by different researchers, from undergraduate students to university readers and professors, conducted in cultures as far apart as Scotland and Kenya, conducted in the early 1970s or the mid-1990s, have agreed on a common instrument for assessing attitude toward Christianity. Since repeated-reliability and factor studies have demonstrated that the scale of attitude toward Christianity has behaved in a consistent fashion, among different age groups, in different cultures, and at different periods in time, it is possible to assume that each of these studies has measured the same construct with the same degree of precision. By drawing these studies together, therefore, the new knowledge generated is more than the sum total of the individual parts.

Looking back over the studies reviewed in the previous chapters, it is now possible to formulate three main types of conclusion. First, it is possible to speak more precisely about the nature of the drift from the churches during childhood and adolescence. There is a sense in which this drift has now been *quantified* in a unique manner and in two dimensions. The drift accelerates progressively during the years of primary and secondary school. The drift has accelerated since the early 1970s into the 1990s. Second, it is possible to speak more precisely about the comparative importance of different factors which may influence and, therefore, help to cause this drift from the churches during childhood and adolescence. Serious attention has been given to social and contextual influences mediated through home and school. Serious attention has been given to individual and personal influences mediated through age, sex and personality. Serious attention has been given to factors like the conflict between science and religion, and the formative power of religious experience. Third, it is possible to speak more precisely about the consequences which may be associated with this drift from the churches during childhood and adolescence. In particular, attention has been drawn to the implications of this drift for young people's attitude toward others, their attitude toward the self, and their views on moral behaviour. The drift from the churches may well be accompanied by a hardening attitude toward others, by an eroding attitude toward self, and by the abandonment of traditional moral values.

Each of these three sets of findings may be fascinating in its own right. In its own way the academic discussion undertaken within each chapter contributes to a developing body of knowledge in an empirical psychology of religion. For example, the discussion on the underlying causes of sex differences in religiosity provides further, and some might say quite conclusive, evidence regarding the superiority of one theory over other theories. At the same time, however, if taken seriously, the findings presented in this book could be of considerable practical benefit to the churches, in planning their pastoral and evangelistic ministry among children and young people who live through this period of accelerating drift from the churches. For example, when churches are deciding how best to resource religious education within the state-maintained sector of schools, the findings that an appreciation of religious experience may enhance the young person's attitude toward Christianity, but that an emphasis on world religions may depress the young person's attitude toward Christianity, may be of some relevance to the outcome of their decision. When churches are evaluating their investment within church schools in the state-maintained sector of education, the findings that church schools *can* exert a positive influence on their pupils' attitude toward Christianity, but that many of them actually exert a negative influence, may be relevant factors to take into account.

The aim of this concluding chapter, therefore, is to examine each of the three types of conclusion emerging from the previous chapters, namely concerning the drift from the churches, concerning the personal and contextual precursors of drift, and concerning the consequences of drift. Having examined these conclusions, the chapter intends to explore the implications of these conclusions for the churches' ministry among children and young people.

Drift from the churches

The churches are by no means unaware of the way in which they lose contact with children and young people. At the anecdotal level, many clergy relate the ability of their churches to recruit children under the age of seven, only to see them disappear again by the age of nine. Although statistics on child attendance at church and Sunday school are often not systematically collected and presented, where they exist these statistics confirm the anecdotal impression.[1] Older clergy may also relate how the situation seems to have become less satisfactory during the years of their ministry. This perspective, however, is less easy to pin down statistically.

Information presented in chapters 3 and 4 adds to this general impression in three important ways. First, these data confirm that the drift from the churches is not simply restricted to the level of behaviour. The drift takes place at the much more fundamental level of attitude. The challenge facing the churches today is not one concerned with changing young people's behaviour, but one concerned with influencing their attitudes. Of course, it is true that behaviour and attitude go hand in hand. Young people who remain in touch with the churches also maintain a more positive attitude toward Christianity. On the other hand, it is unlikely that the churches will influence the religious behaviour of unchurched young people, unless they first influence the attitude toward Christianity of these young people. The churches need to be aware, too, that there are many subtle ways in which the attitudes of children and young people may be influenced. There is a whole industry of marketing, promotion and advertising directed specifically towards influencing the attitudes of children and young people. It may be extremely unwise for the churches not to invest resources in those areas. While the local church remains young people's point of contact with the Christian community, many other wider and more pervasive factors may influence their underlying attitude toward that local church.

Second, these data have been able to test competing theories regarding why it is that young people drift from the churches with increasing age. One group of theories made popular in the 1960s suggested that the drift from the churches was associated with cognitive development and the emergence of a different quality of thinking associated with the ability to deal with abstract thought. A whole new approach to religious education in church and school was promoted on the basis of this theory.[2] If this theory were correct, then there would be clear practical implications for religious education and for catechesis. Another group of theories suggested that the drift from the churches was associated with the transition from the culture of primary school to the culture of secondary school. Again, if this theory were correct, it would provide clues for the churches' ministry. Both theories, however, suggest discontinuity in the child's religious development. Both theories are contradicted by the data from the present research which reveal consistent and persistent linear decline in attitude toward Christianity throughout the years of compulsory schooling, from the age of eight to the age of sixteen.

The theory which makes sense of the linear decline is a socialization theory. What appears to be taking place is this. As young people leave the world of childhood, they are absorbed incrementally into the world of adulthood. Today much of the world of adulthood is characterized by the secular rather than by the religious. If the analysis of social historians like Alan Gilbert is correct, young people in England today are growing up in a post-Christian society.[3] The socialization process is persistently and inevitably drawing young people into the ethos of that post-Christian world. In this sense, to be irreligious is to be normal. The challenge facing the churches today is that of making the gospel message heard among young people in a radically alien social environment.

There is some evidence to suggest that the religious groups which have the greatest influence among young people in such a social context are those which sharpen their distinctiveness over and against the wider social context in which they are placed. Some of the smaller evangelical churches create a distinctive cultural environment for their young people, even to the point of developing distinctive Christian schools.[4] The history of the Roman Catholic church in England, as a persecuted minority, led to a similar distinctiveness in cultural, religious and educational terms.[5] At the same time, there are considerable dangers in seeking the Christian future in such a sectarian form.

Third, these data have been able to monitor the way in which the drift from the churches has fluctuated over the past twenty years. From these data there is clear evidence to suggest that, from the churches' point of view, the situation is not improving. Studies of church membership and attendance over the past twenty years have made it plain that the churches in England are losing progressively more and more contact with the adult population.[6] The information presented in chapter 4 extends this picture from adults to young people, and from religious behaviour to underlying religious attitudes. The precise figures show a persistent and consistent deterioration in attitude toward Christianity between 1974 and 1986, and a subsequent levelling off between 1986 and 1994. Until the next study is completed in 1998, it is impossible to predict whether the plateau will be maintained. What is clear, however, is that the challenge facing the churches in 1994 is greater than the challenge facing them in 1974. Nor is there any evidence to suggest that the crisis addressed by such reports as *The Child in the Church*, published by the British Council of Churches in 1976,[7] has been adequately resolved.

Personal precursors of drift

The preceding chapters have distinguished between two types of variables which may function as predictors of drift from the churches during childhood and adolescence. The first type of variables concern factors which describe the personal characteristics of the individual young people. The second type of variables concern the social or contextual environment in which the young people are placed. Both types of variables have a significant part to play.

The personal precursors of drift from the churches identified by the studies described in this book include sex, personality and personal religious experience. All three of these areas have implications for the churches' ministry among the children and young people.

Sex differences

To begin with, the churches are by no means unaware of the

greater success which they experience among girls and women than among boys and men. This sex difference in church membership and church attendance has been long established.[8] What has been less clear, however, are the underlying reasons for this sex difference in church membership and attendance. The data presented in chapter 2 make three important contributions to this debate. First, these data make it clear that sex differences in relation to Christianity are already well established by the age of eight and persist throughout childhood and adolescence. Second, these data make it clear that sex differences clearly observed in terms of church membership and church attendance extend to the more fundamental area of underlying attitude toward Christianity. Third, these data are able to account for sex differences in religiosity in terms of gender-orientation theory.

Gender-orientation theory suggests that the observed differences in levels of religiosity between men and women are to be accounted for, not in terms of being born male or female, but in terms of the underlying personality dimension of femininity. Both men and women vary considerably in the personality dimension of femininity, although on balance there is a higher-than-average score of femininity among women than among men. What chapter 2 demonstrates is that Christianity appeals more to young women who score high on femininity, than to young women who score low on femininity. At the same time, Christianity appeals more to young men who score high on femininity, than to young men who score low on femininity. The crucial precursor, therefore, to being more religious is not being female, but having a feminine gender orientation. This finding also helps to account for the set of studies which find high levels of psychological femininity among male clergy.[9]

Seen in this light, gender-orientation theory focuses two challenges for the churches' ministry among children and young people. The first challenge concerns capitalizing on the churches' more obvious appeal to young people with a feminine gender orientation. According to the theory, these are young people who value personal qualities like gentleness, tenderness, sympathy, compassion, affection and loyalty. Such qualities will be equally important to the young males as to the young females who are naturally attracted to the churches. The second challenge concerns identifying and responding to the spiritual needs of young people who are not characterized by a feminine gender orientation. This challenge means recognizing the needs of young women who are not characterized by a feminine gender orientation, as much as recognizing the needs of young men who are not characterized by this orientation.

Personality

While the churches have not been unaware of the sex imbalance in their members and attenders, they may have been much less aware of the way in which they attract some personality types rather than others. The data presented in chapter 7 make four important contributions to this debate. First, this chapter reviews the power of different personality theories to account for individual differences in religiosity and concludes that, in the present state of knowledge, Hans Eysenck's dimensional model of personality is likely to provide the most powerful tool to explore the relationship between personality and religion. Since, at present, this is not a tool with which the churches are particularly familiar, there may now be good reason for the theory becoming better known among those responsible for shaping the churches' ministry among children and young people. In essence, Hans Eysenck's dimensional model of personality argues that individual differences can most adequately and economically be described in terms of the three higher-order personality factors of neuroticism–stability, extraversion–introversion, and tender-mindedness–tough-mindedness (psychoticism).[10]

Second, setting Eysenck's theory to work, chapter 7 makes it clear that there is no relationship between religion and neuroticism. Young people are not drawn into the arms of the church as a consequence of their neurotic anxieties or fears. The churches do not need to understand themselves, therefore, essentially as therapeutic communities ministering to disturbed young people. Nor can the churches congratulate themselves on providing safe environments through which young people develop higher levels of stability than enjoyed in society as a whole.

Third, at the same time, chapter 7 makes it very clear that there *is* a consistent relationship between psychoticism and attitude toward Christianity, throughout the whole age range covered by the survey. Children and young people who score high on the psychoticism scale are more inclined to reject Christianity than young people who score low on this dimension. In other words, a positive attitude toward Christianity goes hand in hand with tender-mindedness, while a negative attitude toward Christianity goes hand in hand with tough-mindedness. On the assumption that the Christian gospel is equally available to all people, the challenge faced by the churches is to make that gospel credible among tough-minded young people.

Fourth, chapter 7 also makes it clear that, on some accounts, the churches may appear more attractive to introverts than to extraverts. Again the challenge facing the churches is to recognize how introverts and extraverts differ so radically in their social orientation that they may feel comfortable in very different church-related contexts. While the introverted young person may welcome the opportunity for inward exploration, silence and solitary meditation, he or she may be unnecessarily alienated by pressures to participate in church social functions. Similarly, while the extraverted young person may welcome the social experiences of the church-related youth fellowship, he or she may be unnecessarily alienated by expectations associated with some classic forms of Christian spirituality. To many, it may seem that the public face of the churches favours introverts rather than extraverts.

Religious experience

The work of the Religious Experience Research Unit in Oxford[11] and of David Hay in Nottingham[12] has drawn attention to the fact that many more people report awareness of having religious experiences than claim practising membership of the Christian churches. The churches are not, therefore, unaware of the persistence of the religious experience within predominantly secular society. The data presented in chapter 9 make three contributions to this debate.

First, these data confirm the widespread prevalence of religious experience among young people. The data indicate that many young people are aware of such experiences, recognize them and are able to name them. Although they may be growing up outside the churches, young people are not living with a totally secular world view. The challenge facing the churches is to be able to make connections between what young people appropriately recognize and name as religious experience and what the churches themselves stand for and proclaim.

Second, these data confirm that there is, overall among young people, a positive link between the awareness of religious experience and a positive attitude toward Christianity. It is in the churches' best interests, therefore, for them to be able to encourage young people to become more aware of religious experience and to be able to recognize and name such experiences.

Third, these data also draw attention to the significant part which can be played by conversion experience in the promotion of a positive attitude toward Christianity. While churches will vary greatly, on theological grounds, regarding the emphasis they give to teenage conversion experience, the data presented by this study suggest that such experiences are beneficial, rather than detrimental, to the development of a positive attitude toward Christianity during the teenage years.

Contextual precursors of drift

The social or contextual precursors of drift from the churches identified by the studies described in this book include three key factors which can be associated with the home and three key factors which can be associated with the school. The three key factors associated with home concern the parental religious example, the marital stability of the parents, and social class background. The three key factors associated with school concern the church school issue, the nature of religious education, and the role of science education. These issues will be reviewed in turn.

Parental example
The churches are not unaware of the crucial role of parents in shaping the religious development of their children. It has long been observed that children and young people are unlikely to attend church if their parents fail to do so.[13] What has been less clear concerns the comparative influence of mothers and fathers on the religious development of sons and daughters, and whether it makes any difference if both parents attend or if only one parent attends. The data presented in chapter 6 make four key contributions to this debate.

First, the data make it clear that the mother is the more significant influence on the religious development of both sons and daughters. Second, the data confirm that when both parents attend church regularly, the influence is stronger than when only one parent attends. Third, the data show that, rather than decreasing in significance between the ages of eleven and sixteen, the importance of parental example actually increases over this period. Fourth, the data indicate that the influence of parents is stronger over their children's religious practices, than it is over their children's attitude toward religion. Nevertheless, parental church attendance is able to account for between 9 and 14 percent of variance in the young person's attitude toward Christianity, making this by far the strongest contextual influence on the development of adolescent attitude toward Christianity.

Taken together, these four findings generate two key pointers for the prioritization of resources in the churches' ministry among children and young people. First, if Christian parents are, indeed, so central to the religious formation of their sons and daughters, a major priority within the churches should concentrate on equipping parents to take a more informed and proactive role in the Christian nurture of their young. Parents may need to be helped to understand and to respond appropriately to their children's discontent with aspects of the local church and with the pressure toward secularization which they may experience from their peer group. Second, if pastoral resources for ministry among children and young people are scarce, churches should recognize the importance and value of concentrating such resources among those children and young people who are also appropriately supported by strong parental example. Put starkly, local churches are likely to see longer-term benefit in young lives by collaborating with churchgoing parents to maintain the interest and commitment of their churchgoing children throughout the teenage years, than by recruiting into membership teenagers who remain unsupported by parental example.

Home stability
A great deal of research has drawn attention to the impact of family disruption on many aspects of the lives of children and young people.[14] Much less attention has been given to the impact

of family disruption on the religious development of children and young people. The data presented in chapter 6 make it clear that parental divorce is reflected in a less positive attitude toward Christianity among young people.

The pastoral implication of this finding for the local church is clear. When children already within the church congregation are experiencing or have experienced parental divorce, it is important for the local church to be sensitive to signs of disaffection projected on to church life or on to a more basic and pervasive attitude toward Christianity. Pastoral sensitivity and time invested at such crises in the lives of young churchgoers may be crucial to the positive religious formation of such young people.

Social class
Social class remains a very important factor in British society. One of the most consistent and best-attested correlates of social class remains church attendance.[15] Although there are social-class differences between the denominations, there is much evidence to suggest that the higher social classes are more likely to attend church than the lower social classes. What has not been so clearly documented, however, is the relationship between social class and the religious development of children and young people. The data presented in chapter 6 contribute two main findings to this debate.

First, the data confirm that children and young people from higher-social-class backgrounds are more likely to attend church than children and young people from lower-social-class backgrounds. The mechanism behind this finding is straight-forward. Parents from higher-social-class backgrounds attend church themselves and take their children with them. This finding appears to present the churches with a profound sociological and theological puzzle, when it comes to the deployment of financial and pastoral resources. A theology which emphasizes the servant role of the church may well wish to concentrate resources for ministry among children and young people in lower-social-class areas, without necessarily expecting to recruit from these areas into lifelong church membership. A theology which emphasizes the nurture role of the church may wish to concentrate resources for ministry among children and young people in middle-class areas and properly expect in these areas to recruit the next generation of church members and those capable of financing the next generation of the churches' ministry.

Second, however, the data demonstrate that the link between social class and attitude toward Christianity is quite different from the link between social class and church attendance. While the higher social classes are more likely to attend church, the lower social classes are more likely to hold a positive attitude toward Christianity. The data demonstrate that this is the case even among children and young people. This finding appears to present the churches with a rather different kind of puzzle and one which raises fundamental questions about pastoral strategy. Although it is generally assumed that a positive attitude toward Christianity and church attendance go hand in hand, this correlation is not strong enough to span the divide of social class. For some reason, or set of reasons, children and adults alike from lower-social-class backgrounds are inhibited from translating a positive attitude toward Christianity into church attendance. Likely reasons for this inhibition centre on the discontinuity between the cultural assumptions of a lower-social-class background and the cultural assumptions taken for granted in the lives of many church congregations. In structuring a viable ministry among children and young people in lower-social-class areas, the churches would be mistaken to expect the fruits of such ministry to be reflected in the adoption of middle-class practices of church attendance. Instead, it may be necessary to anticipate an altogether different expression of Christian commitment within different social-class areas.

Church schools
The debate about the purpose and usefulness of church schools has long divided the churches in England.[16] Following the 1944 Education Act, the Roman Catholic Church remained passionately committed to the development of a distinctive system of church schools, while the Free Churches almost entirely withdrew from the church-school system. Within the Church of England there was, and still is, a wide range of opinion. What has, however, been much less easy to pin down is a satisfactory empirical answer to the question whether or not church schools make a distinctive contribution to the religious development of the pupils who attend them. The data presented in chapter 5 make three key contributions to this debate.

First, at the primary school level, the data provide clear evidence that Roman Catholic voluntary aided schools make a significant contribution to the development of a positive attitude toward Christianity among their pupils, in addition to the contribution made by home and church. In other words, through their church schools, the Roman Catholic church is achieving something which would not have been achieved had the Roman Catholic church decided not to continue to invest in the church-school system. All that is demonstrated by these data is that church schools can and do make a significant contribution to one aspect of the religious development of their pupils. If the churches were to regard the promotion of a positive attitude toward Christianity among children and young people as an appropriate aim, then they might want to consider how church schools can best be deployed and developed.

Second, however, the data also provide some evidence to suggest that, although church schools *can* make a positive contribution to their pupils' attitude toward Christianity, not all church schools in fact do so. Three studies indicated that Church of England voluntary aided schools in fact contribute to the development of a *less* positive attitude toward Christianity in their pupils. A fourth study indicated that Church of England voluntary controlled schools contributed to the development of a less positive attitude toward Christianity in their pupils, while Church of England voluntary aided schools made no contribution to their pupils' attitude toward Christianity, in either a positive or a negative direction. This finding has been seen to be controversial within the Church of England and has attracted considerable criticism of the research method.[17] While many Church of England schools may wish to serve the local neighbourhood, rather than influence the religious development of the pupils who attend them, it remains puzzling why a church might wish to discourage a positive attitude toward Christianity among young people.

Third, at the secondary level, the data provide a clear indication that church schools may serve the religious development of their pupils less effectively when there is a conflict between the assumptions on which the school is operated and the assumptions established among the pupils. The assumptions behind many Roman Catholic secondary schools still seem to be that the school functions as a faith community of practising Catholics. The reality among the pupils is that these schools now serve three distinct groups of young people: practising Catholics, lapsed Catholics and practising Christians from other denominational backgrounds. In one sense, it is the practising Christians from other denominational backgrounds who feel disadvantaged in the Catholic school. In another sense, it is the large proportion of lapsed Catholics who undermine the school ethos as a faith community. The challenge facing the Roman Catholic church is how best to develop the Catholic secondary school so that these schools may best promote the religious development of all three groups of pupils. At the same time, if Catholic secondary schools are to continue to recruit a growing number of practising Christian pupils from other denominational backgrounds, it is increasingly important for these schools to address the practical consequences of moving from being denominational institutions to becoming ecumenical faith communities.

Religious education

The nature of religious education taught within the state-maintained schools in England and Wales has undergone radical changes since the subject was so firmly embedded in the 1944 Education Act. The professionalization of religious education means that the subject, as now taught, is very different from what the churches thought they were campaigning for at the time of the 1944 Education Act. Nevertheless, throughout the changes which have taken place in religious education over the past fifty years, the churches have remained supportive of the place of the subject in the school curriculum. What is less clear, however, is whether different approaches to religious education may result in pupils adopting a different attitude toward Christianity. Two pointers emerge from data presented in chapters 5 and 9.

First, the study reported in chapter 5 indicates that pupils who have followed a religious-education syllabus which concentrates on world religions record a significantly less positive attitude toward Christianity than pupils who have followed religious-education syllabuses which concentrate on Christianity and the bible.

Second, the studies reported in chapter 9 indicate that pupils who acknowledge and name religious experience record a significantly more positive attitude toward Christianity than pupils from comparable backgrounds who do not share this experience. In his seminal discussion of the bearing of empirical studies of religious experience on education, David Hay argues that it is a legitimate function of religious education to sharpen pupils' awareness and appreciation of religious experience.[18]

Set side by side, these two findings might help the churches to prioritize the areas in which they may prefer to develop materials and to allocate resources for the promotion of religious education within schools.

Science education

A number of studies have illustrated and discussed the potential conflict between science and religion during childhood and adolescence.[19] What has been less clear, however, are the components of this conflict and the way in which these components may function differently among different age groups of young people. The data presented in chapter 8 make two important contributions to this debate.

First, the findings from several studies make it clear that it is scientism, and not interest in science itself, which militates against a positive attitude toward Christianity. However, scientism is not just bad for religion; scientism is bad for science itself, because it presents a false view of what science is and what science can properly be expected to achieve. Scientism, therefore, is an issue which can and should be addressed as part of the curriculum of science education.

Second, the data confirm the important role still played by the conflict between different accounts of origins in the battle between science and religion. It is on this issue, in particular, that there should be opportunity for collaboration between school departments of science education and departments of religious education. In some cases, it may be appropriate for the churches to encourage this kind of dialogue.

Consequences of drift

As yet, considerably less attention has been given by studies employing the Francis scale of attitude toward Christianity to identifying the possible consequences of a positive attitude toward Christianity during childhood and adolescence, than to identifying the precursors of shaping a positive attitude toward Christianity. Nevertheless, three main sets of consequences of a positive attitude toward Christianity have been identified. These concern a more positive attitude toward others, a more positive attitude toward the self, and a more positive attitude toward traditional moral values. The drift from the churches is, therefore, likely to be accompanied by a significant movement in young people concerning all these areas, with implications both for their own lives and for wider society.

Attitude toward others

One of the major puzzles in research concerning adolescent development has focused on the conflict between theoretical expectations about the development of empathic capabilities during adolescence and clear empirical evidence that such development does not in fact take place. Empathy is a key construct in psychological development, with importance both for the well-being of the individual and the well-being of society. From society's point of view, empathy stands at the heart of pro-social behaviour.[20] From the individual's point of view, empathy stands at the heart of interpreting the relationship between self and others. The data presented in chapter 10 present a unique perspective on this problem.

By using multivariate analysis, these data demonstrate that, during the years of secondary education, two conflicting influences are operating on the development of empathy. On the one hand, in accordance with theoretical expectation, developing intellectual capacity is promoting an increase in empathic capability. On the other hand, declining religiosity is promoting a decline in empathic capability. Such findings suggest that the drift from the churches may well be accompanied by lower levels of empathy among young people and by a hardening attitude toward others.

Attitude toward self

Self-esteem has been shown by a number of studies to be a crucial factor in individual development during childhood, adolescence, and into adulthood.[21] Such research has identified many of the antecedents to the development of positive self-esteem, including the influence of parents, school, peers, personality and ability. The data presented in chapter 10 make a further contribution to the debate by demonstrating that a positive attitude toward Christianity is an additional factor clearly predictive of a higher level of self-esteem, both during childhood and during adolescence.

A whole body of research has documented the relationship between low self-esteem and a range of anti-social or self-harming behaviour. Low self-esteem has been linked to truancy and to bullying. Low self-esteem has been linked to drug abuse and to suicidal behaviour. Such findings suggest that the drift from the churches may well be accompanied by lower levels of self-esteem among young people and by a continued rise in anti-social and self-harming behaviours.[22]

Attitude toward morality
The relationship between morality and religion is complex. While Christian teachings would clearly predict a strong link between religion and morality, the whole history of empirical research in the area has produced conflicting evidence.[23] The data presented in chapter 10 make a further contribution to the debate by demonstrating that a positive attitude toward Christianity is the key predictor of young people's attitude toward traditional Christian moral values. Such findings suggest that the drift from the churches may well be accompanied by the further abandonment of traditional moral values, with a liberalization of attitude toward such issues as alcohol, drugs and sex.

End note

In drawing conclusions from our research data, we have tried to make the best sense of the empirical evidence, as it stands at present. It is of the very nature of the scientific study of religion that each piece of evidence raises new questions and is itself vulnerable to being challenged by new or conflicting findings.

We anticipate that some of our findings will be welcomed. After all, it may, to some people, be good news that religion promotes positive psychological development during childhood and adolescence, increasing empathy and self-esteem. We also anticipate that some of our findings will not be welcomed. After all, it may, to some people, be bad news that Church of England primary schools promote a less positive attitude toward Christianity among their pupils.

Our intention in presenting such findings, however, is to court neither thanks for the good news nor condemnation for the bad news. Rather, our hope is that others may be challenged to join in our quest to check out empirically what is happening in the domain of attitude toward Christianity during childhood and adolescence. After all, what is at stake in this area seems to be nothing less than the mission of the churches and the lives of young people. Our invitation to fellow questers in this field (to undergraduate students, postgraduate students and established researchers alike) is twofold. The first invitation is to pick up our scale of attitude toward Christianity and to set it to work, both to replicate our own studies and to push out the boundaries further into other areas. The second invitation is to criticize our instrument and to put something better in its place. In these ways, the enterprise of research is furthered.

Appendix 1
Scientific study of religion

Objectivity and subjectivity

The history of science and the history of philosophy are separate stories, but they meet and act upon each other in unpredictable ways. Isaac Newton's great scientific work about gravitation, written in Latin, was *Philosophiae Naturalis Principia Mathematica*. Its title in English, *Mathematical Principles of Natural Philosophy*, shows that what we would today call 'physics' was in the seventeenth century 'natural philosophy' and that, to this extent, science and philosophy were the same thing. More recently, some philosophers have seen science as a dehumanizing force which uses objective language as a means of controlling the way human beings think about each other.[1] To this extent, then, philosophy and science may be critics of each other.

Whatever the relationship, however, science has made use of observation, and observation has presumed the existence of an observer. This idea looks easy until it is unpacked by a series of questions. To what extent does the observer bring some sort of interpretation to the events observed? Would different observers have seen different things in the same circumstances? What is it, anyway, which the observer observes? He or she, after all, is only aware of sense impressions and not of the thing itself apart from sense impressions. The most obvious and simple answers to these questions are the common-sense ones, and they are certainly ones which find support in René Descartes's writings.[2] The observer really gains an unbiased impression, albeit a sense impression, of the external world. If the world is external to observers, then they would all observe the same things in the same circumstances. The external world is 'real' and observers detect it, and their thoughts are a pattern of what is 'out there'.

The enormous success of Newton's theory made his scientific approach a pattern to be followed by other types of science. Newton had applied mathematics to explain astronomical observations and, by doing so, formulated a theory of gravitation.

The gravitational force exerted by objects depended not only on their mass but also on their distance from each other. The theory could be applied with great precision to a wide range of phenomena, including the eclipse of the sun, the phases of the moon, the orbit of comets, the trajectory of canon balls, the flow of the tides and the movement of pendulums. Past events could be used to predict future ones, and a model of the universe a little like the workings of a giant clock could be envisaged.

Science diversified in the following centuries, but the Newtonian model remained a powerful incentive to each field which was successively explored. The appeal of scientific laws as robust as those which stemmed from the physical world was strong. Attempts to find laws to describe the development of human society were made by Auguste Comte and Herbert Spencer.[3] Karl Marx, poring over sets of figures in the British Museum, attempted something larger still by trying to find inevitability in the sequence of social structures inherent in the whole course of human history. He saw such structures as being dependent on the economic systems they used. The beauty of this, from Marx's point of view, was that economics lends itself to mathematical analysis because so much of its content is related to wages, trade and currency figures. By analysing economic trends, and then by relating these to social development, Marx was able to argue that he had found a way to predict the future course of society, most famously of capitalist society; just as feudalism had given way to capitalism, so capitalism must give way to communism.

The Marxist view of history is essentially rigid because it incorporates a Newtonian concept of scientific law.[4] There is no sense of probabilistic predictions or of alternative outcomes. Society must develop in certain ways because the laws of history have been uncovered, and these laws are 'iron' and scientific.

Towards the end of the nineteenth century psychology had its more humble beginnings. It dealt with individuals rather than societies. The founding father of psychology is usually said to be Wilhelm Wundt, though a good case can be made in support of Francis Galton.[5] The motivation for Wundt's experiments was partly fuelled by a desire to find mental laws. He had some hope of showing how mental processes were analogous to chemical processes and how perceptions might be broken into constituent sensations or recombined by the association of thoughts.

Wundt's basic method in his early work was to examine the mind through introspection, that is, by asking people under controlled conditions to examine their own thought processes. Galton, who never practised his science in a professional academic setting, linked a long-standing interest in the statistical analysis of religious phenomena (like prayer) to a willingness to probe the internal workings of the mind through word association.

The early mathematical and descriptive approaches to the scientific study of religion led down two paths. The emphasis on what could be counted and measured led to works like Edwin Starbuck's book, *The Psychology of Religion: An Empirical Study of the Growth of Religious Consciousness*, published in 1899.[6] Using a questionnaire, Starbuck reported the mean age at which religious conversion to Christianity usually took place. The emphasis on the inner life of the mind led most famously to William James's classic book, *The Varieties of Religious Experience*, published in 1902. James made use of nearly 200 extracts from the writings of religious individuals.[7] He arranged the extracts according to the topic they covered and then, within each topic, put the extracts into a series to illustrate the early, middle and later phases of its manifestation. James did not rely on any particular method to isolate the topics in the first place, nor did he systematically collect the illustrative material which makes up so large a part of his work. He referred occasionally to Starbuck's findings, and indeed some of his extracts were taken from Starbuck's completed questionnaires. His method is essentially descriptive, though he makes use of larger categories or types, like the healthy-minded soul or the sick soul, by which to make contrasts between opposed ways of looking at life.

Yet, despite the success of James's work, there was an unwillingness on the part of many psychologists to deal with consciousness. Robert Thouless, the Cambridge psychologist, wrote *The Psychology of Religion* in 1923. His book was reprinted with a fresh preface in 1961.[8] Writing nearly forty years after its first publication, Thouless was able to survey the changes which had taken place in his lifetime. He identified the shift from a study of religious consciousness to a study of religious behaviour as being fundamental to what had happened.[9] He suggested that James's book, had it been written later, would have been called

The Varieties of Religious Behaviour. The second change he identified was related to the first: quantitative methods of research had replaced qualitative methods. As a consequence of these changes, however, other alterations had also taken place. In the 1920s, there was a tendency to explain human activity in terms of instincts; by the 1960s, this had disappeared. Instincts appeared to say nothing useful. Religious behaviour could be described and classified, but to say that it was caused by a religious instinct begged questions about where this instinct might be located and how it might be suppressed or developed.

A more broadly based and extensive review of the psychology of religion was made by David Wulff in *Psychology of Religion,* published in 1991.[10] He identified a larger range of approaches to religion than Thouless, and found a larger range of equivalent methods. Broadly speaking, he divided his approaches into the objective and the subjective. Experimentation was found solely in the objective approaches, whereas projective techniques (where individuals are asked, for instance, to describe what thoughts come to them when shown an ambiguous shape), personal documents and phenomenological methods (where attempts are made to describe consciousness) fall within the subjective approaches. Some methods, like the use of questionnaires or interviews or historical-anthropological studies, are to be found within every approach. Though Wulff is generally inclusive in his views, he does offer a critique of each approach, or the main exemplars of each approach, at appropriate points. From this it is clear that objective methods find fault with the subjective methods, and *vice versa.*

This reciprocal critique stems from much more general considerations than those relating specifically to the subject matter under review. It stems from larger changes within society and the changing consensus of philosophical opinion about the status of different types of knowledge, and it is reflected across a spectrum of academic disciplines.

The critique of objective methods by more subjective methods is to be found, for example, both in the discipline of sociology and in literary criticism. It is made most general in the presentation of post-modernist theory, which denies the possibility of a unified world-view, and therefore of any sort of truth which approximates to the absolute. One strand of the quarrel which subjective methods have with objective methods focuses on the question of the existence of an objective observer. Subjective methods break down the distinction between the observer and the external world. This may be by attributing to the observer no fixed identity, but a set of identities which change according to his or her social setting. The self, in other words, is a social construct. Or the distinction may be blurred by the denial that observations can be made with transparent objectivity. Observations are 'theory-laden', coloured and bent by the preconceptions of the observer. By this means, in literary theory, texts may be 'deconstructed' so that their meaning is not fixed and final, but kaleidoscopically shifting in tune with the reader's circumstances.

As a further dismissal of objectivity, the logic prevalent in Western society since Aristotle has been questioned, especially the proposition that an object cannot both be and not be. Once this occurs, it is clear that many logical chains which were thought to be faultless, become undone. The terms used in logical propositions cannot then refer to a reality which exists, and the world has to be 'reconstructed' on a different system.[11] Language becomes an interpretative web which is not related to anything outside itself, since it is by language that the self is defined and things outside language are described. Anything that might be thought to exist outside a text, and to which a text might refer, has no reality. This is because the referent of a text cannot be considered to be independent of a text since it cannot be identified apart from it.[12]

Against this denial of objectivity, numerous counter-arguments have been mounted. Karl Popper has crossed swords with Theodor Adorno over the role of sociological theory.[13] Adorno took the view that sociological theory must, as part of its mission, change society. The conventions which allow scientific activity to take place are, in Adorno's view, social conventions, and any critical activity, like that which is genuinely scientific, must at the same time as it makes theoretical advance also turn its attention to the society in which it is embedded. Such an assertion depends on the Marxist idea that consciousness is a social product and that 'false consciousness' must exist in those sections of society which are adrift from the economic base, the means of production, the proletariat. Yet, Adorno's view of sociology only makes sense if consciousness *is* indissolubly tied to its social base, in other words if there is no consciousness, and therefore no knowledge, which is common to everyone. Without this universal consciousness objective knowledge is impossible. But Adorno's premise is not at all certain. Human beings share a common sensory apparatus and an ability to communicate with each other which counts against the notion of separate socially induced consciousnesses, some of which are true and some of which are incorrigibly false.

More consistently Popper has engaged in a long-standing discussion of the nature of science and of objectivity. He takes issue with those who deny the possibility of objectivity, where objectivity is defined as public and testable agreement between individuals about what is the case. Such a debate goes back into the history of both science and philosophy. It was solved by Kant by pointing to *a priori* concepts, concepts which are true without reference to an observer. Such concepts are those of space, time and causality. To Popper the pursuit of objectivity should be built-in to the methods of science, particularly since experiments allow for evidence to be collected under testable conditions and where public agreement is therefore straightforward. Objectivity, then, may start from subjectivity, but by the process of agreement and criticism it becomes objective knowledge, independent of those who do the agreeing. The whole enterprise of science may be understood as the production of explanatory theories about the world which are subjected to rigorous testing. If a theory fails to meet the tests which it implies (if the eclipse of the sun does not occur when Newton's theory of gravitation says it should), then the theory fails and a new one must be found. If a theory passes the tests which it implies, then the theory passes into the realm of knowledge. Sophisticated relationships between tests and the probability or otherwise of their being passed by scientific theories can be worked out, and the wider the range of content to which the theory refers, the easier it is to find satisfactory tests.

Popper's defence of objectivity is bound up with his examination of scientific methods. He argues that science was once accustomed to try to form its laws by the inductive method, that is, by generalizing from repeated instance of occurrences in the past. The sun rose yesterday, and the day before that, and as far back as anyone can remember, and therefore it is likely to rise tomorrow. This type of reasoning, though it may appeal to common sense, is not watertight. It does not follow *logically* that the sun will rise tomorrow because it has risen innumerable times in the past. Induction is open to the challenge of the sceptic. And, in the scientific endeavour, it fails because, whereas a thousand or a million sightings of a black crow would lead to the inductive law that 'all crows are black', there is always the possibility that the next crow to be sighted will be albino. In other words, countless confirmatory instances of a scientific law can be overthrown by one disconfirmatory instance. There is an asymmetry between proof and disproof and no way of knowing when the disproof may appear.

The only way that science can proceed is to reject induction and to make as much use as possible of deduction. By deductive reasoning, like that involved in mathematics, it is certain that conclusions will truly follow from premises, provided all the steps in between are properly taken. Deductive reasoning must therefore be used to form testable statements from scientific theories. These statements must be tested with a view to disconfirming them, by looking hard for white crows. The failure to find counter-examples allows the scientific theory to be treated as knowledge, though knowledge which is provisional and open to correction.

If this strategy seems to offer no direct route to certainty and, indeed, if 'provisional knowledge' seems paradoxical, Popper argues that it is the best available and, moreover, it conforms to the way that scientific discovery actually takes place. After its discovery scientific knowledge actually exists in the sense that it is recorded in the libraries of the world. It is knowledge which can grow, be criticized and does not depend on any individual's perspective or thoughts. It exists outside human beings as a joint product of the human cultural and scientific heritage. It is objective.

A more radical, but less well-known, defence of objectivity tries to reinstate inductive reasoning.[14] This defence contends that induction, for all practical purposes, works very well. If there are 1,000 tickets in the lottery and a man buys 999 of them, then his confidence in winning the lottery is rightly high, even though the chance of the ticket he does not own being picked does exist. In the same way, it is sensible to disregard the possibility of disconfirmatory instances of scientific laws based on induction. In addition, law based on induction is public and testable, and therefore objective.

Approach adopted in this book

The general critique which subjective and objective methods make of each other is carried on at two levels. The theoretical level relates to the wider background, both historical and cultural, in which science is conducted. The practical level relates to the advantages and disadvantages of the various methods at the disposal of the researcher.

If we start from the large question, 'What can we find out about religion as it affects people's lives today?' we are soon led to the realization that the question is too big to be answered without refinement and rephrasing. Religions are numerous and diverse. So we narrow the question by asking, 'What can we find out about Christianity as it affects people's lives today?' Again we are still led to the realization that the question is too big. Do we want to concentrate on beliefs, behaviours, consciousness, thinking, feelings or attitudes? Are we interested in young or older people? Do we care about the way different aspects of religion change as people grow? Or is our concern with the different way males and females hold their beliefs, if this is in fact the case? Should we turn our attention to what makes people believe or feel or behave or hold an attitude? And, if we turn our attention in this direction, how do we disentangle the effects of one influence from another?

If we look at the methods commonly available for collecting data, then it is evident that a huge number of *interviews* could have been carried out, tape-recorded, classified and summarized. This method, useful though it is for certain categories of question or certain types of people (for example in dealing with very young children or the very elderly), has the drawback, common to many subjective techniques, that it tends to inconsistency. The conversation might turn one way or another. The interviewer might be more or less frightening to the interviewee. Even the *semi-clinical interview* which makes use of a rough schedule of questions and a form of standardized approach fails to avoid these difficulties. In addition this method is time-consuming and subjective to the extent that only those themes and topics which the interviewer thinks worth reporting are picked out and presented to the public.

Second, free and expressive writing in response to *open-ended questions* could be used.[15] But this method, though it is more settled than the interview, does not lend itself easily to objective analysis. Some respondents will write freely and flowingly within the time allowed to them. Others will write very little. Are they embarrassed, bored or incapable of addressing the question? The researcher will have great difficulty in deciding what to make of the mass of information which is collected. Any attempt to classify it will lead to problems because some responses will be carefully nuanced and others forceful and direct. Some pieces of writing may fit into several categories, but if this is so, how can the responses be dealt with mathematically?

It would be possible to combine the semi-clinical interview and the open-ended written question and response. This approach is often used in case studies and yields valuable information. But it cannot easily cope with attempts to deal with the large questions we asked earlier. The case study of one school or one community may or may not be generalizable to a wider context. There is no really objective, or publicly testable, way of deciding whether this is so.

Third, we can ask *written questions that demand a fixed set of responses*. The questions can be phrased simply and the responses on offer to the respondent can be chosen on the basis of interviews or written answers of the type we have already considered. The advantage of this method is that it offers a standard approach to a large number of people. The questionnaire does not change from day to day or year to year. It asks its questions and offers its fixed responses. It lends itself to statistical analysis. For example, in answer to the question, 'Do you believe in God?' there are three basic responses: 'yes', 'no' or 'don't know'. These responses remain the same and the percentage of affirmative replies may be meaningfully compared with uncertain or negative replies. If the questionnaire is answered anonymously, then there is every likelihood that the answers will be truthfully given and, anyway, the whole matter can be tested, as we shall see, by administering the questionnaire under different conditions to discover whether different results follow.

When the difficulties of interviews and open-ended written answers are examined, the advantages of a questionnaire design stand out. It allows for precision and objectivity. Yet, the particular advantage of a questionnaire is that it also allows *both* for measurement of opinions, by gauging responses to individual questions, *and* for the measurement of attitudes, by scaling the interrelationships between individual questions. Neither of the other methods makes this possible. Attitudes, as we have seen, lie at the heart of this book.

For these practical reasons we have made use of the virtues of an *objective approach* to the scientific study of religion. The more theoretical reasons discussed earlier help to confirm this decision.

Concepts within the objective approach

To appreciate in more detail how this approach is carried into action, it is necessary to understand some of the concepts associated with it. These are: measurement, probability, correlation, factor analysis, causation, reliability, validity, variance, t-tests, models and path analysis. Each of these concepts is dealt with in turn.

Measurement
Measurement presumes knowable mathematical relationships and the existence of stable attributes whose characteristics may be observed or inferred. A physical object has height, weight, volume and so on, and these attributes can be recorded in appropriate units against some sort of repeatable standard. An apple can be weighed and its volume and height can be calculated. Each attribute is recorded in different units on a different scale. The different scales may be related to each other so that weight and volume say something together about any particular apple, but it would be foolish to try to say anything precise about height with a weighing machine. Moreover, no one pretends that, by giving the weight or height of an apple, we have said all there is to say about it. There are still other attributes, like taste, which are important but more difficult to specify. The point about measurement, then, is that it does not say everything there is to say about a phenomenon, but it does say important things about it and, providing the measuring instrument is correctly

constructed, it says them accurately. It also says them objectively in the sense that the information so gained is publicly testable; there is no dependence on subjective, transient or personal impressions, however valuable these may be in many circumstances.

Sometimes, especially in psychological studies, an attribute cannot be directly observed, but has to be inferred. We might infer that someone had artistic abilities by looking at their paintings. The paintings are a product of the artistic abilities, though they are not the artistic abilities themselves. Similarly, attitudes are inferred from responses to statements. However, inferred attributes need not be thought of as somehow less real than directly observed attributes. Gravity is an inferred attribute since only its effects can be observed, but no sensible person would doubt its universality or usefulness.

Scales presume that mathematical relationships, even between inferred attributes, may be clearly expressed, and they may be expressed at various levels of sophistication. An *ordinal* scale simply places what is being measured in order of size or intensity. An *(equal-)interval* scale does rather more. It is arranged so that the distance between ten and twenty on the scale, whatever the units employed, is as great as the distance between thirty and forty, or any other points ten units apart. Inches, metres and miles are all interval-scale units. Because an interval scale gives us all the information given by an ordinal scale, and more besides, interval scales are generally preferred.

When measurements are taken, the figures derived will usually show that the collection of things which have been measured vary on the scale that has been used. Whatever varies in this fashion is often referred to as a 'variable'. There is one variable, however, which is often employed in psychological studies in the same way as a scale, although only two points on it may be recorded. This is the variable of sex. If males are scored as 'one' and females as 'two' (or the other way round, the figures are given for the sake of example), then sex can be treated like any other scaled variable.

Probability

Probability theory is complicated and has several branches. The essential notion is that the likelihood of the occurrence of an event or co-occurrence of several events can be calculated. For example, we can calculate that in 600 throws of a conventional dice which has six faces, each number will fall face uppermost 100 times. We can also calculate how frequently we would expect two dice thrown together to produce the same number. For example, the number 3 will be thrown one time in six. This will be the same for both dice. Thus the odds of two dice thrown together showing the same number will be one-in-six multiplied by one-in-six, or one-in-thirty-six. In other words the *conjunction* of two slightly improbable events is *more improbable* than either of the events occurring on its own.

The same idea can be applied to outcomes and characteristics surveyed among a human population. We can illustrate this idea by considering how probable it is that blue eyes go with fair hair and brown eyes with dark hair. Suppose we consider fifty fair-haired people and fifty dark-haired people. If there were no connection between hair colour and eye colour, we should expect that half the fair-haired people would have blue eyes and the other half have brown eyes, and we should expect a similar half-and-half split among the dark-haired people. If we discovered a systematic variation such that there were forty fair-haired people with blue eyes and forty dark-haired people with brown eyes, we could compare our observed frequencies with our expected frequencies. Our expected frequencies would be those which would occur by chance. Our observed frequencies would be those which occurred as a result of a hidden factor (presumably a genetic one).

Notice how, in our example (and it is only an example), both the hair colours are associated with an eye colour. This systematic variation is much more unlikely than one of the hair colours being associated with one eye colour and the other being equally associated with both. In this respect it is similar to our example of two dice both showing the same face.

In essence, we are making four points here. First, chance distributions of outcomes are likely to be evenly distributed. Second, outcomes relating to human populations can be calculated. Third, when these outcomes differ from what would be expected by chance, we look for reasons for this. Fourth, improbabilities increase when they are combined.

By convention, outcomes in sociological and psychological research that are less probable than those which would occur by chance five times in a hundred are said to be *statistically significant*. This means that they are normally worth comment, though the researcher has to judge on the basis of theoretical considerations what sort of substantive significance should be ascribed to them. In general, findings are substantively significant if they contribute to the construction of a new theory or the modification of an existing theory.

Correlation
Correlation refers to the connection between events or variables. Foot-size, for instance, may correlate with height; people with big feet may tend to be taller. A perfect positive correlation is recorded as +1 and lack of correlation is recorded as zero. Negative correlation is observed where two variables are related in the sense that smaller values on one variable are associated with larger values on the other. A perfect negative correlation is recorded as −1.

Correlations are best calculated on interval scales, but ordinal scales will also provide valid results if certain checks are made beforehand. Sex, when treated as a scaled variable, may be correlated with other scales, and the size and direction of the correlation coefficients will then indicate the level of differences between males and females.

Correlation and probability are connected in the sense that higher levels of correlation are necessary to register statistical significance in smaller samples. If the height and weight of the entire adult population of Britain were known, only a very small positive association between the two variables would be necessary for statistical significance. We should be able to say that there was a tendency for heavier people to be taller or for taller people to be heavier. If a small random sample of the entire adult population of Britain were drawn, then a higher correlation between height and weight would be needed to reach the same level of statistical significance. Thus findings derived from samples can be transferred to the larger populations they represent at a calculable level of probability.[16]

Factor analysis
Correlation, however, has a further use. If, for instance, scores on ten variables are correlated together so that each one is correlated

with all the others, a matrix or network of forty-five figures is produced.[17] There will be patterns of variation within this matrix and the process of principal-components analysis, which is a mathematical procedure, reduces the pattern to its simplest form. We might, for example, have a set of figures dealing with children's age, linguistic ability, mathematical ability, parental income, enjoyment of sport, enjoyment of travel, attitude to the environment and attitude to cats and dogs in the home. We might discover that age, linguistic ability, mathematical ability and parental income are closely related and 'load' on to the same factor, but that the other factors (enjoyment of sport, enjoyment of travel, attitude to the environment and attitude to cats and dogs in the home) belonged to a different factor. The technique has many uses but, in an attitude scale, it can be used to see whether the items of the scale hang together in a coherent, or unidimensional, whole. We should expect the majority of items in an attitude scale to load on to the same factor.

Causation

The idea of cause is basic to most people's understanding of the world. A causes B to happen, or B happens because of A. Causal models, at their simplest, set out in a diagram the relationship between A and B. This is very conveniently done in terms of a correlation coefficient. Yet, the existence of a significant correlation does not mean that the direction of causation can simply be read off from the figures. In the case of height and weight, it seems reasonable to believe that height causes weight because, if weight caused height, there would be no short heavy adults. Yet, even this may not be as simple as it looks because we might find that heavy children have a tendency to grow into taller adults than undernourished children. In this case, weight might help to cause height.

Perfect correlation, and therefore perfect causation, in real life is very rare. It is much more common to find that B varies with A, but not exactly. There is some slippage. The slippage may come from errors in measurement or from the effect of another variable, C, which needs to be brought into the picture. The simple rule to remember is that, while causation will be revealed by correlation, correlation will not necessarily point to causation.

Reliability

Reliable scales measure consistently. Scales of any kind will tell us nothing very useful if they give us scores which fluctuate over a brief period of time.

The concept of reliability in measurement theory is often expressed by correlations between a test score and a repetition of the test shortly afterwards. This is known as *test/re-test* reliability. A single scale can produce a similar effect if alternate items are added together and the totals correlated. This is known as *split-half* reliability. Reliability is linked with accuracy. If a scale were inaccurate then test/re-test correlations would vary even if the construct being measured did not change at all. Reliability is also linked with the length of the scale. A scale made up of, say, three items is much more likely to be inaccurate (because a change of response to one item changes the score by a greater proportion than would be the case if there were more items in the scale) and therefore unreliable. Psychologists have calculated various statistics to show the relationship between accuracy and scale length, and between scores on sets of items and other sets of items, or between one item and the rest of the test. The statistic adopted to express reliability throughout this book is Cronbach's 'alpha'.[18] Alpha is the average of all the possible split-half coefficients for the test, that is, the average correlation between all possible combinations of half the items with the other half. By this means the reliability of a test can be calculated without administering it more than once.

Validity

The validity of a scale is defined as the accuracy with which it measures that which it is intended to measure.[19] Obviously a scale which is intended to measure weight but which in fact measures height may have the property of reliability but will in no sense be valid.

Attitude scales are open to external validation in the sense that attitudes may be expected to correlate with, for example, certain behaviours. The trouble with this kind of validation, however, is that if attitude is separate and distinct from behaviour, then we should not, in any case, expect a perfect correlation. There is no way round this problem regarding external validation.

Attitudes are more satisfactorily validated by internal

considerations. There are two methods of this nature. The first may be expressed by the question: Do the items in the scale properly reflect the content of the attitude. For example, does a scale measuring attitude toward war properly reflect all that it should about war? This is known as *content* validity. The second method may be expressed by the question: Does the scale produce scores that correlate with other indices which ought to relate to the one being tested? For example, in a particular population, does a negative attitude toward war correlate with a negative attitude toward violence generally? This second form of validity, which is to be preferred, is dependent on a network of variables which are often related to each other by a single theory. It is known as *construct* validity.

Variance

Suppose that we collect two sets of 250 figures. The first gives the weight of a sample of men aged twenty and the second gives the weight of a sample of women aged twenty. One simple way to compare the weights of the men and women is by averages. To do this, we add the weights for each set together and divide by 250. We can now see at a glance whether, in general, men weigh more than women.

The average is a useful summary of the two sets. We have turned the 250 figures for men into one figure which expresses them all. And the same applies to the 250 figures for women. The trouble with an average, though, is that it may not give a particularly good overall idea of what our men weigh. There may be a group of heavyweight wrestlers in our sample, all of whom weigh more than twenty stone. The average for male weights will be raised by this unusual subgroup. What we need is a figure to tell us how varied our set of 250 men are. The best way to do this is to calculate the *variance*.

The variance is really the squared average distance of each weight from the average of the group. In order to calculate it we have to subtract the average from each weight, square the result (thus eliminating negative figures from the below average people), add the squares together and then divide by the number in the group. The resulting number shows whether the group is clustered closely round its average or spread out with a lot of very heavy and very light people at the extremities of the distribution.

A proper comparison is not quite as simple as this because the distribution of scores may fit various patterns. There may be one extremely heavy person and ten extremely light ones, or there may be an even number of light and heavy people. Both distributions could have the same variance, but the basic idea of variance expressing the *general dispersion of scores* around the average should be grasped.

What happens when there are two sets of scores which correlate? How do the variances relate to each other? Without going into the mathematics of this, it is simple to remember that the correlation coefficient (called 'r') of the two sets of scores, if squared, expresses the percentage of variance the two sets have in common. (If one variable causes the other, then the percentage shows how strong the causal link is.) If the correlation coefficient is 0·80, then the square of this is 0·64 and this means that 64 per cent of the variance in one set is determined by the variance in the other set.

It may be helpful to think about extreme cases to visualize the relationship properly. Suppose the correlation was +1, then the square of this would be one, showing that 100 per cent of variance in one set of figures was caused by the other set. The highest figure in one set would correspond with the highest figure in the second set, the second-highest figures would also correspond, and so on throughout the whole set. Now suppose that each set were turned into a graph to show the distribution of scores. The two graphs would be linked, not in the shape (because the distributions would be different) but in the sense that changes in one graph (as the sample was increased, for instance) would be exactly reflected by changes in the other graph. They would look like two hump-shaped lines that moved together.

If, on the other hand, the correlation were 0, then 0% of the variance in one set would be determined by variance in the other set. As one set changed, it would be unrelated to changes in the other set. The two graphs would fluctuate independently of each other. They would look like two hump-shaped lines that moved without synchronization.

T-tests

One comparison between two groups tests for the significance of the difference between their means (or averages). The principle is the same for that of other statistical tests in the sense that chance differences in means are compared with observed differences. If the observed differences are less likely to have come about than would have been the case by chance five times in a hundred, then the differences are significant. There is one further feature of this test which needs to be taken into account if the difference between means is to be properly compared. The variance of scores within the two groups must also be inspected.

Models

One feature of an acceptance of objective knowledge is that it becomes sensible to build models. Models are normally precisely proportioned representations of something bigger. They are constructed to show how the separate parts of the thing being modelled fit together and work together. By looking at the model, it is possible to understand the real thing better, and if the model and the real thing do not behave in the same way, then the model can be altered. But the reason that models are compatible with an objective view of knowledge is that the model and the real thing both exist 'out there' in the external world and can be related to each other through this shared existence. A subjective view of knowledge, which blurs or denies the distinction between the external world and the observer, has much greater difficulty in showing how the model relates to the reality it is designed to describe. This is because there is no external reality on which the subjectivist may obtain a hold.

The models which are constructed in this text are generally causal. They try to show how one thing has an effect on another. The things in the model, however, need not exist in a physical and concrete way. For example, if we tried to build a model to show how eating, body weight and exercise were connected, we might show that eating caused an increase in weight unless there were an appropriate increase in exercise. And even then the model would be complicated because exercise would, for a while, cause an increase in weight while fat was turned to muscle. The basic components of the model could be related in a diagram and the causal relations between them expressed visually. The variable describing eating, though, would best be transformed into numbers, perhaps by giving all foods a calorific value. In the same way, the variables expressing weight and exercise would be given a numeric descriptor. The variables, however, are not things, not objects, but quantifications of behaviour or weight. Nevertheless the model could show, and could predict, increases or decreases in body weight for anyone whose behaviour was put into it.

Path analysis

Correlation coefficients show how two variables relate together. But it is possible to correlate many more than two things together by the process of 'multiple regression'. This is done by making one variable the 'dependent' variable and then correlating a set of other variables with it. Here, for example, we might make the reading age of a child the dependent variable and correlate it with the child's chronological age, his or her mathematical ability, parental income, interest in the environment expressed on a scale and the number of books in the home. All these variables can be expressed in figures. They may be of different kinds, in the sense that the child's mathematical ability may be expressed on an ordinal scale while his or her chronological age is recorded on an interval scale. Nevertheless, all the variables may be correlated together, and a joint correlation calculated. This joint correlation is called R and is distinguished from individual correlations which are called r. We can then check to see if the joint correlation is more than each of the individual correlations. For instance, we might find that the child's chronological age and the number of books in the parental home correlated more highly with reading age than any other combination of variables. We might, however, find that all the variables are needed to give the best result.

What complicates the issue is that the 'predictor' variables, those which correlate with reading age, may correlate with each other, and some may correlate negatively with each other. It might be the case that mathematical ability and interest in the environment correlate negatively so that, when both variables are put into the equation, some of the positive correlation between mathematical ability and reading ability is cancelled out by the interest in the environment variable. All these possibilities must be explored.

In building the path model the coefficients from regression analysis are used, though they are converted to a standardized form, that is, the figures which take account of the different units in which the variables may be measured.[20] In their standardized form the individual coefficients from regression analysis are called beta weights. The researcher, having obtained the regression coefficients, has to decide how to place the variables in a causal sequence. The path model shows the standardized regression coefficients next to an arrow which represents the direction of causation. What this means is that variables near the arrow head change in response to changes in the variable at the other end of the arrow. An example makes clearer how the model is put together.

Suppose church attendance is found to be correlated with personal prayer and personal prayer with a positive attitude toward Christianity, it is arguable that church attendance, mediated through personal prayer, causes a positive attitude toward Christianity. The line of correlation might take the opposite direction, however. A positive attitude toward religion might cause personal prayer and this might lead to church attendance. In establishing the direction of causation it is usually helpful to see the *temporal* sequence in a set of variables. The variable that takes place first is clearly more likely to be the cause of the second variable, rather than the other way round. More sophisticated techniques allow for the removal of the effects of the intervening variables in a causal model. In the example given, we might be able to remove the effects of personal prayer and by this means to judge the effects of church attendance on its own on attitude toward Christianity (or *vice versa*). The removal of the effects of personal prayer is effectively done by calculating the connection between church attendance and attitude toward Christianity among people whose level of personal prayer is identical.

These sophisticated techniques make use of the fact that the variance due to the first variable to be entered in a multiple-regression equation 'has first bite of the cherry'. It removes variance and leaves less variance for subsequent variables to account for. In the example we have given, we would remove the effects of personal prayer by entering that variable first into the multiple-regression equation. Afterwards we would enter church attendance. Any variance church attendance accounted for would then be uncontaminated by the effects of differences in personal prayer among church attenders. All these manipulations may be made using multiple-regression techniques because statistical packages routinely allow researchers to fix the order in which variables will be entered to the equation.

Studies reported in this book include a number of path models, which can be conveniently divided into four main groups. In each of the first three groups attitude toward Christianity is the dependent variable, the one at the end of the causal line which is altered by the others in the model.

In the first group of models there is a straightforward attempt to predict differences in attitude toward Christianity from basic knowledge about the young person's age and sex and from the contexts of home, school and church. For age and gender will influence attitude toward Christianity, but attitude toward Christianity will not affect age or gender. Where the effects of differences in parental church attendance or school are the focus of the enquiry, it makes sense to see how children's attitude toward Christianity varies as a consequence of the school or church or home, and the causal model allows a figure to be put on the contribution to children's attitudes of each of the factors in the model. In this way, the effects of Anglican and Roman Catholic schools, for example, on children's attitudes may be discovered, and this calculation can take into account the differences which might exist between Anglican and Roman Catholic homes. The model allows the causal contribution of each variable to be assessed in relation to all the others so that, in effect, the result of any one variable may be isolated.

In the second group of models attitude toward Christianity is considered as a function of personality. In these studies the Eysenckian description of personality is used. Individuals are located along each of the three major dimensions of personality: extraversion–introversion, neuroticism–stability and tender-mindedness–tough-mindedness (psychoticism). Here again attitude toward Christianity is thought of as being dependent on personality, though in this instance the question of causal direction is more open. If a negative relationship were to be found between attitude toward Christianity and neuroticism, this could be explained in two different ways. It may be that a positive attitude toward Christianity reduces tendencies to neuroticism, or that stable people adopt a more favourable attitude toward

Christianity. This debate can only be partly settled by *assumptions* about the permanence and stability of individual differences in personality which argue for the priority of personality over individual differences in religiosity.

In a third group of models attitude toward Christianity is related to wider societal variables like pop culture, religious television and denominational identity. Again it is the wider societal variables that are assumed to influence attitude toward Christianity.

The final group of models place attitude toward Christianity as one of the causal factors. Can a positive attitude toward Christianity be said to be a cause of prejudice or identifiable moral values? Does a positive attitude toward Christianity lead to a favourable attitude toward school or to particular subjects on the curriculum, especially science? Does a positive attitude toward Christianity lead to a rejection of drug-taking?

Finally, there is a group of models where the direction of causation needs to be tested both ways. What is the relationship between religious experience and attitude toward Christianity? Are those who have had a religious experience also more open to Christianity, or are those who have a positive attitude toward Christianity more likely to have a religious experience?

Interdisciplinary research

The issue of interdisciplinary research underlies many of the investigations which are reported. To appreciate this issue, it is helpful to understand the way academic work is divided into disciplines. An economist works in the discipline of economics and a historian in the discipline of history. The distinction between an economist and a historian may look straightforward. The first deals with money and the second deals with the past. Yet in order to understand the way money behaves today, the economist needs to know how it used to behave. Trade cycles, fluctuations in currency values and other factors relevant to today's problems have been observed before. So the economist must also have an understanding of the economics of the past. In the same way, the historian may best be able to understand the pattern of historical events by taking economic data into consideration. Perhaps the price of corn or the value of land was at the root of a particular historical disturbance. So, though the various studies within academic life are separate, they are also relevant to each other and may overlap and intermingle.

A philosophical approach to academic disciplines suggests that each one is made distinct by particular concepts and criteria which belong where they do and nowhere else. The characteristic concepts of economics function according to the criteria used within that discipline. By using these concepts according to these criteria, the economist may operate on the data of the past or the present. The age of the data is not relevant to the definition of the discipline. In the same way, though a historian may take an interest in economic matters, he or she operates as a historian by using the characteristic criteria and concepts of history.

But what of work which is done at the boundary between two disciplines? There really may be issues where the division between academic disciplines is difficult to apply. If this is the case, Francis and Kay have argued that any effective piece of inter-disciplinary work should be acceptable to practitioners of all the various disciplines who might rightfully claim the area as their own.[21] If the interdisciplinary investigation, for example, addresses an area of religion which is of concern to religious education, then *both* religious practitioners (especially theologians) *and* educationalists should recognize that the investigation has taken the concepts and criteria of their respective disciplines seriously. Or, to put the matter the other way, what an interdisciplinary piece of work should *not* do is to address the problems of one discipline by reducing concepts and criteria distinctive to that discipline to those established by another discipline.

What this approach, of course, presumes is that each discipline is sharply demarcated and sufficiently similarly structured to other disciplines to allow studies of this kind to take place. When these presumptions are met, interdisciplinary work can solve problems inaccessible to practitioners of a single discipline. Occasionally, when the problems are too large or the questions being asked are too complicated, interdisciplinary work must give way to multi-disciplinary approaches which allow several investigations, each within a single discipline, to proceed in parallel. The presumption under these conditions is that complementary explanations of phenomena are equally valid and that none of the contributing disciplines supersedes the others in explanatory power.

Whereas multi-disciplinary studies often used different methods, interdisciplinary studies are characterized by a unity of method within the contributing disciplines. These methods are those of the social sciences. They depend on the concepts which belong to the objective approach and, for this reason, have a family resemblance to each other.

Appendix 2
Assessing attitudes

Introduction

This appendix explores how an instrument to measure *attitude toward Christianity* was constructed.

Once a decision has been taken to study religion in an objective way, then the number of methods which are suitable for this type of data collection become limited to those which produce measurable and testable variables. Moreover, if objectivity is to be pursued rigorously, then samples large enough to be representative of the population as a whole, or worthwhile subsections of it, must be drawn. These two considerations alone point in the direction of a questionnaire-based research project, or series of projects. Questionnaires allow for the generation of measurable and testable variables since each response to a questionnaire item may be counted, and a re-administration of the questionnaire allows for the testing of any conclusions which have been drawn. Questionnaires also allow for the drawing of large samples. We know, for example, that there are approximately half a million pupils in year nine in England and Wales[1] so that, if we wish to say anything specific about them all, we need to draw a reasonably large sample. We cannot say exactly how large the sample will need to be in each instance, but we know from sampling theory that the size of the sample will be determined by how widely the particular variable we are interested in fluctuates and whether its distribution is normal. What sampling theory tells us quite clearly is that a very small sample, especially if it is not drawn randomly, is likely to be unrepresentative.

There are other practical advantages of using a questionnaire. Questionnaires can provide, in addition to the information necessary to construct and apply attitude scales, information about personal and social variables which may influence attitudes. In other words, the variables necessary for building path models can be collected at one and the same time as attitudes are measured.

In addition to these advantages, there is another, perhaps more crucial one. Questionnaires allow for the measurement of attitudes, and attitudes appear central to the study of religious development. This is because attitudes stand as variables which have a personal, psychological dimension and as variables which have a social, collective dimension. Thus attitudes appear to be related to perception, learning, behaviour, emotions and cognition as well as to factors like sex and personality which are all personal variables. They are also related to membership of social groups and social behaviour. Like religion itself, then, attitudes stand astride more than one discipline and lend themselves to interdisciplinary studies.

Lastly, though the sociological and psychological literature on attitudes has not stopped developing, it has at least reached a point where a wide consensus exists. As we shall see, attitudes have been measured scientifically since the late 1920s. The fifty years which passed before Francis initiated the series of studies reported in this book allowed teething problems in measurement theory to take place and be largely resolved. The sub-discipline of psychometrics, in which attitude measurement falls, was ripe for application to the field of religion in a way which it had not been in the 1940s or 1950s. Furthermore and fortuitously, the development of main-frame and later desktop computers took place from the late 1960s onwards. In terms of attitude measurement and the calculation of coefficients involving samples of thousands, a revolution began to take place. Thus theoretical advances in psychometrics and technological advances in computational power converged in the 1970s and permitted rapid gains to be made in our understanding of attitudes and related variables. As we have seen, these gains allowed for the first time an accurate estimation to be made of matters as diverse as the impact of church schools and the effects of the apparent conflict between science and religion on the religious development of young people.

Attitudes

What, in brief, are attitudes? Two main ideas about attitudes exist. The first notion takes attitudes to be multi-dimensional constructs (or attributes). According to this notion, attitudes are made up of cognitive, affective and conative components.[2] The cognitive components are beliefs, the affective components are evaluations, and the conative components are made up of behaviour in some way associated with the attitude under consideration. The second notion takes attitudes to be unidimensional constructs (or attributes) only made up of affective components.[3] Francis favoured the unidimensional construct, partly on the basis of Fishbein's argument that the link between the components of the multi-dimensional notion of attitudes is unsatisfactory. The affective measure of attitude is usually broad, while the behavioural component is narrow. This means that correlations between these two components can be unstable. In addition the unidimensional notion has greater 'empirical feasibility'; it is likely to be turned into a more valid and reliable scale.[4]

Once the unidimensional notion of attitudes is chosen, it is necessary to ask how wide the affective component should be. Fishbein, in an important paper, argued that attitudes are made up from evaluative responses to beliefs about an object or concept.[5] Someone's attitude toward an object or concept comprises the sum total of his or her evaluative responses to these beliefs. But these evaluative responses are intellectually formed and emotionally expressed; they have a cognitive and an affective aspect. To take an example, a person who evaluates football negatively is likely to express this evaluation by agreeing with the emotional statements, 'I hate football' or 'football is boring.' The evaluation co-exists with an emotional tone and is in some respects mixed with it.

Before beginning work on the construction of an attitude scale, Francis was careful to exclude six other psychological constructs which might confuse the picture. Previous research using questionnaires had shown that 'sets' (which are unconscious perceptual predispositions) may sometimes influence responses recorded in questionnaires. People simply mark positive or negative responses without properly understanding the statement being put to them. The way to deal with this, however, is to make sure that statements are balanced between positives and negatives so as to engage the mind of the respondent. For example, 'I hate football' would be balanced by an item like, 'football is a great game'.

Then, it is important to distinguish between attitudes and opinions (opinions are held without emotional commitment or desire). Opinions are by this definition inherently unstable. They are elicited by single items. Attitudes, by contrast, are measured by groups of items and research has shown that, because attitudes are underlying dispositions, they are much less inclined to change from day to day. In order to penetrate behind ephemeral opinions to the underlying deep-seated attitudes, attitude scales must be composed of reasonably large numbers of items which hang together.

Beliefs are also clearly different from attitudes. In general, beliefs are related to the existence of something or its relations with other things. A belief is modifiable in the light of evidence but, in this context, it is not held with emotional force. Attitude scales will include references to beliefs, but not simply bald statements about belief like, 'I believe in religion' or 'I believe in God.'

Traits are related to more specific referents than attitudes, and often refer to types of behaviour. People may exhibit the trait of laziness or punctuality, but these are not a measure of their underlying attitude to anything. Attitude scales will not, therefore, refer to the *way* in which particular behaviour is carried out.

Values refer to some aspect of an object and are linked with goal achievement. For example, a person who values the environment may be careful to buy ecologically sound products and to avoid pollution. The value is linked with an aim or goal and operates as a guide to behaviour. Attitude scales will avoid linking questions or statements about current behaviour with long-term goals.

Motives are associated with drives towards behaviour. They function like values, although they 'push' people towards certain behaviour, while values 'pull' them. Attitude scales will avoid linking questions or statements about current behaviour with internal drives.

In the light of this consideration, Francis defined an attitude toward religion as:

A relatively permanent and enduring evaluative predisposition to a positive cr negative response of an affective nature which is based upon and reflects to some extent evaluative concepts or beliefs learned about the characteristics of a referent or group of referents which come within a definition of the religious.[6]

Having established a general definition of attitude toward religion, this definition was next specifically applied to attitude toward Christianity as one example of a religious tradition. This application took into account the fact that the operational form of the definition was to be set to work among young people as young as eight years of age. Attitude toward Christianity was, therefore, to be assessed by reference to six components of the Christian tradition accessible even to eight-year-olds, namely reference to God, Jesus, bible, prayer, church services and Christian worship and education as experienced in school.

Constructing a scale
In his foundation studies, Francis realised that a first-class scale measuring attitude toward Christianity could only be constructed if the best possible practice were observed at each stage in the process. Where the literature on scale construction had not achieved consensus it would be necessary to test each possible option systematically. If necessary, he was aware that he would have to construct several scales by several methods and to test each against the others until the result showed unequivocally that one was better than the rest. All this would involve a long and painstaking procedure, but it was one that could be hoped to lead to substantial results. An accurate interval scale measuring attitude toward Christianity, that was both reliable and valid, would be the outcome.

A careful review of the literature revealed that five main methods of attitude-scale construction have been proposed. Thurstone,[7] Likert[8] and Guttman[9] all put forward quite distinctive methods. Edwards,[10] in a modification of the Thurstone and Likert methods, suggested a technique which combined aspects of both methods. Finally Osgood, in a technique which was originally proposed in the context of the objective meaning of language, developed a method that has also been used in attitude scaling.[11]

Thurstone

Thurstone's method of attitude scaling requires six steps. First, a set of statements is collected and printed on separate cards. Second, a number of judges are asked to sort these statements into equal-appearing intervals, traditionally arranged along a continuum of eleven points from extreme unfavourability through neutrality to extreme favourability. Third, the scale value of each statement is computed by seeing which point on the scale the fiftieth percentile of judges place it. Fourth, the scale value assigned by the twenty-fifth and seventy-fifth percentiles is regarded as the index of variability (Q) and is taken as a measure of the ambiguity of the statements. Statements with a high Q value are eliminated from the final scale. Fifth, a selection of statements with a low Q value is made in such a way that they represent the whole continuum of the scale. Sixth, the scale is pilot-tested and statistically analysed to check its internal consistency.

It is important that the initial bank of statements represents the full range of attitudinal responses and that the judges who sort the statements are similar in age and outlook to the population whose attitudes are to be measured. In addition, items should express one idea, be comprehensible to the target population, should avoid words or syntax that introduce ambiguity and statements that are likely to be endorsed by everyone. Negatively worded and positively worded statements should both be included in the final scale to avoid the possibility of a response set and to minimize fatigue or boredom.

In order to test the usefulness of the Thurstone technique of attitude scaling, Francis began by assembling a bank of 110 statements from four places: existing attitude scales used among children and young people, published texts of children's writing and conversation, a series of individual interviews and a set of children's essays.

Moreover, Francis appears to be the first person to use primary-school pupils (aged nine to eleven) as sorters, on the grounds that the sorters should be drawn from the same population as those among whom the scale was to be employed. He tested the competence of children in this task against that of adults. He particularly wanted to know whether the scale values assigned by children would be the same as those assigned by adults and whether the Q values would be the same. What he did, therefore, was to enlist the help of 120 children from four classes in two primary schools. The class teacher and the researcher were present throughout the exercise. The children were asked to sort the statements, typed on pieces of paper, into three piles: favourable, neutral and unfavourable. After a school break, the children were then asked to take their three piles and to subdivide each set of statements into three further piles, in order to generate a greater differentiation of favourableness and unfavourableness. This was achieved using nine numbered pockets. The children were allowed as much time as they needed.

Each class teacher was asked to mark the responses of the children in each class who, on the grounds of ability, were most likely to have had difficulty with the exercise. The remaining 100 children's responses were then compared with those of a group of twenty-five primary school teachers. Correlations between the scale values of the children and the teachers were highly significant. However, the Q values resulting from the two groups differed considerably, implying that children and adults had difficulty with the meaning of different items. All items which had a high Q value for either children or adults were removed and this depleted the pool of items to such an extent that it proved to be impossible to construct a scale made up in exactly the way specified by the Thurstone technique. Instead a scale was constructed made up of items which had been judged by the adults. This scale was administered to both children and adults and tested on both populations for reliability.

The split-half reliability coefficient, when applied to the scale completed by 100 nine- to eleven-year-olds and 100 primary-school teachers, showed little difference, but in the case of the children this comparison alone would have been misleading because many of the children marked the middle or 'neutral' category. A further statistical test confirmed that adults and children understood the scale differently: they recorded a different range of scores and checked a different number of items. Francis concluded that the scale produced by this method could not be recommended for use with children in the primary age range.

Thurstone and Likert
Using the same items which had been previously collected and

sorted by the primary-school children, Francis carried out a second analysis using the Likert technique. This Likert system of scoring items is to allocate (usually) a five-point set of possible responses ranging from 'agree strongly', and 'agree', through 'not certain', to 'disagree' and 'disagree strongly'. Sixty items which had low Q values according to both the adult and child sorters were presented to four classes of ten- to eleven-year-olds. Each item was scored on the five point scale and then all the responses to the individual items were added up to give an overall score. Again the least able, those with reading difficulties, were eliminated, and this left 110 completed questionnaires.

Statistical item analysis followed and the sixty items were reduced in stages. At each point in the reduction of the number of items, the alpha coefficient was kept as high as possible. In the end there was very little difference between the alpha coefficient of the sixty-item scale and that of the final twenty-four-item scale, thus demonstrating that the best twenty-four items had been selected. The alpha coefficient reported for the final twenty-four-item scale was 0·977. Once this phase of the analysis was complete, the items were factor-analysed to discover whether they constituted a single dimension. In other words, though the items might inter-correlate satisfactorily overall, they might break down into groups of items which correlated more strongly with each other than with all the others. In the event, the first factor of the unrotated solution proposed by principal-component analysis accounted for 65·8 per cent of the variance, and it was easily more than four times greater than the next largest factor. The scale was therefore shown to be unidimensional.

When the final scale was examined, it was found to contain a third of its items which were scored in a negative direction, but none of these items included the words 'not', 'never' or 'none'. Thus the empirical process of item selection had produced items which showed desirable properties: they were simple, comprehensible, direct, avoided a fixed response set and were known to function reliably and unidimensionally among primary-aged pupils.

Reliability of the Thurstone–Likert scale
In order to be sure that the Thurstone–Likert scale of attitude toward Christianity, described above, functioned with the same

characteristics of reliability and unidimensionality among different age groups of children and young people, this instrument was administered to a hundred pupils in each of the year groups from year two in the primary school (six- to seven-year-olds) to year eleven in the secondary school (fifteen- to sixteen-year-olds). For each year group separate alpha coefficients were computed and the results of principal component analysis were examined. The scale functioned very similarly from year three (seven- to eight-year-olds) to year eleven (fifteen- to sixteen-year-olds). The main difficulty found by children in year two (six- to seven-year-olds) was in distinguishing between positive and negative statements. Alpha varied between 0.93 among the seven- to eight-year-olds to 0·97 among the fifteen- to sixteen-year-olds. Unidimensionality was satisfactory throughout.

Validity of the Thurstone–Likert scale
Validity was checked by seeing how the scores derived from the Thurstone–Likert scale of attitude toward Christianity fitted theoretical expectations in four ways. More favourable attitude toward religion had been found among younger children and among girls. More favourable attitude toward religion had been found among pupils whose religious behaviour and religious involvement was high. This accords with theoretical expectations. Age, sex, religious behaviour and religious involvement function, therefore, to support the construct validity of the scale.

Likert
In order to be certain that he had selected the best set of items from the pool, Francis constructed a scale that made use of the Likert method alone, and did not use the Thurstone sorting procedure with its elimination of ambiguous (high-Q-value) items. The whole of the original bank of 110 items were administered to over 100 ten- to eleven-year-old pupils and gradually whittled down by reference to the item rest of test correlations and the alpha coefficient. Twenty-four items were selected by this method, but they were not the same ones which had been selected previously. Only fourteen were common to both selection procedures.

After an inspection of the items and a minor modification, the two scales were administered to four classes of ten- to eleven-year-old pupils drawn from five schools. Approximately half the pupils in each class completed each of the two scales. Statistics were computed and these showed that a slightly better scale had been constructed by the joint Thurstone-Likert method than by the Likert method on its own. The alpha coefficient of the scale produced by the joint Thurstone–Likert method was higher, and the percentage of variance accounted for by the first factor of the unrotated solution proposed by principal component analysis was also higher.

Guttman

Despite the satisfactoriness of the scale produced by the Thurstone–Likert method, Francis decided to see if it would be possible to secure an improvement using Guttman's technique. In particular he wanted to know if this technique might enable attitudes to be measured with greater precision at a younger age than had proved possible using the Thurstone–Likert method.

Guttman had worked out his technique for scale construction after considering the theoretical features which he considered ought to be found in a perfect scale. In his view, the perfect scale should be both unidimensional and cumulative. The uni-dimensional feature may be checked by principal-components analysis, as is done with other methods of scale construction. The cumulative nature of a scale is achieved by writing items with a distinct direction (either positive or negative) which the respondent must either accept or reject. Once this is done, Guttman considered that perfect scalability implies that respondents who score, say, 80 per cent on the scale will mark the first 80 per cent of the items on the scale, while respondents who score 20 per cent will mark the first 20 per cent, and so on. In other words, the total score registered by an individual is matched by the precise items which he or she selects. In the Likert system, by contrast, since respondents may select one of five responses to each item, this does not happen. If it functions correctly, however, the Guttman scale will measure attitude with a much shorter scale than is needed by other methods. This might be an additional benefit when considering the scaling of attitudes among particularly young children.

In order to test the Guttman technique, Francis subdivided the main scale into six four-item subscales (on the bible, church, God, Jesus, prayer and school religion). When the figures were computed and examined, it became clear that the youngest group of children, aged six to seven years, were in many instances unable to distinguish between positively and negatively worded statements; or in more technical terms they were much more susceptible to 'response setting' than those older than themselves. After further tests and validation exercises, it was concluded that the Guttman scale was *not* preferable to the Thurstone–Likert scale.

Osgood

Finally, Francis explored the advantages and disadvantages of Osgood's techniques of attitude-scale construction in comparison with the scale produced by the joint Thurstone–Likert method. Osgood's 'semantic differential' works by measuring a person's reaction to a word by offering pairs of contrasting adjectives. For example, in the context of attitude toward Christianity, a child might be asked to react to the word 'church'. In order to test Osgood's technique the existing set of attitudinal statements would have been put aside and adjectival pairs like good/bad, interesting/boring would have been drawn up and then presented in this format:

| good | 3 | 2 | 1 | 0 | 1 | 2 | 3 | bad |
| interesting | 3 | 2 | 1 | 0 | 1 | 2 | 3 | boring |

On this scale the 1 positions are generally labelled 'slightly', the 2 positions 'quite' and the 3 positions 'extremely'. A number of studies have shown that adjectival pairs are meaningful opposites and do provide unidimensional scales. A person's attitude score can be calculated as either the total or the average of the pairs of adjectives.

Nevertheless, there have been criticisms of the Osgood technique. One of the strongest of these refers to the middle position on the scale. On the one hand, it may indicate that the respondent rates the concept exactly half-way between the contrasting adjectives. On the other hand, it may show that the respondent does not know his or her mind or considers the adjectival pair irrelevant to the stimulus word which is being tested.

For the purposes of constructing the attitude-toward-religion scale, there are practical difficulties with the method. The six aspects of Christianity identified to form the basis of the Thurstone–Likert scale cannot be treated satisfactorily with the same set of adjectives. The adjectival pairs most appropriate to assess attitude toward 'church' would only apply to 'God' by artificially limiting the set of adjectives. While Francis found that the Osgood technique generated a satisfactory measure of attitude toward religious education, which could be set alongside measures of attitude toward other aspects of the school curriculum,[12] it was not conducive to providing a more broadly based measure of attitude toward Christianity appropriate for use among younger primary school children.

Conditions of administration

As a result of all these considerations, therefore, the Thurstone–Likert scale is the one which is used in the studies in the body of this book. Before setting the scale to work, however, one further matter needed attention. Would test scores be influenced by the conditions under which the scale was completed?

Lie scale
The idea of a 'lie scale' has been developed to try to detect whether or not the respondent to a questionnaire is completing the instrument honestly. To discover if this is so, several items are interspersed with the main scale which put forward unrealistic statements about honest behaviour. For example, a person might be asked to respond to the statement, 'I have never told a lie in my life'. Since the vast majority of people are guilty of telling lies from time to time, however minor, it is assumed that anyone who agrees with this statement must be trying to project a socially desirable but inaccurate image of himself or herself. Francis drew up a four-item lie scale which was shown to function reliably and validly with the age group in question. It was then used to test the conditions under which the scale was administered to children. Particular attention was given to the influence of the test administrator and to the influence of anonymity on the responses to the attitude test.

Test administrator

It was clearly important to make sure that the scale of attitude toward Christianity functioned in the same way whoever administered it. By way of experiment the questionnaire was administered to nine- and ten-year-old children in county schools under three conditions: first, by the class teacher, second, by someone dressed and introduced as a lay person and, third, by the same person dressed and introduced as a member of the clergy. The attitude scores were not found to be significantly different on the three occasions, though they were slightly higher when administered by the member of the clergy. The lie-scale scores also were not very different when the test was administered by the class teacher or the visiting lay person, but they did change when administered by a member of the clergy.[13] There was a slight tendency for a few children to attempt to gain the approval of the priest by exaggerating their favourable disposition to religion, and this was detected by the lie scale. For most purposes, however, this set of checks suggests that the administrator of the tests makes no practical difference to the way children respond to the statements on the attitude scale. Similar responses to the questionnaire can be expected whether it is administered by the class teacher, whom the pupils know, or by a visitor to the school, whom the pupils do not know. On the other hand, it does not appear advisable to place the administration of the instrument in the hands of a visiting priest, whom some pupils may set out to impress.

Anonymity

It was also important to discover if the guarantee of anonymity is an essential part of the accurate measurement of attitude toward Christianity by questionnaire.[14] Although on the majority of occasions it is perfectly easy and sensible to guarantee anonymity, there may be other occasions when it would be helpful to identify the completed questionnaires in order to link the responses with other information about the pupils or with questionnaires completed on another occasion. In order to explore the importance of anonymity, therefore, 300 children aged ten and eleven years of age were tested under three conditions: first, a hundred children were asked to write their names on the questionnaire; second, a hundred children were asked to write their initials on the questionnaire; third, a hundred children completed the form anonymously. No significant differences were found either on the attitude-scale scores or on the lie scale scores. For practical purposes, this study demonstrates that during the large-scale administration of this attitude scale within schools, the anonymity or otherwise of children is unimportant.

Technical details

Since the level of confidence which can be placed in the findings of the studies detailed in later chapters hinges on the confidence which can be placed in the scale of attitude toward Christianity itself, a series of studies have been carried out to check the reliability and homogeneity of the scale in different contexts. These studies have usually reported two kinds of statistics. First, they have reported the correlations between each item and the sum of the rest of the items. This provides a clear measure of the extent to which each item and the rest of the scale co-vary. The lower the correlation, the less well the individual item contributes to the overall scale score. At the same time, the alpha coefficient provides a measure of the homogeneity of the whole set of items. Second, these studies have reported the loadings of each item on the first factor of the unrotated solution proposed by principal-component analysis. These statistics provide another indication of how well each item contributes to the overall scale. The lower the factor loading, the less well the individual item contributes to the overall scale score. At the same time, the percentage of variance explained by the first factor provides another index of the homogeneity and unidimensionality of the scale items.

Tables A2.1 and A2.2 provide both sets of statistics from a study published by Francis in 1988.[15] This study employed data from 200 boys and 200 girls for each of the nine year groups from the first year of the junior school (year three) through the fifth year of the secondary school (year eleven). All the pupils were attending non-church-related state-maintained schools in England.

Table A2.1 demonstrates that a very similar pattern of item–rest-of-test correlation coefficients, ranging from 0·50 to 0·87, emerge for year five through year eleven. Similarly, the alpha coefficients for these seven year groups remain stable between

Table A2.1 Item–rest-of-test correlation coefficients for each year group

Item	Year 3	Year 4	Year 5	Year 6	Year 7	Year 8	Year 9	Year 10	Year 11
I find it boring to listen to the bible	0.4052	0.5003	0.5501	0.6477	0.5605	0.5719	0.4982	0.6130	0.6668
I know that Jesus helps me	0.5942	0.6191	0.7321	0.7323	0.7250	0.7394	0.7527	0.7637	0.7924
Saying my prayers helps me a lot	0.5780	0.5783	0.6974	0.6907	0.6869	0.7303	0.7366	0.7433	0.7706
The church is very important to me	0.5490	0.5840	0.6494	0.6377	0.6413	0.6907	0.5987	0.6243	0.7066
I think going to church is a waste of my time	0.4717	0.5732	0.6517	0.6660	0.5730	0.6503	0.6079	0.6398	0.7027
I want to love Jesus	0.6120	0.6914	0.7532	0.7734	0.7353	0.7766	0.7308	0.8062	0.8016
I think church services are boring	0.5012	0.5886	0.6137	0.6188	0.4565	0.6089	0.5089	0.5303	0.6206
I think people who pray are stupid	0.5059	0.5611	0.6280	0.6524	0.6446	0.5674	0.6205	0.5365	0.6228
God helps me to lead a better life	0.6242	0.6906	0.7355	0.7638	0.7458	0.7708	0.7315	0.8085	0.8374
I like school lessons about God very much	0.6389	0.6611	0.7277	0.6785	0.6525	0.6229	0.5954	0.6138	0.7178
God means a lot to me	0.7156	0.7746	0.8362	0.8263	0.7884	0.8110	0.8132	0.8675	0.8723
I believe that God helps people	0.6552	0.6901	0.7389	0.7490	0.7425	0.7269	0.7631	0.7551	0.8020
Prayer helps me a lot	0.6277	0.7116	0.7656	0.7683	0.7329	0.7687	0.8055	0.8240	0.8045
I know that Jesus is very close to me	0.6206	0.6822	0.7575	0.7856	0.7072	0.7824	0.7588	0.8239	0.8376
I think praying is a good thing	0.6223	0.7591	0.7678	0.7668	0.7386	0.7852	0.8032	0.7821	0.8372
I think the bible is out of date	0.3279	0.4713	0.5785	0.5939	0.6238	0.6333	0.6148	0.5666	0.6608
I believe that God listens to prayers	0.6519	0.6879	0.6713	0.7375	0.7463	0.7514	0.7607	0.7864	0.8284
Jesus doesn't mean anything to me	0.4622	0.6556	0.7083	0.7729	0.7279	0.7540	0.7389	0.7926	0.7734
God is very real to me	0.6761	0.7358	0.7836	0.7782	0.7745	0.7928	0.7757	0.8351	0.8301
I think saying prayers in school does no good	0.4421	0.6144	0.7388	0.6499	0.6232	0.6144	0.5901	0.6350	0.6617
The idea of God means much to me	0.6458	0.7473	0.8005	0.8198	0.7586	0.7613	0.7744	0.8136	0.8366
I believe that Jesus still helps people	0.6492	0.6900	0.7782	0.7034	0.7336	0.6996	0.7164	0.7616	0.8150
I know that God helps me	0.6697	0.7209	0.7968	0.8150	0.7960	0.8075	0.8158	0.8167	0.8601
I find it hard to believe in God	0.4121	0.5575	0.6519	0.5610	0.6428	0.6471	0.7146	0.7587	0.6948
alpha coefficient	0.9258	0.9490	0.9638	0.9641	0.9589	0.9630	0.9610	0.9668	0.9727

Note: In order to produce the item–rest-of-test correlation coefficients the negative items were reverse-scored.

Table A2.2 Factor loadings on unrotated principal factor for each year group

Item	Year 3	Year 4	Year 5	Year 6	Year 7	Year 8	Year 9	Year 10	Year 11
I find it boring to listen to the bible	0.4117	0.5285	0.5737	0.6707	0.5810	0.5910	0.5168	0.6316	0.6853
I know that Jesus helps me	0.6832	0.6598	0.7655	0.7629	0.7632	0.7683	0.7834	0.7944	0.8191
Saying my prayers helps me a lot	0.6330	0.6185	0.7285	0.7207	0.7257	0.7650	0.7709	0.7722	0.7965
The church is very important to me	0.5918	0.6155	0.6789	0.6662	0.6635	0.7135	0.6178	0.6432	0.7291
I think going to church is a waste of my time	0.4785	0.5979	0.6709	0.6841	0.5872	0.6677	0.6206	0.6575	0.7198
I want to love Jesus	0.6654	0.7264	0.7839	0.7994	0.7683	0.8027	0.7656	0.8283	0.8245
I think church services are boring	0.5095	0.6139	0.6351	0.6393	0.4709	0.6241	0.5223	0.5489	0.6379
I think people who pray are stupid	0.5125	0.5835	0.6510	0.6784	0.6706	0.5930	0.6505	0.5622	0.6440
God helps me to lead a better life	0.6876	0.7334	0.7692	0.7926	0.7812	0.8036	0.7651	0.8344	0.8605
I like school lessons about God very much	0.6997	0.6937	0.7525	0.7076	0.6782	0.6466	0.6149	0.6381	0.7404
God means a lot to me	0.7734	0.8085	0.8607	0.8513	0.8202	0.8387	0.8440	0.8898	0.8907
I believe that God helps people	0.7245	0.7327	0.7690	0.7818	0.7750	0.7604	0.7944	0.7835	0.8242
Prayer helps me a lot	0.6851	0.7485	0.7904	0.7947	0.7686	0.7999	0.8337	0.8362	0.8307
I know that Jesus is very close to me	0.6848	0.7205	0.7880	0.8108	0.7476	0.8127	0.7932	0.8477	0.8592
I think praying is a good thing	0.6732	0.7906	0.7903	0.7923	0.7657	0.8119	0.8290	0.8039	0.8540
I think the bible is out of date	0.3390	0.4973	0.6039	0.6167	0.6447	0.6522	0.6350	0.5881	0.6789
I believe that God listens to prayers	0.7150	0.7296	0.7066	0.7678	0.7804	0.7852	0.7958	0.8162	0.8500
Jesus doesn't mean anything to me	0.4737	0.6842	0.7330	0.7950	0.7500	0.7788	0.7641	0.8140	0.7906
God is very real to me	0.7365	0.7730	0.8114	0.8064	0.8091	0.8204	0.8087	0.8606	0.8528
I think saying prayers in school does no good	0.4547	0.6463	0.7593	0.6742	0.6441	0.6349	0.6146	0.6590	0.6826
The idea of God means much to me	0.7010	0.7845	0.8241	0.8448	0.7930	0.7929	0.8059	0.8373	0.8556
I believe that Jesus still helps people	0.7186	0.7314	0.8059	0.7359	0.7670	0.7350	0.7532	0.7905	0.8355
I know that God helps me	0.7414	0.7631	0.8244	0.8401	0.8295	0.8393	0.8461	0.8462	0.8811
I find it hard to believe in God	0.4293	0.5899	0.6763	0.5889	0.6693	0.6761	0.7418	0.7864	0.7190
% of variance	39%	47%	55%	56%	52%	55%	54%	58%	62%

Note: In order to calculate these factor loadings the negative items were reverse-scored.

0·96 and 0·97. The pattern among year three and year four is slightly less impressive, with item–rest-of-test correlations dropping to 0·40 and the alpha coefficients dropping to 0·93 and 0·95. Nevertheless, these statistics still outperform the levels of reliability, homogeneity and unidimensionality achieved by the majority of psychometric instruments intended for use among pupils of this age.

The statistics presented in table A2.2 confirm the view derived from table A2.1 and provide some extra detail. The proportion of variance accounted for by the first factor varies between 52 per cent and 62 per cent from year five through year eleven. The proportion of variance accounted for by the first factor in year three and year four drops to 39 per cent and 47 per cent respectively. Again, many would argue that these proportions of variance remain highly satisfactory indices of homogeneity and unidimensionality.

Closer inspection of the item–rest-of-test correlation coefficients and the factor loadings among the pupils in year three indicates that the more problematic items are the eight negatively phrased items. The same problem concerning the negatively phrased items tends to emerge among the pupils in year four, although with considerable less clarity.

On balance these statistics confirm that the scale of attitude toward Christianity can be employed with complete confidence from year five to year eleven in non-denominational state-maintained schools in England, and with only slightly less confidence among year three to year four within the same schools.

Since it is dangerous simply to assume that a scale which works in one context works equally well in another, other studies have tested these findings in different contexts. For example, another study by Francis confirms the reliability of the scale among 3,114 pupils attending Roman Catholic state-maintained secondary schools in England.[16] Greer and Francis tested the scale among 935 pupils in Roman Catholic maintained schools in Northern Ireland,[17] while Francis and Greer tested the scale among 1,189 pupils in Protestant secondary schools in Northern Ireland.[18] Gibson and Francis tested the scale among 1,431 pupils in Roman Catholic state-maintained secondary schools in Scotland,[19] while Gibson tested the scale among 4,405 pupils in non-denominational state-maintained secondary schools in Scotland.[20] The scale has also been tested in Kenya by Fulljames and Francis[21] and in Nigeria by Francis and McCarron.[22]

Further developments

Research employing the Francis scale of attitude toward Christianity has also benefited from three further developments. First, a study by Francis, Greer and Gibson recognized that there may be occasions when a twenty-four-item scale takes too long to complete.[23] This may especially be the case when a measure of attitude toward Christianity is required as part of a much larger battery of instruments. Re-analysing data from studies of secondary-school pupils in England, Scotland and Northern Ireland, they conducted a series of analyses to select the set of seven items which most consistently predicted the scores recorded on the whole set of twenty-four items. In a second study, Francis confirmed that the same subset of seven items provided an effective short form of the scale among nine- to eleven-year-olds.[24]

Second, a study by Francis and Stubbs recognized the advantages of developing the scale of attitude toward Christianity for use among adults, so that patterns of relationships established among school children could be checked among an older population using a comparable instrument.[25] This modification simply required the rewording of the two original items which had referred to aspects of school. The reliability and validity of the adult form of the scale of attitude toward Christianity has been confirmed by studies in England,[26] Ireland,[27] the USA,[28] Canada and Australia.[29]

Third, a series of studies is now under way to explore other-language editions of the instrument including, Chinese, Dutch, French, German, Greek, Hebrew, Norwegian and Russian.

Appendix 3
Tables and figures

Table 2.1 Correlations between attitude toward Christianity, sex, masculinity and femininity among 16–18-year-olds

	Attitude	Masculinity	Femininity
Sex	+0·1473	−0·1875	+0·2875
	0·05	0·001	0·001
Femininity	+0·2563	−0·0490	
	0·001	NS	
Masculinity	-0·0069		
	NS		

Table 2.2 Multiple regression significance tests exploring influence of masculinity, femininity and sex on attitude toward Christianity among 16–18-year-olds

Dependent variables	R^2	Increase R^2	F	P<	Beta	T	P<
Masculinity	0·0000	0·0000	0·0	NS	+0·0203	+0·4	NS
Femininity	0·0657	0·0657	20·3	0·001	+0·2331	+3·9	0·001
Sex	0·0720	0·0063	1·9	NS	+0·0841	+1·4	NS

Table 2.3 Correlations between attitude toward Christianity, sex, masculinity and femininity among 13–15-year-olds

	Attitude	Masculinity	Femininity
Sex	+0·2682	−0·1783	+0·3371
	0·001	0·001	0·001
Femininity	+0·3371	−0·0552	
	0·001	NS	
Masculinity	-0·1783		
	0·001		

Table 2.4 Multiple regression significance tests exploring influence of masculinity, femininity and sex on attitude toward Christianity among 13–15-year-olds

Dependent variables	R^2	Increase R^2	F	P<	Beta	T	P<
Masculinity	0·0328	0·0328	23·1	0·001	-0·1201	-3·1	0·01
Femininity	0·1390	0·1062	84·0	0·001	+0·2859	+7·4	0·001
Sex	0·1482	0·0093	7·4	0·01	+0·1133	+2·7	0·01

Table 3.1 Mean attitude scale scores by sex and year group: non-denominational schools in England

Year group	Male			Female		
	Mean	SD	N	Mean	SD	N
Year three	87·9	21·4	200	96·0	16·5	200
Year four	84·1	22·2	200	96·1	18·1	200
Year five	84·6	22·7	200	93·3	20·3	200
Year six	77·9	21·9	200	81·4	21·7	200
Year seven	8·6	20·8	200	84·1	16·7	200
Year eight	71·5	20·0	200	83·7	18·5	200
Year nine	68·9	18·8	200	79·2	18·2	200
Year ten	62·2	21·2	200	74·3	16·7	200
Year eleven	55·7	20·9	200	70·4	19·3	200

Table 3.2 Mean attitude scale scores by sex and age: non-denominational schools in Scotland

Age groups	Male			Female		
	Mean	SD	N	Mean	SD	N
Eleven-year-olds	73·5	19·3	133	81·7	18·9	208
Twelve-year-olds	73·0	20·0	524	81·3	17·7	547
Thirteen-year-olds	72·6	20·2	520	78·3	18·7	479
Fourteen-year-olds	67·0	19·5	466	73·1	18·7	427
Fifteen-year-olds	63·5	21·1	442	69·9	19·0	400
Sixteen-year-olds	59·1	20·4	138	66·5	20·7	121

Table 3.3 Mean attitude scale scores by sex and year group: Protestant schools in Northern Ireland

Year group	Male			Female		
	Mean	**SD**	**N**	**Mean**	**SD**	**N**
Year seven	90·3	19·7	162	100·5	14·3	100
Year eight	87·9	21·5	146	92·6	17·4	95
Year nine	84·0	21·2	164	88·8	18·7	95
Year ten	81·3	22·1	118	87·6	20·2	102
Year eleven	81·5	22·7	127	91·4	20·0	80

Table 3.4 Mean attitude scale scores by sex and year group: Roman Catholic schools in England

Year group	Male			Female		
	Mean	**SD**	**N**	**Mean**	**SD**	**N**
Year seven	97·9	15·0	305	100·5	13·7	267
Year eight	91·6	14·4	278	96·1	13·2	278
Year nine	86·5	17·9	301	90·2	13·4	302
Year ten	82·6	17·8	293	88·3	15·6	313
Year eleven	80·8	17·9	278	89·3	15·7	277

Table 3.5 Mean attitude scale scores by sex and age: Roman Catholic schools in Scotland

Age groups	Male			Female		
	Mean	**SD**	**N**	**Mean**	**SD**	**N**
Eleven-year-olds	94·7	14·3	30	96·4	12·5	42
Twelve-year-olds	89·1	16·5	128	91·5	12·5	135
Thirteen-year-olds	85·7	18·4	143	89·4	13·7	169
Fourteen-year-olds	82·6	16·1	155	87·1	15·1	144
Fifteen-year-olds	76·5	16·4	164	83·1	16·4	173
Sixteen-year-olds	81·2	19·3	72	84·7	15·1	76

Table 3.6 Mean attitude scale scores by sex and year group: Roman Catholic schools in Northern Ireland

Year group	Male			Female		
	Mean	SD	N	Mean	SD	N
Year seven	102·8	12·2	126	105·9	11·2	84
Year eight	96·9	13·2	108	102·6	12·9	105
Year nine	97·3	15·5	96	100·3	12·5	90
Year ten	94·2	12·0	109	98·8	11·7	82
Year eleven	90·9	16·2	76	95·5	12·6	59

Table 4.1 Mean attitude scale scores: 1974–1994 by church attendance

Year	Overall		Unchurched		Churchgoers	
	Mean	SD	Mean	SD	Mean	SD
1974	77·8	21·6	63·6	18·5	93·6	17·6
1978	74·9	20·3	62·8	16·7	93·0	15·3
1982	70·4	20·9	59·1	16·3	93·7	14·7
1986	68·4	19·8	57·4	15·6	86·8	17·1
1990	70·4	18·3	60·1	14·9	87·6	14·2
1994	68·5	19·3	60·6	15·9	90·1	14·9

Table 4.2 Percentage responses to the individual attitude items in 1974, 1978, 1982, 1986, 1990 and 1994

Attitude item	1974 % Agree	1978 % Agree	1982 % Agree	1986 % Agree	1990 % Agree	1994 % Agree
I find it boring to listen to the bible	33	34	40	49	48	51
I know that Jesus helps me	42	30	22	23	20	22
Saying my prayers helps me a lot	36	29	24	18	20	19
The church is very important to me	27	19	13	15	13	14
I think going to church is a waste of my time	26	30	37	39	31	33
I want to love Jesus	39	34	26	23	18	22
I think church services are boring	39	49	53	56	54	56
I think people who pray are stupid	11	6	11	11	8	10
God helps me to lead a better life	39	33	27	29	27	22
I like school lessons about God very much	32	28	23	21	13	18
God means a lot to me	39	31	28	24	25	25
I believe that God helps people	59	58	44	42	46	41
Prayer helps me a lot	36	29	22	19	22	20
I know that Jesus is very close to me	36	28	20	20	18	18
I think praying is a good thing	55	47	40	37	40	39
I think the bible is out of date	20	21	30	30	24	28
I believe that God listens to prayers	47	37	33	29	36	31
Jesus doesn't mean anything to me	16	17	21	23	20	23
God is very real to me	41	33	26	22	25	25
I think saying prayers in school does no good	36	37	41	41	40	42
The idea of God means much to me	40	33	28	25	27	24
I believe that Jesus still helps people	49	49	36	38	40	38
I know that God helps me	42	34	27	25	28	25
I find it hard to believe in God	36	40	43	50	41	41

Note: The sample contains an equal number of pupils in each year of study.

Table 4.3 Mean attitude scale scores: 1974–1994 by year groups

Year group	1974		1978		1982		1986		1990		1994	
	Mean	SD	Mean	SD	Mean	SD	Mean	SD	Mean	SD	Mean	SD
Year seven	82·0	21·4	82·7	19·1	80·6	17·0	80·3	18·6	74·1	18·1	77·1	19·6
Year eight	83·3	22·2	80·2	19·1	71·9	20·3	75·1	17·2	72·7	15·8	71·7	20·6
Year nine	79·0	20·5	77·7	14·6	71·8	20·6	67·7	18·5	71·7	17·0	66·5	16·1
Year ten	78·8	18·8	68·5	20·3	64·2	18·1	61·5	18·4	68·3	18·7	64·4	18·0
Year eleven	66·0	21·0	65·3	22·3	63·6	23·6	57·2	17·4	65·5	10·5	63·3	18·5

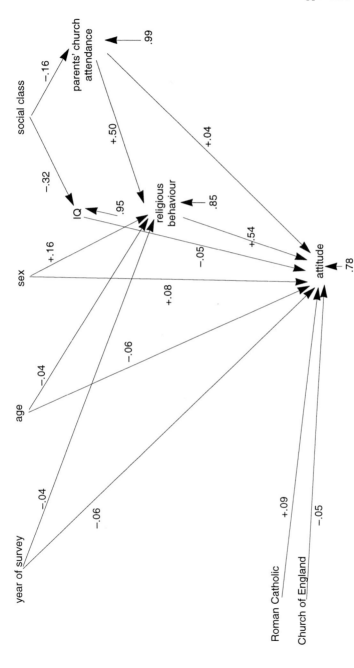

Figure 5.1 Path model exploring influence of church primary schools on pupils' attitude toward Christianity in East Anglia

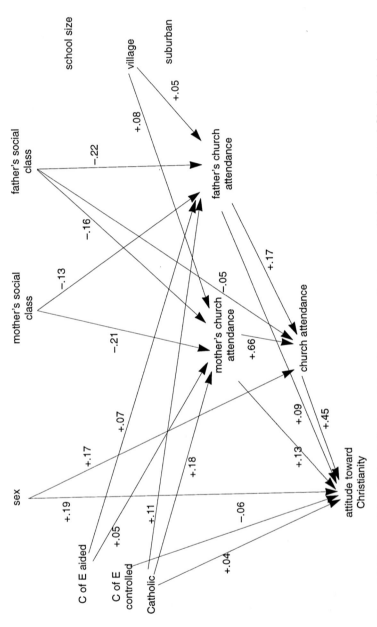

Figure 5.2 Path model exploring influence of church primary schools on pupils' attitude toward Christianity in Gloucestershire

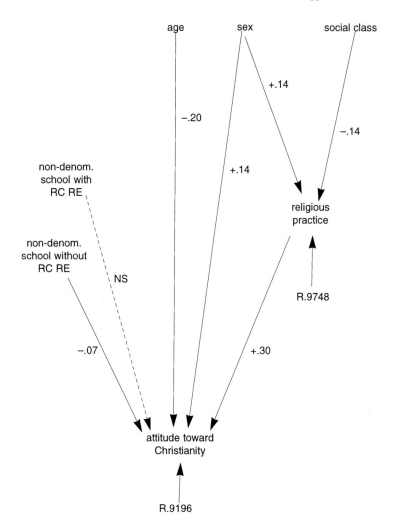

Figure 5.3 Path model exploring influence of Roman Catholic secondary schools on pupils' attitude toward Christianity in Scotland

Table 6.1 Multiple regression significance tests exploring influence of parental church attendance on children's church attendance and attitude toward Christianity by sex and age group

Dependent variables	Independent variables	R^2	Increase R^2	F	P<	Beta	T	P<
11–12-year-old males								
Church attendance	father's church	0·3608	0·3608	356·2	0·001	+0·3011	+8·2	0·001
	mother's church	0·4939	0·1331	165·8	0·001	+0·4721	+12·9	0·001
Attitude toward Christianity	church attendance	0·3591	0·3591	353·5	0·001	+0·4858	+11·0	0·001
	father's church	0·3768	0·0177	17·9	0·001	+0·1554	+3·6	0·001
	mother's church	0·3772	0·0004	0·4	NS	+0·0303	+0·7	NS
15–16-year-old males								
Church attendance	father's church	0·3900	0·3900	474·4	0·001	+0·3292	+10·8	0·001
	mother's church	0·5537	0·1637	271·8	0·001	+0·5009	+16·5	0·001
Attitude toward Christianity	church attendance	0·3419	0·3419	385·5	0·001	+0·5085	+11·4	0·001
	father's church	0·3445	0·0026	3·0	NS	+0·0493	+1·2	NS
	mother's church	0·3466	0·0020	2·3	NS	+0·0653	+1·5	NS
11–12-year-old females								
Church attendance	father's church	0·2874	0·2874	299·2	0·001	+0·1637	+5·0	0·001
	mother's church	0·5075	0·2201	331·2	0·001	+0·5990	+18·2	0·001
Attitude toward Christianity	church attendance	0·3014	0·3014	320·2	0·001	+0·4947	+11·3	0·001
	father's church	0·3057	0·0042	4·5	0·05	+0·0685	+1·7	NS
	mother's church	0·3059	0·0003	0·3	NS	+0·0251	+0·5	NS
15–16-year-old females								
Church attendance	father's church	0·3449	0·3449	388·5	0·001	+0·2379	+7·6	0·001
	mother's church	0·5492	0·2044	334·1	0·001	+0·5713	+18·3	0·001
Attitude toward Christianity	church attendance	0·3617	0·3617	418·1	0·001	+0·5349	+12·2	0·001
	father's church	0·3661	0·0044	5·1	0·05	+0·0722	+1·9	NS
	mother's church	0·3666	0·0005	0·6	NS	+0·0337	+0·8	NS

Table 7.1 Correlations between personality variables and attitude toward Christianity in the UK, USA, Australia and Canada

Scale	UK	USA	Australia	Canada
Extraversion	+0·0420 NS	+0·0915 NS	+0·1072 NS	+0·0816 NS
Neuroticism	+0·0070 NS	-0·0945 NS	-0·0075 NS	-0·0893 NS
Psychoticism	-0·3084 ·001	-0·2077 ·01	-0·2733 ·001	-0·1726 ·01
Lie scale	+0·1340 ·01	+0·0988 NS	+0·0498 NS	-0·0401 NS

Table 8.1 Correlations between attitude toward Christianity, parental church attendance, parental occupational status, parental encouragement, church attendance, scientism, perception of Christianity as creationist and interest in science

	Attitude toward Christianity	Interest in science	Perception of Christianity as creationist	Scientism	Parental encouragement	Church attendance	Mother's occupation	Father's occupation	Mother's church attendance	Father's church attendance
Sex	+0·1884 0·001	-0·1280 0·001	-0·0465 NS	-0·0617 0·05	+0·0260 NS	+0·1075 0·01	-0·0392 NS	-0·1138 0·01	-0·0044 NS	+0·0103 NS
Father's church attendance	+0·4573 0·001	-0·0179 NS	-0·1276 0·001	-0·1930 0·001	+0·6209 0·001	+0·6089 0·001	-0·1077 0·05	-0·1065 0·01	+0·6680 0·001	
Mother's church attendance	+0·4823 0·001	-0·0170 NS	-0·1262 0·001	-0·2397 0·001	+0·6655 0·001	+0·6835 0·001	-0·1489 0·001	-0·0657 0·05		
Father's occupation	-0·0344 NS	-0·0837 0·05	+0·1379 0·001	+0·0443 NS	-0·0211 NS	-0·0634 NS	-0·4931 0·001			
Mother's occupation	-0·0448 NS	-0·0259 NS	+0·1025 0·05	+0·0787 0·05	-0·0623 NS	+0·6587 0·001				
Church attendance	+0·6553 0·001	-0·0555 NS	-0·1439 0·001	-0·2953 0·001	+0·6587 0·001					
Parental encouragement	+0·5843 0·001	+0·0277 NS	-0·1144 0·001	-0·2729 0·001						
Scientism	-0·4219 0·001	+0·0524 NS	+0·2626 0·001							
Perception of Christianity as creationist	-0·1451 0·001	-0·0709 0·05								
Interest in science	-0·0926 0·01									

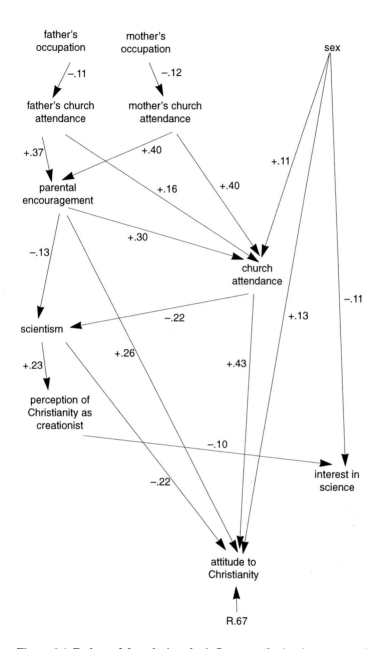

Figure 8.1 Path model exploring the influences of scientism, perception of Christianity as creationist and interest in science on pupils' attitude toward Christianity, after controlling for other factors

Table 8.2 Correlations between attitude toward Christianity, the perception of Christianity as creationist and sex among three age groups

Age band	Attitude with sex	Creationism with sex	Attitude with creationism
11–13 years	+0·1701 0·001	−0·0407 0·05	+0·1670 0·001
14–15 years	+0·1562 0·001	−0·0211 NS	+0·0673 0·001
16–17 years	+0·1671 0·001	+0·0154 NS	−0·1036 0·05

Table 9.1 Correlations between attitude toward Christianity, Christian moral values, church attendance, personal prayer, belief in God and religious experience

	Sex	Attitude toward Christianity	Christian moral values	Church attendance	Personal prayer	Belief in God
Religious experience	+0·1817 0·001	+0·4876 0·001	+0·2726 0·001	+0·2862 0·001	+0·3897 0·001	+0·3700 0·001
Belief in God	+0·1671 0·001	+0·7486 0·001	+0·4190 0·001	+0·4518 0·001	+0·4686 0·001	
Personal prayer	+0·2193 0·001	+0·6699 0·001	+0·3930 0·001	+0·4166 0·001		
Church attendance	+0·1378 0·001	+0·5440 0·001	+0·3997 0·001			
Christian moral values	+0·2057 0·001	+0·5564 0·001				
Attitude toward Christianity	+0·2385 0·001					

Table 10.1 Correlations between attitude toward Christianity, empathy, age and sex

	Attitude	Empathy
Age	-0·3031 0·001	+0·0159 NS
Sex	+0·1004 0·01	+0·3610 0·001
Empathy	+0·3342 0·001	

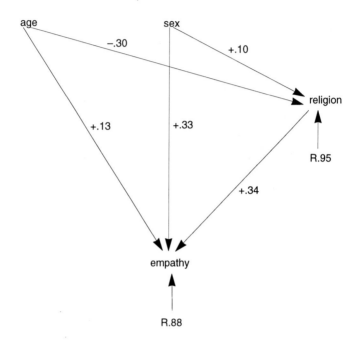

Figure 10.1 Path model exploring the influence of attitude toward Christianity on empathy after controlling for age and sex

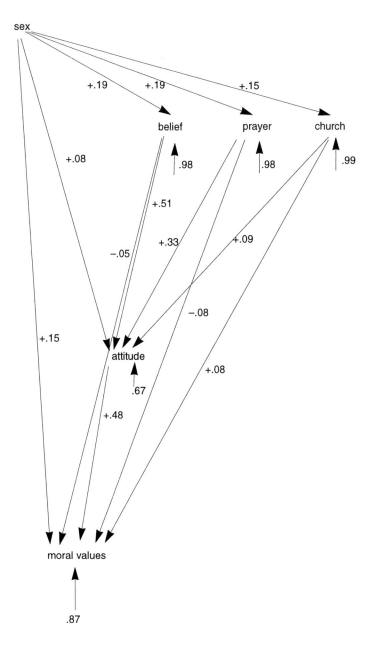

Figure 10.2 Path model exploring the influence of attitude toward Christianity on Christian moral values

Notes

Notes to chapter 1: Introduction

[1] L. J. Francis, 'An enquiry into the concept "Readiness for Religion"' (Univ. of Cambridge Ph.D. thesis, 1976).

[2] L. J. Francis, 'Measurement reapplied: research into the child's attitude towards religion', *British Journal of Religious Education*, 1 (1978), 45–51.

[3] W. K. Kay, 'Religious thinking, attitudes and personality amongst secondary pupils in England and Ireland' (Univ. of Reading Ph.D. thesis, 1981).

[4] L. J. Francis and Y. J. Katz, 'The relationship between personality and religiosity in an Israeli sample', *Journal for the Scientific Study of Religion*, 31 (1992), 153–62.

Notes to chapter 2: Sex differences

[1] See, for example, P. Brierley and V. Hiscock (eds.), *UK Christian Handbook: 1994/95 Edition* (London, Christian Research Association, 1993); Gallup Report, *Political, Social and Economic Trends* (Princeton, Gallup, 1987); E. M. Gee, 'Gender differences in church attendance in Canada: the role of labor force participation', *Review of Religious Research*, 32 (1991), 267–73.

[2] A. C. Webster and P. E. Perry, *The Religious Factor in New Zealand Society* (Palmerston North, New Zealand, Alpha Publications, 1989).

[3] G. D. Bouma and B. R. Dixon, *The Religious Factor in Australian Life* (Melbourne, MARC Australia, 1987).

[4] J. Harrison, *Attitudes to Bible, God, Church* (London, Bible Society, 1983).

[5] D. Hay and A. Morisy, 'Reports of ecstatic, paranormal or religious experience in Great Britain and the United States: a comparison of trends', *Journal for the Scientific Study of Religion*, 17 (1978), 255–68.

[6] Gallup Report, *Political, Social and Economic Trends*, op. cit.

[7] L. J. Francis and W. K. Kay, *Teenage Religion and Values* (Leominster, Gracewing, 1995).

[8] S. Harding, D. Phillips and M. Fogarty, *Contrasting Values in Western Europe: Unity, Diversity and Change* (Basingstoke, Macmillan, 1986).

[9] A. Greeley, 'Religion in Britain, Ireland and the USA', in R. Howell,

L. Brook, G. Prior and B. Taylor (eds.), *British Social Attitudes: 9th Report* (Aldershot, Dartmouth Publishers, 1992), 51– 70.

[10] A. S. Miller, 'Conventional religious behaviour in modern Japan: a service industry perspective', *Journal for the Scientific Study of Religion*, 31 (1992), 207–14.

[11] M. Abrams, 'Demographic correlates of values', in M. Abrams, D. Gerard and N. Timms (eds.), *Values and Social Change in Britain* (Basingstoke, Macmillan, 1985), 21–49.

[12] Notes 1–11 above are related to all these countries except Scotland, Wales and Ireland. Scottish data are to be found in P. Brierley and F. Macdonald, *Prospects for Scotland: Report of the 1984 Census of the Churches* (London, MARC Europe, 1985); Welsh data are to be found in P. Brierley and B. Evans (eds.), *Prospects for Wales: A Report of the 1982 Census of the Churches* (London, Bible Society and MARC Europe, 1983); Irish data are to be found in J. E. Greer, *A Questioning Generation* (Belfast, Church of Ireland Board of Education, 1972).

[13] See for example, H. Mol, *The Faith of Australians* (Sydney, George Allen and Unwin, 1985).

[14] H. M. Nelson and R. H. Potvin, 'Gender and regional differences in the religiosity of Protestant adolescents', *Review of Religious Research*, 22 (1981), 268–85.

[15] For example, D. O. Moberg, *The Church as a Social Institution* (Englewood Cliffs, Prentice-Hall, 1962)

[16] D. A. Martin, *The Sociology of English Religion* (London, SCM, 1967).

[17] C. Y. Glock, B. B. Ringer and E. R. Babbie, *To Comfort and to Challenge* (Berkeley, University of California Press, 1967).

[18] H. M. Nelsen and A. K. Nelsen, *Black Church in the Sixties* (Lexington, University Press of Kentucky, 1975).

[19] D. A. De Vaus, 'The impact of children on sex related differences in church attendance', *Sociological Analysis*, 43 (1982), 145–54.

[20] See, G. E. Lenski, 'Social correlates of religious interest', *American Sociological Review*, 18 (1953), 533–44; Martin, *The Sociology of English Religion* and T. Luckman, *The Invisible Religion* (New York, Macmillan, 1967).

[21] For example, Moberg, *The Church as a Social Institution* and J. M. Yinger, *The Scientific Study of Religion* (New York, Macmillan, 1970).

[22] D. A. De Vaus, 'Workforce participation and sex differences in church attendance', *Review of Religious Research*, 25 (1984), 247–56.

[23] Glock et al., *To Comfort and to Challenge*, op. cit.

[24] De Vaus, 'Workforce participation', op. cit.

[25] See B. Lazerwitz, 'Some factors associated with church attendance', *American Sociological Review*, 18 (1961), 301–9 and L. J. Francis, *Young and Unemployed* (Tunbridge Wells, Costello, 1984).

[26] M. Y. Morgan and J. Scanzoni, 'Religious orientations and women's expected continuity in the labor force', *Journal of Marriage and the Family*, 49 (1987), 367–79.

[27] S. L. Bem, *Bem Sex Role Inventory: Professional Manual* (Palo Alto, California, Consulting Psychologists Press, 1981).

[28] E. H. Thompson, 'Beneath the status characteristics: gender variations in religiousness', *Journal for the Scientific Study of Religion*, 23 (1991), 381–94.

[29] J. E. Gaston and L. B. Brown, 'Religious and gender prototypes', *International Journal for the Psychology of Religion*, 1 (1991), 233–41; J. K. Antill, J. D. Cunningham, G. Russell and N. L. Thompson, 'An Australian sex-role scale', *Australian Journal of Psychology*, 33 (1981), 169–83.

[30] L. J. Francis, 'The personality characteristics of Anglican ordinands: feminine men and masculine women?' *Personality and Individual Differences*, 12 (1991), 1133–40 and L. J. Francis, 'Male and female clergy in England: their personality differences, gender reversal?' *Journal of Empirical Theology*, 5(2) (1992), 31–8.

[31] S. Freud, *Totem and Taboo* (London, Routledge and Kegan Paul, 1950).

[32] S. Freud, *New Introductory Lectures on Psychoanalysis* (London, The Hogarth Press, 1946).

[33] See, for example, M. Argyle and B. Beit-Hallahmi, *The Social Psychology of Religion* (London, Routledge and Kegan Paul, 1975).

[34] A. Vergote, A. Tamayo, L. Pasquali, M. Bonami, M.-R. Pattyn and A. Custers, 'Concept of God and parental images', *Journal for the Scientific Study of Religion*, 8 (1969), 79–97.

[35] H. M. Gibson, 'Adolescents' images of God', *Panorama*, 6(1) (1994), 104–14.

[36] A. Tamayo and A. Dugas, 'Conceptual representation of mother, father, and God according to sex and field of study', *Journal of Psychology*, 97 (1977), 79–84. See also M. O. Nelson and E. M. Jones, 'Application of the Q-technique to the study of religious concepts', *Psychological Reports*, 3 (1957), 293–97.

[37] Argyle and Beit-Hallahmi, *The Social Psychology of Religion*, op. cit.

[38] B. Reed, *The Dynamics of Religion* (London, Darton, Longman and Todd, 1978).

[39] T. Walter, 'Why are most churchgoers women?' *Vox Evangelica*, 20 (1990), 73–90.

[40] See L. J. Francis, 'Is psychoticism really a dimension of personality fundamental to religiosity?' *Personality and Individual Differences*, 13 (1992), 645–52 and L. J. Francis, 'Personality and religion among college students in the UK', *Personality and Individual Differences*, 14 (1993), 619–22.

[41] See L. J. Francis, 'The development of a scale of attitude towards Christianity among 8–16 year olds', *Collected Original Resources in Education*, 12(3) (1988), fiche 1, A04.

[42] L. J. Francis and J. E. Greer, 'Measuring attitudes towards Christianity among pupils in Protestant secondary schools in Northern Ireland', *Personality and Individual Differences*, 11 (1990), 853–56.

[43] L. J. Francis, 'Measuring attitudes towards Christianity among 12- to 18-year-old pupils in Catholic schools', *Educational Research*, 29 (1987), 230–3.

[44] H. M. Gibson, 'Measuring attitudes towards Christianity among 11- to 16-year-old pupils in non-denominational schools in Scotland', *Educational Research*, 31 (1989), 221–7.

[45] P. Fulljames and L. J. Francis, 'The measurement of attitudes towards Christianity among Kenyan secondary school students', *The Journal of Social Psychology*, 127 (1987), 407–9.

[46] L. J. Francis and C. Wilcox, 'Religion and gender orientation' (in press).

[47] L. J. Francis, 'Religiosity and femininity: are women really more religious?' (in press).

[48] H. J. Eysenck and S. B. G. Eysenck, *Psychoticism as a Dimension of Personality* (London, Hodder and Stoughton, 1976).

[49] A. F. Jorm, 'Sex differences in neuroticism: a quantitative synthesis of published research', *Australian and New Zealand Journal of Psychiatry*, 21 (1987), 501–6.

[50] L. J. Francis and D. W. Lankshear, *Continuing in the Way: Children, Young People and the Church* (London, National Society, 1991).

Notes to chapter 3: Age trends

[1] L. J. Francis, 'The decline in attitudes towards religion among 8–15 year olds', *Educational Studies*, 13 (1987), 125–34.

[2] For an introduction to Piaget's own writings, see for example J. Piaget, *The Moral Judgment of the Child* (London, Routledge and Kegan Paul, 1932); J. Piaget, *The Child's Conception of Movement and Speed* (London, Routledge and Kegan Paul, 1970); J. Piaget, *The Principles of Genetic Epistemology* (London, Routledge and Kegan Paul, 1972); J. Piaget and B. Inhelder, *The Origin of the Idea of Chance in Children* (London, Routledge and Kegan Paul, 1975).

[3] R. J. Goldman, *Religious Thinking from Childhood to Adolescence* (London, Routledge and Kegan Paul, 1964), 58.

[4] R. J. Goldman, *Readiness for Religion* (London, Routledge and Kegan Paul, 1965), 160, 162.

[5] Ibid., 62.

[6] Goldman, *Religious Thinking*, op. cit., 242.

[7] Ibid., 240.

[8] Goldman, *Readiness for Religion*, op. cit.,165.

[9] Details for both these trends are given in L. J. Francis, 'The development of a scale of attitude toward Christianity among 8–16 year olds', *Collected Original Resources in Education*, 29(3) (1988), fiche 1, A04; L. J. Francis, 'Measuring attitude towards Christianity during childhood and adolescence', *Personality and Individual Differences*, 10 (1989), 695–8.

[10] L. J. Francis, 'An enquiry into the concept "readiness for religion"' (Univ. of Cambridge Ph.D. thesis, 1976).

[11] H. M. Gibson, 'Measuring attitudes towards Christianity among 11-16 year old pupils in non-denominational schools in Scotland', *Educational Research*, 31 (1989), 221–7.

[12] L. J. Francis and J. E. Greer, 'Measuring attitudes towards Christianity among pupils in Protestant secondary schools in Northern Ireland', *Personality and Individual Differences*, 11 (1990), 853–6.

[13] W. K. Kay, 'Religious thinking, attitudes and personality amongst secondary pupils in England and Ireland' (Univ. of Reading Ph.D. thesis, 1981).

[14] L. J. Francis and A. Montgomery, 'Personality and attitudes towards Christianity among eleven to sixteen year old girls in a single sex Catholic school', *British Journal of Religious Education*, 14 (1992), 114–19.

[15] L. J. Francis, 'Measuring attitudes towards Christianity among 12- to 18 year-old pupils in Catholic schools', *Educational Research*, 29 (1987), 230–3.

[16] H. M. Gibson and L. J. Francis, 'Measuring attitudes towards Christianity among 11- to 16-year old pupils in Catholic schools in Scotland', *Educational Research*, 31 (1989), 65–9.

[17] J. E. Greer and L. J. Francis, 'Measuring attitudes towards Christianity among pupils in Catholic secondary schools in Northern Ireland', *Educational Research*, 33 (1991), 70–3.

[18] L. J. Francis, 'The decline in attitude towards religion among 8-15 year olds', Educational Studies, 13 (1987), 125–34.

[19] This method was proposed by Osgood and discussed in chapter 3. It uses a different sort of attitude scale from that which is used in the majority of this book.

[20] W. K. Kay, 'RE and assemblies: pupils' changing views', in L. J. Francis (ed.), *Research in Religious Education* (Leominster, Gracewing, in press).

[21] Francis, ' "Readiness for Religion" '; see also K. E. Hyde, *Religious Learning in Adolescence*, Educational Monographs no.7 (University of Birmingham, Institute of Education, 1965).

[22] A. E. Siegel and S. Siegel, 'Reference groups, membership groups and attitude change', *Journal of Abnormal and Social Psychology*, 55 (1957), 360–4.

[23] L. J. Francis and H. M. Gibson, 'Television, pop culture and the drift from Christianity during adolescence', *British Journal of Religious Education*, 15 (1993), 31–7.

[24] See, for example, D. Cohen, *Piaget: Critique and Reassessment* (London, Croom Helm, 1983), particularly in his comments on children's egocentrism.

Notes to chapter 4: Generation changes

[1] D. Wright and E. Cox, 'Religious belief and co-education in a sample of sixth form boys and girls', *British Journal of Social and Clinical Psychology*, 6 (1967), 23–31; D. Wright and E. Cox, 'A study of the relationship between moral judgement and religious belief in a sample of English adolescents', *Journal of Social Psychology*, 72 (1967), 135–44.

[2] D. Wright and E. Cox, 'Changes in attitudes towards religious education and the bible among sixth form boys and girls', *British Journal of Educational Psychology*, 41 (1971), 328–31; D. Wright and E. Cox, 'Changes in moral belief among sixth form boys and girls over a seven year period in relation to religious belief, age and sex differences', *British Journal of Social and Clinical Psychology*, 10 (1971), 332–41.

[3] E. B. Turner, 'Religious understanding and religious attitudes in male urban adolescents' (The Queen's Univ. of Belfast Ph.D. thesis, 1970).

[4] E. B. Turner, I. F. Turner and A. Reid, 'Religious attitudes in two types of urban secondary schools: a decade of change?' *Irish Journal of Education*, 14 (1980), 43–52.

[5] I. F. Turner and C. J. Crossey, 'Stability and change over 21 years in the religious attitudes of adolescents', *British Journal of Religious Education*, 16 (1993), 58–64.

[6] J. E. Greer, *A Questioning Generation* (Belfast, Church of Ireland Board of Eduction, 1972).

[7] J. E. Greer, 'The persistence of religion: a study of adolescents in Northern Ireland', *Character Potential*, 9(3) (1980), 139–49.

[8] J. E. Greer, 'The persistence of religion in Northern Ireland: a study of sixth form religion, 1968–1988', *Collected Original Resources in Education*, 13(2) (1989), fiche 20, G9.

9 The results of the original study conducted in 1974 are reported in L. J. Francis, 'An enquiry into the concept "readiness for religion"' (Univ. of Cambridge Ph.D. thesis, 1976). The first replication in 1978 is discussed by L. J. Francis, C. B. Wesley and J. N. Rust, 'An account of the religious attitude research project at the London Institute of Education', *Area*, 11 (1978), 10–15. The results of the first four studies are discussed by L. J. Francis, 'Monitoring changing attitudes towards Christianity among secondary school pupils between 1974 and 1986', *British Journal of Educational Psychology*, 59 (1989), 86–91 and L. J. Francis, 'Drift from the churches: secondary school pupils' attitudes towards Christianity', *British Journal of Religious Education*, 11 (1989), 76–86. The results of the 1990 study are discussed by L. J. Francis, 'Monitoring attitudes towards Christianity: the 1990 study', *British Journal of Religious Education*, 14 (1992), 178–82. The results of the 1994 study are discussed by L. J. Francis, 'Monitoring attitudes toward Christianity between 1974 and 1994 among secondary school pupils in England', in M. Bar-Lev and W. Shaffir (eds.), *Leaving Religion and Religious Life: Patterns and Dynamics* (in press).

10 I. Ajzen and M. Fishbein, *Understanding Attitudes and Predicting Social Behaviour* (Englewood Cliffs, Prentice-Hall, 1980).

Notes to chapter 5: School influence

1 See for example, J. A. Comber and J. P. Keeves, *Science Education in Nineteen Countries*, International Studies in Evaluation, vol.1 (Stockholm, Almqvist Wiksell, 1973).

2 Further details of these studies are given in: J. S. Coleman, 'Methods and results of IEA studies of effects of school on learning', *Review of Educational Research*, 45 (1975), 335–86 and C. Jencks, M. Smith, H. Acland, M. J. Bane, D. Cohen, H. Gintis, B. Heyns and S. Michelson, *Inequality: A Reassessment of the Effect of Family and Schooling in America* (New York, Basic Books, 1972).

3 For a full history of this area see M. Cruickshank, *Church and State in English Education* (London, Macmillan, 1963) and J. Murphy, *Church, State and Schools in Britain 1800–1970* (London, Routledge and Kegan Paul, 1971).

4 J. Murphy, *The Education Act 1870* (Newton Abbot, David and Charles, 1972).

5 D. A. De Vaus, 'The impact of Catholic schools on the religious orientation of boys and girls', *Journal of Christian Education*, 71 (1981), 44–51.

6 For further details see M. P. Hornsby-Smith, *Catholic Education: The Unobtrusive Partner* (London, Sheed and Ward, 1978).

[7] See the Report of the Bishops of England and Wales, *Signposts and Homecomings: The Educative Task of the Catholic Community* (Middlegreen, St Paul Publications, 1981).

[8] I. Ramsey, Durham Report, *The Fourth R: The Report of the Commission on Religious Education in Schools* (London, National Society and SPCK, 1970).

[9] L. J. Francis, 'School influence and pupil attitude towards religion', *British Journal of Educational Psychology*, 49 (1979), 107–23.

[10] Office of Population Censuses and Surveys, *Classification of Occupations 1980* (London, HMSO, 1980).

[11] L. J. Francis, C. B. Wesley and J. N. Rust, 'An account of the religious attitude research project at the London Institute of Education', *Area*, 11 (1978), 10–15.

[12] L. J. Francis, 'Denominational schools and pupil attitudes towards Christianity', *British Educational Research Journal*, 12 (1986), 145–52.

[13] L. J. Francis, *Religion in the Primary School* (London, Collins Liturgical Publications, 1987).

[14] L. J. Francis and M. Carter, 'Church aided secondary schools, religious education as an examination subject and pupil attitudes towards religion', *British Journal of Educational Psychology*, 50 (1980), 297–300.

[15] L. J. Francis and A. Jewell, 'Shaping adolescent attitude towards the church: comparison between Church of England and county secondary schools', *Evaluation and Research in Education*, 6 (1992), 13–21.

[16] L. J. Francis, 'Measuring attitudes towards Christianity among 12- to 18-year-old pupils in Catholic schools', *Educational Research*, 29 (1987), 230–3.

[17] H. M. Gibson and L. J. Francis, 'Measuring attitudes towards Christianity among 11- to 16-year old pupils in Catholic schools in Scotland', *Educational Research*, 31 (1989), 65–9.

[18] J. E. Greer and L. J. Francis, 'Measuring attitudes towards Christianity among pupils in Catholic secondary schools in Northern Ireland', *Educational Research*, 33 (1991), 70–3.

[19] L. J. Francis, 'Measuring attitude towards Christianity during childhood and adolescence', *Personality and Individual Differences*, 10 (1989), 695–8.

[20] H. M. Gibson 'Measuring attitudes towards Christianity among 11–16 year old pupils in non-denominational schools in Scotland', *Educational Research*, 31 (1989), 221–7.

[21] L. J. Francis and J. E. Greer, 'Measuring attitudes towards Christianity among pupils in Protestant secondary schools in Northern Ireland', *Personality and Individual Differences*, 11 (1990), 853–6.

22 J. Rhymer, 'Religious attitudes of Roman Catholic secondary school pupils in Strathclyde region' (Univ. of Edinburgh Ph.D. thesis, 1983).

23 J. Rhymer and L. J. Francis, 'Roman Catholic secondary schools in Scotland and pupil attitude towards religion', *Lumen Vitae*, 40 (1985), 103–10.

24 W. A. L. Blyth and R. Perricott, *The Social Significance of Middle Schools* (London, Batsford, 1977).

25 J. J. Boyle, 'Catholic children's attitudes towards Christianity' (Univ. of Bradford M.Sc. thesis, 1984).

26 J. J. Boyle and L. J. Francis, 'The influence of differing church aided school systems on pupil attitude towards religion', *Research in Education*, 35 (1986), 7–12.

27 L. J. Francis, 'Roman Catholic secondary schools: falling rolls and pupil attitudes', *Educational Studies*, 12 (1986), 119–27.

28 J. Egan, *Opting Out: Catholic Schools Today* (Leominster, Fowler Wright, 1988).

29 J. Egan and L. J. Francis, 'School ethos in Wales: the impact of non-practising Catholic and non-Catholic pupils on Catholic secondary schools', *Lumen Vitae*, 41 (1986), 159–71.

30 L. J. Francis and J. Egan, 'The Catholic school as "faith community": an empirical enquiry', *Religious Education*, 85 (1990), 588–603.

31 L. J. Francis and J. Egan, 'Catholic schools and the communication of faith', *Catholic School Studies*, 60, 2 (1987), 27–34.

32 Francis, 'School influence and pupil attitude towards religion'. See also, L. J. Francis, 'Paths of holiness? Attitudes towards religion among 9-11 year old children in England', *Character Potential: A Record of Research*, 9 (1980), 129–38.

33 W. K. Kay, 'Religious thinking, attitudes and personality amongst secondary pupils in England and Ireland' (Univ. of Reading Ph.D. thesis, 1981).

34 See W. K. Kay, 'Subject preference and attitude to religion in secondary school', *Educational Review*, 33 (1981), 47–51.

Notes to chapter 6: Home influence

1 M. Rutter, B. Maughan, P. Mortimore, J. Ouston and A. Smith, *Fifteen Thousand Hours: Secondary Schools and their Effects on Children* (London, Open Books, 1979).

2 D. G. MacRae, *Weber* (London, Fontana, 1974); R. H. Tawney, *Religion and the Rise of Capitalism* (Harmondsworth, Penguin, 1938). First edition in March 1926.

3 D. Lawton, *Social Class, Language and Education* (London, Routledge and Kegan Paul, 1968).

[4] See, for example, H. J. Eysenck, 'Social attitudes and social class', *British Journal of Social and Clinical Psychology*, 10 (1971), 201–12.

[5] See, for example, M. Argyle, *The Psychology of Social Class* (London, Routledge, 1994).

[6] L. J. Francis, P. R. Pearson and D. W. Lankshear, 'The relationship between social class and attitude towards Christianity among ten and eleven year old children', *Personality and Individual Differences*, 11 (1990), 1019–27.

[7] H. M. Gibson, L. J. Francis and P. R. Pearson, 'The relationship between social class and attitude towards Christianity among fourteen- and fifteen-year-old adolescents', *Personality and Individual Differences*, 11 (1990), 631–5.

[8] W. K. Kay, 'Religious thinking, attitudes and personality amongst secondary pupils in England and Ireland' (Univ. of Reading Ph.D. thesis, 1981).

[9] M. Jennings and R. Niemi, 'The transmission of political values from parent to child', *American Political Science Review*, 42 (1968), 169–84.

[10] G. Homans, *Social Behaviour: Its Elementary Forms* (New York, Harcourt, Brace, Jovanovich, 1974).

[11] A. C. Acock and V. L. Bengtson, 'On the relative influence of mothers and fathers: a covariance analysis of political and religious socialisation', *Journal of Marriage and the Family*, 40 (1978), 519–30.

[12] J. S. Coleman, *The Adolescent Society* (New York, Free Press, 1971).

[13] L. J. Francis and H. M. Gibson, 'Parental influence and adolescent religiosity: a study of church attendance and attitude towards Christianity among 11–12 and 15–16 year olds', *International Journal for the Psychology of Religion*, 3 (1993), 241–53.

[14] L. J. Francis, H. M. Gibson and D. W. Lankshear, 'The influence of Protestant Sunday schools on attitude towards Christianity among 11–15 year olds in Scotland', *British Journal of Religious Education*, 14 (1991), 35–42.

[15] A. Greeley, 'Religion in Britain, Ireland and the USA', in R. Jowell, L. Brook, G. Prior and B. Taylor (eds.), *British Social Attitudes: the 9th report* (Aldershot, Dartmouth Publishers, 1992), 51–70.

[16] L. J. Francis and D. W. Lankshear, 'Asking about baptism: straw polls and fenced fonts', *Modern Churchman*, 34(5) (1993), 88–92.

[17] L. J. Francis, 'The religious significance of denominational identity among eleven year old children in England', *Journal of Christian Education*, 97 (1990), 23–8.

[18] W. K. Kay, 'Marital happiness and children's attitudes to religion', *British Journal of Religious Education*, 3 (1981), 102–5.

[19] Kay, 'Religious thinking', op. cit.

[20] More details of the IEA study are given in chapter 7.

[21] É. Durkheim, 'The social foundations of religion', in R. Robertson (ed.), *Sociology of Religion* (Harmondsworth, Penguin, 1969). This chapter is an extract from, *The Elementary Forms of Religious Life*, first published in 1912 as *Les Formes élémentaires de la vie religieuse*.

Notes to chapter 7: Personality and religion

[1] Much more detailed information is given in, C. G. Jung, *Psychological Types* (London, Kegan Paul, Trench, Trubner and Co. Ltd, 1944). (First German edition 1920).

[2] See H. J. Eysenck and G. D. Wilson, *The Experimental Study of Freudian Theories* (London, Methuen, 1973) and H. J. Eysenck, *Decline and Fall of the Freudian Empire* (London, Viking, 1985).

[3] A short but scathing attack is to be found in, H. J. Eysenck, 'An experimental study of Freudian concepts', *Bulletin of the British Psychological Society*, 25 (1972), 261–7.

[4] See H. J. Eysenck and S. B. G. Eysenck, *Manual of the Eysenck Personality Questionnaire* (London, Hodder and Stoughton, 1975).

[5] S. B. G. Eysenck, *Manual of the Junior Eysenck Personality Inventory* (London, Hodder and Stoughton, 1965).

[6] Eysenck first developed measures of neuroticism through the Maudsley Medical Questionnaire, the Maudsley Personality Inventory and the Eysenck Personality Inventory. The psychoticism scale first appeared in the 'PEN' (Psychoticism, Extraversion and Neuroticism) Inventory and was refined in the Eysenck Personality Questionnaire and the Revised Eysenck Personality Questionnaire.

[7] Some of these criticisms are the same as those used against the construction of attitude scales in appendix 2. They include: the tendency of people to endorse socially desirable responses, the tendency to agree or disagree with items regardless of whether they are positively or negatively worded, and the alleged mismatch between questionnaires and 'real-life situations'. To all these criticisms replies have been given, usually by carefully testing questionnaire answers against answers given in other situations and by administering questionnaires under varying conditions. The clear advantage of questionnaires over other forms of information-gathering is that the same statements are presented to each respondent.

[8] The work of Cattell, carried out independently in the United States, is in many respects parallel to that of Eysenck; see R. B. Cattell, *The Scientific Analysis of Personality* (Harmondsworth, Penguin, 1965). Both men used questionnaires. Cattell isolated sixteen factors but, when these factors are submitted to a higher-order analysis, it is possible to extract two, corresponding to extraversion-introversion

and neuroticism–stability, which are similar to those identified by Eysenck.

⁹ For example in M. W. Eysenck and H. J. Eysenck, 'Mischel and the concept of personality', *British Journal of Psychology*, 71 (1980), 191–204 and J. Block, 'Advancing the psychology of personality: paradigmatic shift or improving the quality of research', in D. Magnusson and N. S. Endler (eds.), *Personality at the Crossroads* (London, John Wiley and Sons, 1977).

¹⁰ L. J. Francis and W. K. Kay, *Teenage Religion and Values* (Leominster, Gracewing, 1995).

¹¹ H. J. Eysenck, *The Psychology of Politics* (London, Routledge and Kegan Paul, 1954) and H. J. Eysenck 'Personality and social attitudes', *Journal of Social Psychology*, 53 (1961), 243–9.

¹² G. W. Allport, *The Individual and his Religion: A Psychological Interpretation* (New York, Macmillan, 1950).

¹³ Evidence for this is summarized by D. M. Wulff, *Psychology of Religion: Classic and Contemporary Views* (Chichester, John Wiley and Sons, 1991).

¹⁴ See note 1.

¹⁵ S. B. G. Eysenck and H. J. Eysenck, 'The place of impulsiveness in a dimensional system of personality', *British Journal of Social and Clinical Psychology*, 16 (1977), 57–68 discuss impulsivity fully. Analysis is complicated by the breakdown of impulsiveness into four sub-traits which correlated slightly differently to the other personality dimensions. However, P. R. Pearson, L. J. Francis and T. J. Lightbown, 'Impulsivity and religiosity', *Personality and Individual Differences*, 7 (1986), 89–94, show that it is the component of impulsivity related to doing things on the spur of the moment rather than the one relating to calculated risk-taking which is related to psychoticism, which supports the explanation about psychoticism's imperviousness to conditionability.

¹⁶ L. J. Francis, P. R. Pearson, M. Carter and W. K. Kay, 'Are introverts more religious?' *British Journal of Social Psychology*, 20 (1981), 101–4.

¹⁷ L. J. Francis, P. R. Pearson and W. K. Kay, 'Are introverts still more religious?', *Personality and Individual Differences*, 4 (1983), 211–12. About 1 per cent of variance was accounted for after age and sex had made their contributions.

¹⁸ L. J. Francis and P. R. Pearson, 'Extraversion and religiosity', *Journal of Social Psychology*, 125 (1985), 269–70.

¹⁹ L. J. Francis, P. R. Pearson and W. K. Kay, 'Neuroticism and religiosity among English school children', *Journal of Social Psychology*, 121 (1983), 149–50.

²⁰ Ibid.

[21] L. J. Francis and P. R. Pearson, 'Religiosity, gender and the two faces of neuroticism', *Irish Journal of Psychology*, 12 (1991), 60–8.

[22] L. J. Francis, 'Neuroticism and intensity of religious attitudes among clergy in England', *Journal of Social Psychology*, 132 (1992), 577–80; L. J. Francis, 'Personality and attitude towards religion among adult churchgoers in England', *Psychological Reports*, 69 (1991) 791–4.

[23] L. J. Francis, P. R. Pearson and M. T. Stubbs, 'Personality and religion among low ability children in residential special schools', *British Journal of Mental Subnormality*, 31 (1985), 41–5.

[24] L. J. Francis, P. R. Pearson and W. K. Kay, 'Eysenck's personality quadrants and religiosity', *British Journal of Social Psychology*, 21 (1982), 262–4.

[25] W. K. Kay, 'Psychoticism and attitude to religion', *Personality and Individual Differences*, 2 (1981), 249–52.

[26] L. J. Francis and P. R. Pearson, 'Psychoticism and religiosity among 15 year olds', *Personality and Individual Differences*, 6 (1985), 397–8.

[27] L. J. Francis, 'Is psychoticism really a dimension of personality fundamental to religiosity?' *Personality and Individual Differences*, 13 (1992), 645–52.

[28] Pearson, Francis and Lightbown, 'Impulsivity and religiosity', op. cit.

[29] L. J. Francis, P. R. Pearson and W. K. Kay, 'Are religious children bigger liars?' *Psychological Reports*, 52 (1983), 551–4.

[30] L. J. Francis, P. R. Pearson and W. K. Kay, 'Religiosity and lie scores: a question of interpretation', *Social Behaviour and Personality*, 16 (1988), 91–5.

[31] P. R. Pearson and L. J. Francis, 'The dual nature of the Eysenckian lie scales: are religious adolescents more truthful?' *Personality and Individual Differences*, 10 (1989), 1041–8.

[32] L. J. Francis and P. R. Pearson, 'Religiosity and the short-scale EPQ-R indices of E, N and L, compared with the JEPI, JEPQ and EPQ', *Personality and Individual Differences*, 9 (1988), 653–7.

[33] L. J. Francis, D. W. Lankshear and P. R. Pearson, 'The relationship between religiosity and the short form JEPQ (JEPQ-S) indices of E, N, L and P among eleven year olds', *Personality and Individual Differences*, 10 (1989), 763–9.

[34] L. J. Francis and A. Montgomery, 'Personality and attitudes towards Christianity among eleven to sixteen year old girls in a single sex Catholic school', *British Journal of Religious Education*, 14 (1992), 114–19.

[35] L. J. Francis and G. A. Bennett, 'Personality and religion among female drug misusers', *Drug and Alcohol Dependence*, 30 (1992), 27–31.

[36] L. J. Francis, 'Personality and religion among college students in the UK', *Personality and Individual Differences*, 14 (1993), 619–22.

37 L. J. Francis, J. M. Lewis, L. B. Brown, R. Philipchalk and D. Lester, 'Personality and religion among undergraduate students in the United Kingdom, United States, Australia and Canada', *Journal of Psychology and Christianity* (in press).

38 D. Fontana, 'Some standardization data for the Sandler–Hazari Obsessionality Inventory', *British Journal of Medical Psychology*, 53 (1980), 267–75.

39 C. A. Lewis and S. Joseph, 'Obsessive actions and religious practices', *Journal of Psychology*, 128 (1994), 699–700.

40 C. A. Lewis, 'Religiosity and obsessionality: the relationship between Freud's "Religious Practices"', *Journal of Psychology*, 128 (1994), 189–96.

41 C. A. Lewis and S. Joseph, 'Religiosity: psychoticism and obsessionality in Northern Irish university students', *Personality and Individual Differences*, 17 (1994), 685–7.

Notes to chapter 8: Science and religion

1 See G. Eastman, 'Scientism in science education', *The Science Teacher*, 36 (1969), 19–22; P. A. Rubba, J. K. Horner and J. M. Smith, 'A study of two misconceptions about the nature of science among junior high school students', *School Science and Mathematics*, 81 (1981), 113–21; and M. Poole, 'An investigation into aspects of the interplay between science and religion at sixth form level' (Univ. of London M.Phil. thesis, 1983).

2 See, for example, M. B. Roberts, 'The roots of creationism', *Faith and Thought*, 112(1) (1986), 21–36; H. M. Morris, *The Biblical Basis for Modern Science* (Grand Rapids, Baker, 1984); H. M. Morris, *A History of Modern Creationism* (San Diego, Master Book Publishers, 1984); H. M. Morris and J. Whitcomb, *The Genesis Flood* (Grand Rapids, Baker, 1961).

3 R. Forster and P. Marston, *Reason and Faith* (Eastbourne, Monarch Publications, 1989) give an account of the rise of creationism from a non-creationist position. They show how creationism is a relatively new phenomenon.

4 Commentaries on Genesis from a range of theological standpoints draw attention to these structural patterns.

5 5 See H. Reich, 'Between religion and science: complementarity in the religious thinking of young people', *British Journal of Religious Education*, 11(2) (1989), 62–9.

6 P. Fulljames and L. J. Francis, 'The influence of creationism and scientism on attitudes towards Christianity among Kenyan secondary school students', *Educational Studies*, 14 (1988), 77–96.

[7] P. Fulljames, H. M. Gibson and L. J. Francis, 'Creationism, scientism, Christianity and science: a study in adolescent attitudes', *British Educational Research Journal*, 17 (1991), 171–90.

[8] L. J. Francis, P. Fulljames and H. M. Gibson, 'Does creationism commend the gospel? A developmental study among 11–17 year olds', *Religious Education*, 87 (1992), 19–27.

[9] L. J. Francis and W. K. Kay, *Teenage Religion and Values* (Leominster, Gracewing, 1995), 148, 149.

[10] M. F. Belenky, B. M. Clinch, N. R. Goldberger and J. M. Tarule, *Women's Ways of Knowing: The Development of Self, Voice, and Mind* (New York, Basic Books, 1986).

[11] See Fulljames, Gibson and Francis, op. cit., on which this part of the discussion is based.

Notes to chapter 9: Religious experience

[1] B. Spilka, R. W. Hood and R. L. Gorsuch, *The Psychology of Religion: An Empirical Approach* (Englewood Cliffs, Prentice-Hall, 1985).

[2] J. H. Leuba, 'Religious beliefs of American scientists', *Harper's*, 169 (1934), 297, quoted by M. Argyle and B. Beit-Hallahmi, *The Social Psychology of Religion* (London, Routledge and Kegan Paul, 1975), 90.

[3] See A. Hardy, *The Divine Flame* (London, Collins, 1966).

[4] E. Robinson, *The Original Vision* (Oxford, Religious Experience Research Unit, 1977); E. Robinson, *This Time-bound Ladder* (Oxford, Religious Experience Research Unit, 1977); E. Robinson, *Living the Questions* (Oxford, Religious Experience Research Unit, 1978).

[5] D. Hay, *Exploring Inner Space: scientists and religious experience* (London, Mowbray, 1987).

[6] Spilka, Hood and Gorsuch, op. cit., 184.

[7] Ibid., 185.

[8] Ibid., 187.

[9] T. R. Miles, *Religious Experience* (Basingstoke, Macmillan, 1972).

[10] See Argyle and Beit-Hallahmi, op. cit., 61.

[11] D. M. Wulff, *Psychology of Religion: Classic and Contemporary Views* (Chichester, John Wiley and Sons, 1991), 51.

[12] W. James, *The Varieties of Religious Experience* (Glasgow, William Collins, 1979), 122. First delivered as the Gifford Lectures in 1901.

[13] Compare Spilka, Hood and Gorsuch, *Psychology of Religion*, 208, with Wulff, op. cit., 502.

[14] Spilka, Hood and Gorsuch, op. cit., 208.

[15] G. A. Coe, *The Psychology of Religion* (Chicago, University of Chicago Press, 1916).

[16] L. W. Grensted, *The Psychology of Religion* (London, Oxford University Press, 1952), 72ff.

[17] L. Festinger, *A Theory of Cognitive Dissonance* (Evanston, Row Peterson, 1957).

[18] M. Rokeach, *The Open and Closed Mind* (New York, Basic Books, 1960) and R. J. Lifton, *Thought Reform and the Psychology of Totalism: A Study of 'Brainwashing' in China* (London, Gollancz, 1961).

[19] L. J. Francis and J. E. Greer, 'The contribution of religious experience to Christian development: a study among fourth, fifth and sixth year pupils in Northern Ireland', *British Journal of Religious Education*, 15 (1993), 38–43.

[20] J. E. Greer and L. J. Francis, 'The religious profile of pupils in Northern Ireland: a comparative study of pupils attending Catholic and Protestant secondary schools', *Journal of Empirical Theology*, 3(2) (1990), 35–50.

[21] J. E. Greer and L. J. Francis, 'Religious experience and attitude towards Christianity among secondary school children in Northern Ireland', *Journal of Social Psychology*, 132 (1992), 277–9.

[22] W. K. Kay, 'Conversion among 11–15 year olds', *Spectrum*, 13(2) (1981), 26–33.

[23] See for example, K. Lang and G. E. Lang, 'Decisions for Christ: Billy Graham in New York', in M. Stein, A. J. Vidich and O. M. White (eds.), *Identity and Anxiety* (Chicago, Free Press, 1960).

Notes to chapter 10: Religion and life

[1] See the discussion by F. Watts and M. Williams, *The Psychology of Religious Knowing* (London, Geoffrey Chapman, 1988).

[2] J. Wilson, N. Williams and B. Sugarman, *Introduction to Moral Education* (Harmondsworth, Penguin, 1967).

[3] See both D. Wright, *The Psychology of Moral Behaviour* (Harmondsworth, Penguin, 1971) and J. Bowlby, *Child Care and the Growth of Love* (Harmondsworth, Penguin, 1953).

[4] L. J. Francis and P. R. Pearson review the empirical literature in 'Empathic development during adolescence: religiosity, the missing link?' *Personality and Individual Differences*, 8 (1987), 145–8.

[5] S. B. G. Eysenck, 'Impulsiveness and antisocial behaviour in children', *Current Psychological Research*, 1 (1981), 31–7.

[6] See C. D. Batson, 'Religion as prosocial: agent or double agent?' *Journal for the Scientific Study of Religion*, 15 (1976), 29–45 and C. D. Batson and P. A. Gray, 'Religious orientation and helping behaviour: responding to one's own or to the victim's needs?' *Journal of Personality and Social Psychology*, 40 (1981), 511–20.

7 For further and original discussion of personal valuation systems see D. Bannister and F. Fransella, *Inquiring Man: The Theory of Personal Constructs* (Harmondsworth, Penguin, 1971).

8 See L. J. Francis and W. K. Kay, *Teenage Religion and Values* (Leominster, Gracewing, 1995).

9 See W. K. Kay and L. J. Francis, 'Well-being and its educational consequences', *Spectrum* 26(1) (1994), 8–14.

10 K. Chamberlain and S. Zika, 'Religiosity, meaning in life and well-being', in J. F. Schumaker (ed.), *Religion and Mental Health* (Oxford, Oxford University Press, 1992), 138–48.

11 J. Piaget, *The Moral Judgement of the Child* (Harmondsworth, Penguin, 1977). The first edition was published under the title *Le Jugement moral chez l'enfant* in 1932.

12 See for example K. Bergling, *Moral Development: The Validity of Kohlberg's Theory* (Stockholm, Almqvist and Wiksell International, 1981). We have described here stages 3, 4 and 5 in the sixth version of Kohlberg's scheme.

13 Empathy was measured by the Eysenck Impulsiveness Inventory, form I_6 Junior. Full details of the instrumentation used are given in Francis and Pearson, op. cit.

14 J. E. Greer, 'Viewing "the other side" in Northern Ireland: openness and attitude to religion among Catholic and Protestant Adolescents', *Journal for the Scientific Study of Religion*, 24 (1985), 275–92.

15 S. H. Jones and L. J. Francis, 'Religiosity and self-esteem during childhood and adolescence', in L. J. Francis, W. K. Kay and W. S. Campbell (eds.), *Research in Religious Education*, Leominster, Fowler Wright Books (1996).

16 L. P. Lipsitt, 'A self-concept scale for children and its relationship to the children's form of the Manifest Anxiety Scale', *Child Development*, 29 (1958), 463–72.

17 Jones and Francis, op. cit.

18 S. Coopersmith, *Self-Esteem Inventories* (Palo Alto, Consulting Psychologists Press, 1981).

19 C. Wilcox, L. J. Francis and S. H. Jones, 'Religiosity and happiness: a study among 15–16 year olds' (in press).

20 M. Argyle, M. Martin and J. Crossland, 'Happiness as a function of personality and social encounters', in J. P. Forgas and J. M. Innes (eds.), *Recent Advances in Social Psychology: An International Perspective* (North Holland, Elsevier Science Publishers, 1989), 189–203.

21 L. J. Francis and J. E. Greer, 'Measuring Christian moral values among Catholic and Protestant adolescents in Northern Ireland', *Journal of Moral Education*, 21 (1992), 59–65.

22 L. J. Francis and J. E. Greer, 'Catholic schools and adolescent

religiosity in Northern Ireland: shaping moral values', *Irish Journal of Education*, 24(2) (1990), 40–7.

[23] L. J. Francis and W. K. Kay, op. cit.

[24] For example those put forward by A. Maslow, *Toward a Psychology of Being* (New York, Van Nostrand Reinhold, 1968). D. M. Wulff in *Psychology of Religion: Classic and Contemporary Views* (New York, John Wiley and Sons, 1991) lists the characteristics of Maslow's self-actualizers. These characteristics are easily assimilated to a concept of well-being that makes use of traditional Christian theological ideas. For example, the self-actualizer has a more accurate perception of reality including human nature, enjoys a relative detachment from the immediate physical culture and social environment, is empathic, is centred on problems lying outside him- or herself, has clear ethical standards and feels able to reconcile apparent dichotomies or pairs of opposites.

Notes to chapter 11: Conclusion

[1] L. J. Francis and D. W. Lankshear, *Continuing in the Way: Children, Young People and the Church* (London, National Society, 1991).

[2] See, for example, R. J. Goldman, *Readiness for Religion* (London, Routledge and Kegan Paul, 1965).

[3] A. D. Gilbert, *The Making of Post-Christian Britain* (London, Longman, 1980).

[4] See B. O'Keeffe, 'A look at the Christian schools movement', in B. Watson (ed.), *Priorities in Religious Education* (London, Falmer Press, 1992), 92–112.

[5] See M. P. Hornsby-Smith, *Catholic Education: The Unobtrusive Partner* (London, Sheed and Ward, 1978).

[6] See P. Brierley and V. Hiscock, *UK Christian Handbook: 1994/95 Edition* (London, Christian Research Association, 1993).

[7] British Council of Churches, *The Child in the Church* (London, British Council of Churches, 1976).

[8] See, for example, C. D. Field, 'Adam and Eve: gender in the English Free Church constituency', *Journal of Ecclesiastical History*, 44 (1993), 63–79.

[9] See, for example, L. J. Francis, 'The personality characteristics of Anglican ordinands: feminine men and masculine women?' *Personality and Individual Differences*, 12 (1991), 1133–40.

[10] See, H. J. Eysenck and M. W. Eysenck, *Personality and Individual Differences: A Natural Science Approach* (New York, Plenum Press, 1985).

[11] See, for example, E. Robinson, *The Original Vision* (Oxford, Religious

Experience Research Unit, 1977); E. Robinson, *This Time-Bound Ladder* (Oxford, Religious Experience Research Unit, 1977); E. Robinson, *Living the Questions* (Oxford, Religious Experience Research Unit, 1978).

12 D. Hay, *Exploring Inner Space: Scientists and Religious Experience* (London, Mowbray, 1987); D. Hay, *Religious Experience Today: Studying the Facts* (London, Mowbray, 1990).

13 See, for example, L. J. Francis, *Teenagers and the Church: A Profile of Church-going Youth in the 1980s* (London, Collins, 1984).

14 See, for example, L. Burghes, *Lone Parenthood and Family Disruption: The Outcome for Children* (London, Family Policy Studies Centre, 1994).

15 See, for example, M. Argyle, *The Psychology of Social Class* (London, Routledge, 1994).

16 The debate is rehearsed in L. J. Francis, *Religion in the Primary School: Partnership between Church and State?* (London, Collins, 1987).

17 See, for example, M. Levitt, ' "The church is very important to me." A consideration of the relevance of Francis's Attitude towards Christianity scale to the aims of Church of England aided schools', *British Journal of Religious Education*, 17 (1995), 100–7.

18 D. Hay, 'The bearing of empirical studies of religious experience on education', *Research Papers in Education*, 5(1) (1990), 3–28.

19 See, for example, M. W. Poole, 'An investigation into aspects of the interplay between science and religion at sixth form level' (Univ. of London M.Phil. thesis, 1983).

20 See, for example, N. Eisenberg and P. H. Mussen, *The Roots of Pro-social Behaviour in Children* (Cambridge, Cambridge University Press, 1989).

21 See, for example, S. Coopersmith, *The Antecedents of Self-esteem* (San Francisco, W. H. Freeman, 1967).

22 A similar pattern linking the absence of religion with anti-social and self-harming behaviours is reported in L. J. Francis and W. K. Kay, *Teenage Religion and Values* (Leominster, Gracewing, 1995).

23 See, for example, D. Wright, *The Psychology of Moral Behaviour* (Harmondsworth, Penguin, 1971).

Notes to Appendix 1: Scientific study of religion

1 See the conversation between Bryan Magee and Ernest Gellner recorded in B. Magee (ed.), *Men of Ideas* (Oxford, Oxford University Press, 1982).

2 Particularly in the *Meditations of First Philosophy*.

[3] Further details are given by G. Duncan Mitchell, *Sociology: The Study of Social Systems* (London, University Tutorial Press, 1959).

[4] See, for example, Marx's preface to the first edition of *Capital* where he states, 'it is not a question of the higher or lower degree of development of social antagonisms that spring from the *natural laws* of capitalist production. It is a question of these *laws* themselves, of these tendencies winning their way through and working themselves out with *iron necessity*' (emphasis added). The quotation is found in *Capital* (Harmondsworth, Penguin, 1976), I, 91.

[5] See H. J. Eysenck, *Sense and Nonsense in Psychology* (Harmondsworth, Penguin, 1958), 158.

[6] E. D. Starbuck, *The Psychology of Religion: An Empirical Study of the Growth of Religious Consciousness* (New York, Charles Scribner's Sons, 1899).

[7] W. James, *The Varieties of Religious Experience* (Glasgow, William Collins, 1979).

[8] R. H. Thouless, *The Psychology of Religion* (Cambridge, Cambridge University Press, 1961).

[9] L. S. Hearnshaw, *The Shaping of Modern Psychology* (London, Routledge and Kegan Paul, 1987) suggests that Wundt's desire to analyse consciousness led to a 'dead end', and that most psychologists realized this by the beginning of the 1930s.

[10] D. M. Wulff, *Psychology of Religion: Classic and Contemporary Views* (New York, John Wiley and Sons, 1991).

[11] J. Derrida, *Of Grammatology*, Eng. trans. G. C. Spivak (London, Johns Hopkins University Press, 1976).

[12] See B. Vickers, *Appropriating Shakespeare* (London, Yale University Press, 1993), who quotes V. Descombes, *Objects of All Sorts: A Philosophical Grammar*, Eng. trans. L. Scott-Fox and J. M. Harding (Oxford, Oxford University Press, 1986).

[13] See D. Frisby, 'The Popper–Adorno Controversy: the methodological dispute in German sociology', *Philosophy of Social Science*, 2 (1972), 105–19.

[14] D. Stove, *Popper and After: Four Modern Irrationalists* (Oxford, Pergamon Press, 1982).

[15] As has been done by D. Hay, *Exploring Inner Space: Scientists and Religious Experience* (Harmondsworth, Penguin, 1982).

[16] J. P. Keeves (ed.), *Educational Research, Methodology, and Measurement: An International Handbook* (Oxford, Pergamon Press, 1988).

[17] In fact 100 figures would be produced (10 multiplied by 10), but 10 of them would be produced by multiplying each variable by itself. In addition each remaining coefficient would be produced twice because, for example, variable three's correlation with variable four would be

the same as variable four's correlation with variable three, and so on.

[18] This statistic is fully discussed by L. J. Cronbach, 'Coefficient alpha and the internal structure of tests', *Psychometrika*, 16 (1951), 297–334.

[19] See R. A. Zeller, 'Validity', in Keeves, op. cit., 322–30.

[20] F. N. Kerlinger and E. J. Pedhauser, *Multiple Regression in Behavioral Research* (London, Holt, Rinehart and Winston, 1973) give a full account of the method.

[21] The issue was addressed by L. J. Francis, 'The psychology of religion: revived, not yet reborn', *Bulletin of the British Psychological Society*, 31 (1978), 44–5 and by L. J. Francis, 'Psychological studies of religion head for derailment', *Religion*, 13 (1983), 127–36. L. J. Francis and W. K. Kay took note of the topic in 'Attitude towards religion: definition, measurement and evaluation', *British Journal of Educational Studies*, 32 (1984), 45–50. It was also addressed by W. K. Kay and L. J. Francis in 'The seamless robe: interdisciplinary enquiry in religious education', *British Journal of Religious Education*, 7 (1985), 64–7.

Notes to Appendix 2: Assessing attitudes

[1] *Annual Abstract of Statistics* (London, HMSO, 1994).

[2] D. Krech, R. S. Crutchfield and E. L. Ballackey, *Individual in Society* (New York, McGraw-Hill, 1962).

[3] M. Fishbein, 'An investigation of the relationships between beliefs about an object and the attitude toward that object', *Human Relations*, 16 (1963), 233–40.

[4] L. J. Francis and W. K. Kay, 'Attitude towards religion: definition, measurement and evaluation', *British Journal of Educational Studies*, 32 (1984), 45–50. See also I. Ajzen and M. Fishbein, 'Attitude-behaviour relations: a theoretical analysis and a review of empirical research', *Psychological Bulletin*, 84 (1977), 888–918.

[5] M. Fishbein, 'An investigation of the relationships between beliefs about an object and the attitude toward that object', op. cit.

[6] L. J. Francis, 'An enquiry into the concept "readiness for religion"' (Univ. of Cambridge Ph.D. thesis, 1976).

[7] L. L. Thurstone, 'Attitudes can be measured', *American Journal of Sociology*, 33 (1928), 529–54. More details of this are given by L. L. Thurstone and E. J. Chave, *The Measurement of Attitude* (Chicago, University of Chicago Press, 1929).

[8] R. A. Likert, 'A technique for the measurement of attitudes', *Archives of Psychology*, 140 (1932), 1–55.

[9] L. Guttman, 'The quantification of a class of attributes: a theory and

method of scale construction', in P. Horst et al. (eds.), *The Prediction of Personal Adjustment* (New York, Social Science Research Council, 1941). This is amplified in L. Guttman, 'A basis for scaling qualitative data', *American Sociological Review*, 9 (1944), 139–50.

[10] A. L. Edwards, *Techniques of Attitude Scale Construction* (New York, Appleton-Century-Crofts, 1957) makes use of previous work to suggest modifications.

[11] C. E. Osgood, G. J. Suci and P. H. Tannenbaum, *The Measurement of Meaning* (Urbana, University of Illinois Press, 1957). See also J. G. Snider and C. E. Osgood, *Semantic Differential: A Source Book* (Chicago, Aldine, 1969).

[12] L. J. Francis, 'The decline in attitude towards religion among 8–15 year olds', *Educational Studies*, 13 (1987), 125–34.

[13] The results were statistically significant. See L. J. Francis, 'The priest as test administrator in attitude research', *Journal for the Scientific Study of Religion*, 18 (1979), 78–81.

[14] L. J. Francis, 'Anonymity and attitude scores among ten and eleven year old children', *Journal of Experimental Education*, 49 (1981), 74–6.

[15] L. J. Francis, 'The development of a scale of attitude towards Christianity among 8–16 year olds', *Collected Original Resources in Education*, 12 (1988), fiche 1, A04.

[16] L. J. Francis, 'Measuring attitudes towards Christianity among 12–18 year old pupils in Catholic schools', *Educational Research*, 29 (1987), 230–3.

[17] J. E. Greer and L. J. Francis, 'Measuring attitudes towards Christianity among pupils in Catholic secondary schools in Northern Ireland', *Educational Research*, 33 (1991), 70–3.

[18] L. J. Francis and J. E. Greer, 'Measuring attitudes towards Christianity among pupils in Protestant secondary schools in Northern Ireland', *Personality and Individual Differences*, 11 (1990), 853–6.

[19] H. M. Gibson and L. J. Francis, 'Measuring attitudes towards Christianity among 11- to 16-year-old pupils in Catholic schools in Scotland', *Educational Research*, 31 (1989), 65–9.

[20] H. M. Gibson, 'Measuring attitudes towards Christianity among 11–16 year old pupils in non-denominational schools in Scotland', *Educational Research*, 31 (1989), 221–7.

[21] P. Fulljames and L. J. Francis, 'The measurement of attitudes towards Christianity among Kenyan secondary school students', *Journal of Social Psychology*, 127 (1987), 407–9.

[22] L. J. Francis and M. M. McCarron, 'The measurement of attitudes towards Christianity among Nigerian secondary school students', *Journal of Social Psychology*, 129 (1989), 569–71.

[23] L. J. Francis, J. E. Greer and H. M. Gibson, 'Reliability and validity of

a short measure of attitude towards Christianity among secondary school pupils in England, Scotland and Northern Ireland', *Collected Original Resources in Education*, 15(3) (1991), fiche 2, G09.

24 L. J. Francis, 'Reliability and validity of a short measure of attitude towards Christianity among nine to eleven year old pupils in England', *Collected Original Resources in Education*, 16(1) (1992), fiche 3, A02.

25 L. J. Francis and M. T. Stubbs, 'Measuring attitudes towards Christianity: from childhood to adulthood', *Personality and Individual Differences*, 8 (1987), 741–3.

26 L. J. Francis, 'Reliability and validity of the Francis scale of attitude towards Christianity (adult)', *Panorama*, 4(1) (1992), 17–19.

27 J. Maltby, 'The reliability and validity of the Francis scale of attitude towards Christianity among Republic of Ireland adults', *Irish Journal of Psychology*, 15 (1994), 595–8.

28 C. A. Lewis and J. Maltby, 'The reliability and validity of the Francis scale of attitude towards Christianity among US adults', *Psychological Reports* 76 (1995), 1243–7.

29 L. J. Francis, J. M. Lewis, R. Philipchalk, L. B. Brown and D. Lester, 'The internal consistency reliability and construct validity of the Francis scale of attitude towards Christianity (adult) among undergraduate students in the UK, USA, Australia and Canada', *Personality and Individual Differences*, 19 (1995), 949–53.

References

The following list is a citation of studies employing or discussing the Francis scale of attitude toward Christianity available at April 1995.

Al Mossawi, M., 'Factors mediating the effectiveness of TV advertisements' (Univ. of Manchester Ph.D. thesis, 1992).

Bennett, G. and K. Rigby, 'Psychological change during residence in a rehabilitation centre for female drug misusers', *Drug and Alcohol Dependence*, 27 (1991), 149–57.

Boyle, J. J., 'Catholic children's attitudes towards Christianity' (Univ. of Bradford M.Sc. thesis, 1984).

Boyle, J. J. and L. J. Francis, 'The influence of differing church aided school systems on pupil attitude towards religion', *Research in Education*, 35 (1986), 7–12.

Carter, M., 'The development of aspects of self in adolescence with reference to religious and moral education' (Univ. of Nottingham M.Phil. thesis, 1979).

Curran, M. B., 'The distinctive nature and ethos of the Catholic school and the effect of the admission of non-Catholic pupils' (Roehampton Institute of Higher Education MA thesis, 1992).

Francis, L. J., 'An enquiry into the concept "Readiness for Religion"' (Univ. of Cambridge Ph.D. thesis, 1976).

Francis, L. J., 'Readiness for research in religion', *Learning for Living*, 16 (1977), 109–14.

Francis, L. J., 'Attitude and longitude: a study in measurement', *Character Potential: A Record of Research*, 8 (1978), 119–30.

Francis, L. J., 'Measurement reapplied: research into the child's attitude towards religion', *British Journal of Religious Education*, 1 (1978), 45–51.

Francis, L. J., 'The priest as test administrator in attitude research', *Journal for the Scientific Study of Religion*, 18 (1979), 78-81.

Francis, L. J., 'School influence and pupil attitude towards religion', *British Journal of Educational Psychology*, 49 (1979), 107–23.

Francis, L. J., 'Christianity and the child today', *Occasional Papers: Farmington Institute for Christian Studies*, 6 (1980).

Francis, L. J., 'Paths of holiness: attitudes towards religion among 9–11 year old children in England', *Character Potential: A Record of Research*, 9 (1980), 129–38.

Francis, L. J., 'Anonymity and attitude scores among ten and eleven year old children', *Journal of Experimental Education*, 49 (1981), 74–6.

Francis, L. J., 'Roman Catholic schools and pupil attitudes in England', *Lumen Vitae*, 39 (1984), 99–108.

Francis, L. J., 'Personality and religion: theory and measurement', in L.B. Brown (ed.), *Advances in the Psychology of Religion* (Oxford, Pergamon Press, 1985), 171–84.

Francis, L. J., 'Denominational schools and pupil attitudes towards Christianity', *British Educational Research Journal*, 12 (1986), 145–52.

Francis, L. J., 'Roman Catholic secondary schools: falling rolls and pupil attitudes', *Educational Studies*, 12 (1986), 119–27.

Francis, L. J., 'The decline in attitudes towards religion among 8-15 year olds', *Educational Studies*, 13 (1987), 125–34.

Francis, L. J., 'Measuring attitudes towards Christianity among 12–18 year old pupils in Catholic schools', *Educational Research*, 29 (1987), 230–3.

Francis, L. J., *Religion in the Primary School* (London, Collins Liturgical Publications, 1987).

Francis, L. J., 'The development of a scale of attitude towards Christianity among 8-16 year olds', *Collected Original Resources in Education*, 12(3) (1988), fiche 1, A04.

Francis, L. J., 'Monitoring attitude towards Christianity during childhood and adolescence', in M. Pyysiainen (ed.), *Kasvatus ja Uskonto: Professori Kalevi Tammisen Juhlakirja* (Helsinki, Werner Soderstrom Osakeghtio, 1988), 230–47.

Francis, L. J., 'Drift from the churches: secondary school pupils' attitudes towards Christianity', *British Journal of Religious Education*, 11 (1989), 76–86.

Francis, L. J., 'Measuring attitude towards Christianity during childhood and adolescence', *Personality and Individual Differences*, 10 (1989), 695–8.

Francis, L. J., 'Monitoring changing attitudes towards Christianity among secondary school pupils between 1974 and 1986', *British Journal of Educational Psychology*, 59 (1989), 86–91.

Francis, L. J., 'The religious significance of denominational identity among eleven year old children in England', *Journal of Christian Education*, 97 (1990), 23–8.

Francis, L. J., 'Personality and attitude towards religion among adult churchgoers in England', *Psychological Reports*, 69 (1991), 791–4.

Francis, L. J., 'Is psychoticism really the dimension of personality fundamental to religiosity?' *Personality and Individual Differences*, 13 (1992), 645–52.

Francis, L. J., 'Christianity today: the teenage experience', in J. Astley and D. V. Day (eds.) *The Contours of Christian Education* (Great Wakering, McCrimmons, 1992), 340–68.

Francis, L. J., 'Monitoring attitude towards Christianity: the 1990 study', *British Journal of Religious Education*, 14 (1992), 178–82.

Francis, L. J., 'Neuroticism and intensity of religious attitudes among clergy in England', *Journal of Social Psychology*, 132 (1992), 577–80.

Francis, L. J., 'Reliability and validity of a short measure of attitude towards Christianity among nine to eleven year old pupils in England', *Collected Original Resources in Education*, 16(1) (1992), fiche 3, A02.

Francis, L. J., 'Religion, neuroticism, and psychoticism', in J. F. Schumaker (ed.), *Religion and Mental Health* (New York, Oxford University Press, 1992), 149–60.

Francis, L. J., 'Reliability and validity of the Francis scale of attitude towards Christianity (adult)', *Panorama*, 4(1) (1992), 17–19.

Francis, L. J., 'Attitudes towards Christianity during childhood and adolescence: assembling the jigsaw', *Journal of Beliefs and Values*, 14(2) (1993), 4-6.

Francis, L. J., 'The identity of Anglicanism: the teenage experience', *Collegium*, 2(1) (1993), 4–12.

Francis, L. J., 'Personality and religion among college students in the UK', *Personality and Individual Differences*, 14 (1993), 619–22.

Francis, L. J., 'Reliability and validity of a short scale of attitude towards Christianity among adults', *Psychological Reports*, 72 (1993), 615–18.

Francis, L. J., 'Church schools and pupils' attitudes towards Christianity: a response to Mairi Levitt', *British Journal of Religious Education* (in press).

Francis, L. J., 'Monitoring attitudes toward Christianity between 1974 and 1994 among secondary school pupils in England', in M. Bar-Lev and W. Shaffir (eds.), *Leaving Religion and Religious Life: Patterns and Dynamics* (in press).

Francis, L. J., 'Religiosity and femininity: are women really more religious?' (in press).

Francis, L. J. and G. A. Bennett, 'Personality and religion among female drug misusers', *Drug and Alcohol Dependence*, 30 (1992), 27–31.

Francis, L. J. and M. Carter, 'Church aided secondary schools, religious education as an examination subject and pupil attitude towards religion', *British Journal of Educational Psychology*, 50 (1980), 297–300.

Francis, L. J., P. Fulljames and H. M. Gibson, 'Does creationism commend the gospel? A developmental study among 11–17 year olds', *Religious Education*, 87 (1992), 19–27.

Francis, L. J. and H. M. Gibson, 'Popular religious television and adolescent attitudes towards Christianity', in J. Astley and D. V. Day (eds.), *The Contours of Christian Education* (Gt Wakering, McCrimmons, 1992), 369-381.

Francis, L. J. and H. M. Gibson, 'Parental influence and adolescent religiosity: a study of church attendance and attitude towards Christianity among 11–12 and 15–16 year olds', *International Journal for the Psychology of Religion*, 3 (1993), 241–253.

Francis, L. J. and H. M. Gibson, 'Television, pop culture and the drift from Christianity during adolescence', *British Journal of Religious Education*, 15 (1993), 31–7.

Francis, L. J., H. M. Gibson and P. Fulljames, 'Attitude towards Christianity, creationism, scientism and interest in science', *British Journal of Religious Education*, 13 (1990), 4–17.

Francis, L. J., H. M. Gibson and D. W. Lankshear, 'The influence of Protestant Sunday schools on attitudes towards Christianity among 11–15 year olds in Scotland', *British Journal of Religious Education*, 14 (1991), 35–42.

Francis, L. J., H. M. Gibson and D. W. Lankshear, 'Do Sunday schools make a difference?' *Crosscurrent*, 37 (1992), 10–11.

Francis, L. J. and J. E. Greer, 'Catholic schools and adolescent religiosity in Northern Ireland: shaping moral values', *Irish Journal of Education*, 24 (1990), 40–7.

Francis, L. J. and J. E. Greer, 'Measuring attitudes towards Christianity among pupils in Protestant secondary schools in Northern Ireland', *Personality and Individual Differences*, 11 (1990), 853–6.

Francis, L. J. and J. E. Greer, 'Measuring Christian moral values among Catholic and Protestant adolescents in Northern Ireland', *Journal of Moral Education*, 21 (1992), 59–65.

Francis, L. J. and J. E. Greer, 'The teenage voice: the religious profile of pupils attending Catholic and Protestant secondary schools in Northern Ireland', in P. Brierley (ed.), *The Irish Christian Handbook* (London, MARC Europe, 1992), 20–3.

Francis, L. J. and J. E. Greer, 'The contribution of religious experience to Christian development: a study among fourth, fifth and sixth year pupils in Northern Ireland', *British Journal of Religious Education*, 15 (1993), 38–43.

Francis, L. J., J. E. Greer and H. M. Gibson, 'Reliability and validity of a short measure of attitude towards Christianity among secondary school pupils in England, Scotland and Northern Ireland', *Collected Original Resources in Education*, 15(3) (1991), fiche 2, G09.

Francis, L. J. and W. K. Kay, 'Attitude towards religion: definition, measurement and evaluation', *British Journal of Educational Studies*, 32 (1984), 45–50.

Francis, L. J., D. W. Lankshear and P. R. Pearson, 'The relationship between religiosity and the short form JEPQ (JEPQ-S) indices of E, N, L and P among eleven year olds', *Personality and Individual Differences*, 10 (1989), 763–9.

Francis, L. J., J. M. Lewis, L. B. Brown, R. Philipchalk and D. Lester, 'Personality and religion among undergraduate students in the United Kingdom, United States, Australia and Canada', *Journal of Psychology and Christianity*, 14 (1995), 250–62.

Francis, L. J., J. M. Lewis, R. Philipchalk, L. B. Brown and D. Lester, 'The internal consistency reliability and construct validity of the Francis scale of attitude towards Christianity (adult) among undergraduate students in the UK, USA, Australia and Canada', *Personality and Individual Differences*, 19 (1995), 949–53.

Francis, L. J., J. M. Lewis, R. Philipchalk, D. Lester and L. B. Brown, 'Reliability and validity of a short scale of attitude toward Christianity among students in the UK, USA, Australia and Canada' , *Psychological Reports*, 77 (1995), 431–34.

Francis, L. J. and M. M. McCarron, 'The measurement of attitudes towards Christianity among Nigerian secondary school students', *Journal of Social Psychology*, 129 (1989), 569–71.

Francis, L. J. and A. Montgomery, 'Personality and attitudes towards Christianity among eleven to sixteen year old girls in a single sex Catholic school', *British Journal of Religious Education*, 14 (1992), 114–19.

Francis, L. J. and P. R. Pearson, 'Extraversion and religiosity', *Journal of Social Psychology*, 125 (1985), 269–70.

Francis, L. J. and P. R. Pearson, 'Psychoticism and religiosity among 15 year olds', *Personality and Individual Differences*, 6 (1985), 397–8.

Francis, L. J. and P. R. Pearson, 'Empathic development during adolescence: religiosity, the missing link?' *Personality and Individual Differences*, 8 (1987), 145–8.

Francis, L. J. and P. R. Pearson, 'The development of a short form of the JEPQ (JEPQ-S): its use in measuring personality and religion', *Personality and Individual Differences*, 9 (1988), 911–16.

Francis, L. J. and P. R. Pearson, 'Religiosity and the short-scale EPQ-R indices of E, N and L, compared with the JEPI, JEPQ and EPQ', *Personality and Individual Differences*, 9 (1988), 653–7.

Francis, L. J. and P. R. Pearson, 'Religiosity, gender and the two faces of neuroticism', *Irish Journal of Psychology*, 12 (1991), 60–8.

Francis, L. J., P. R. Pearson, M. Carter and W. K. Kay, 'Are introverts more religious?' *British Journal of Social Psychology*, 20 (1981), 101–4.

Francis, L. J., P. R. Pearson, M. Carter and W. K. Kay, 'The relationship between neuroticism and religiosity among English 15–16 year olds', *Journal of Social Psychology*, 114 (1981), 99–102.

Francis, L. J., P. R. Pearson and W. K. Kay, 'Eysenck's personality quadrants and religiosity', *British Journal of Social Psychology*, 21 (1982), 262–4.

Francis, L. J., P. R. Pearson and W. K. Kay, 'Are introverts still more religious?' *Personality and Individual Differences*, 4 (1983), 211–12.

Francis, L. J., P. R. Pearson and W. K. Kay, 'Are religious children bigger liars?' *Psychological Reports*, 52 (1983), 551–4.

Francis, L. J., P. R. Pearson and W. K. Kay, 'Neuroticism and religiosity among English school children', *Journal of Social Psychology*, 121 (1983), 149–50.

Francis, L. J., P. R. Pearson and W. K. Kay, 'Religiosity and lie scores: a question of interpretation', *Social Behaviour and Personality*, 16 (1988), 91–5.

Francis, L. J., P. R. Pearson and D. W. Lankshear, 'The relationship between social class and attitude towards Christianity among ten and eleven year old children', *Personality and Individual Differences*, 11 (1990), 1019–27.

Francis, L. J., P. R. Pearson and M. T. Stubbs, 'Personality and religion among low ability children in residential special schools', *British Journal of Mental Subnormality*, 31 (1985), 41–5.

Francis, L. J. and M. T. Stubbs, 'Measuring attitudes towards Christianity: from childhood to adulthood', *Personality and Individual Differences*, 8 (1987), 741–3.

Francis, L. J., C. B. Wesley and J. N. Rust, 'An account of the religious attitude research project of the London Institute of Education', *Area*, 11 (1978), 10–15.

Francis, L. J. and C. Wilcox, 'Religion and gender orientation', in *Personality and Individual Differences*, 20 (1996), 119–21.

Fulljames, P. and L. J. Francis, 'Creationism and student attitudes towards science and Christianity', *Journal of Christian Education*, 90 (1987), 51–5.

Fulljames, P. and L. J. Francis, 'The measurement of attitudes towards Christianity among Kenyan secondary school students', *Journal of Social Psychology*, 127 (1987), 407–9.

Fulljames, P. and L. J. Francis, 'The influence of creationism and scientism on attitudes towards Christianity among Kenyan secondary school students', *Educational Studies*, 14 (1988), 77–96.

Fulljames, P., H. M. Gibson and L. J. Francis, 'Creationism, scientism, Christianity and science: a study in adolescent attitudes', *British Educational Research Journal*, 17 (1991), 171–90.

Gibson, H. M., 'Attitudes to religion and communication of Christian truth' (Univ. of St Andrews Ph.D. thesis, 1989).

Gibson, H. M., 'Attitudes to religion and science among school children aged 11 to 16 years in a Scottish city', *Journal of Empirical Theology*, 2 (1989), 5–26.

Gibson, H. M., 'Measuring attitudes towards Christianity among 11-16 year old pupils in non-denominational schools in Scotland', *Educational Research*, 31 (1989), 221–7.

Gibson, H. M., 'Christianity and young people today', *Life and Work* (October, 1990), 30–1; (November 1990), 18–19.

Gibson, H. M. and L. J. Francis, 'Measuring attitudes towards Christianity among 11- to 16-year old pupils in Catholic schools in Scotland', *Educational Research*, 31 (1989), 65–9.

Gibson, H. M., L. J. Francis and P. R. Pearson, 'The relationship between social class and attitude towards Christianity among fourteen and fifteen year old adolescents', *Personality and Individual Differences*, 11 (1990), 631–5.

Greer, J. E., 'Religious attitudes and thinking in Belfast pupils', *Educational Research*, 23 (1981), 177–89.

Greer, J. E., 'A comparison of two attitude to religion scales', *Educational Research*, 24 (1982), 226–7.

Greer, J. E., 'Growing up in Belfast: a study of religious development', *Collected Original Resources in Education*, 6(1) (1982), fiche 1, A14.

Greer, J. E., 'Attitude to religion reconsidered', *British Journal of Educational Studies*, 31 (1983), 18–28.

Greer, J. E., 'Viewing "the other side" in Northern Ireland: openness and attitudes to religion among Catholic and Protestant adolescents', *Journal for the Scientific Study of Religion*, 24 (1985), 275–92.

Greer, J. E. and L. J. Francis, 'The religious profile of pupils in Northern Ireland: a comparative study of pupils attending Catholic and Protestant secondary schools', *Journal of Empirical Theology*, 3 (1990), 35–50.

Greer, J. E. and L. J. Francis, 'Measuring attitudes towards Christianity among pupils in Catholic Secondary schools in Northern Ireland', *Educational Research*, 33 (1991), 70–3.

Greer, J. E. and L. J. Francis, 'Religious experience and attitude towards Christianity among secondary school children in Northern Ireland', *Journal of Social Psychology*, 132 (1992), 277–9.

Greer, J. E. and J. Long, 'Religion in rural Ulster', *Education North*, 1(2) (1989), 15–19.

Hyde, K. E., *Religion in Childhood and Adolescence: A Comprehensive Review of the Research* (Birmingham, Alabama, Religious Education Press, 1990).

Jones, S. H. and L. J. Francis, 'Religiosity and self-esteem during childhood and adolescence', in L. J. Francis, W. K. Kay and W. S. Campbell (eds.), *Research in Religious Education* (Leominster, Fowler Wright Books, 1996).

Kay, W. K., 'Conversion among 11–15 year olds', *Spectrum*, 13(2) (1981), 26–33.

Kay, W. K., 'Marital happiness and children's attitudes to religion', *British Journal of Religious Education*, 3 (1981), 102–5.

Kay, W. K. 'Psychoticism and attitude to religion', *Personality and Individual Differences*, 2 (1981), 249–52.

Kay, W. K., 'Religious thinking, attitudes and personality amongst secondary pupils in England and Ireland' (Univ. of Reading Ph.D. thesis, 1981).

Kay, W. K., 'Subject preference and attitude to religion in secondary schools', *Educational Review*, 33 (1981), 47–51.

Kay, W. K., 'Syllabuses and attitudes to Christianity', *The Irish Catechist*, 5(2) (1981), 16–21.

Lester, D. and L. J. Francis, 'Is religiosity related to suicidal ideation after personality and mood are taken into account?' *Personality and Individual Differences*, 15 (1993), 591–2.

Levitt, M., 'The influence of a church primary school on children's religious beliefs and practices: a Cornish study' (Univ. of Exeter Ph.D. thesis, 1993).

Levitt, M., ' "The church is very important to me." A consideration of the relevance of Francis' attitude towards Christianity scale to the aims of Church of England aided schools', *British Journal of Religious Education*, 17 (1995), 100–7.

Lewis, C. A., 'Religiosity and obsessionality: the relationship between Freud's "religious practices" ', *Journal of Psychology*, 128 (1994), 189–96.

Lewis, C. A. and S. Joseph, 'Obsessive actions and religious practices', *Journal of Psychology*, 128 (1994), 699–700.

Lewis, C. A. and S. Joseph, 'Religiosity: psychoticism and obsessionality in Northern Irish university students', *Personality and Individual Differences*, 17 (1994), 685–7.

Lewis, C. A. and J. Maltby, 'Religiosity and preoedipal fixation: a refinement', *Journal of Psychology*, 126 (1992), 687–8.

Lewis, C. A. and J. Maltby, 'Religious attitudes and obsessional personality traits among UK adults', *Psychological Reports*, 75 (1994), 353–4.

Lewis, C. A. and J. Maltby, 'Religiosity and personality among US adults', *Personality and Individual Differences*, 18 (1995), 293–5.

Lewis, C. A. and J. Maltby, 'The reliability and validity of the Francis scale of attitude towards Christianity among US adults', *Psychological Reports*, 76 (1995), 1243–7.

Long, J. F., 'A study of Catholic secondary schools in the Archdiocese of Armagh with special reference to RE' (Univ. of Ulster D.Phil. thesis, 1989).

Maltby, J., 'The reliability and validity of the Francis scale of attitude towards Christianity among Republic of Ireland adults', *Irish Journal of Psychology*, 15 (1994), 595–8.

Maltby, J., 'Is there a denominational difference in scores on the Francis scale of attitude towards Christianity among Northern Irish adults?' *Psychological Reports*, 76 (1995), 88–90.

Maltby, J., P. McCollam and D. Millar, 'Religiosity and obsessionality: a refinement', *Journal of Psychology*, 128 (1994), 609–11.

Miller, J. D., 'Conversion, confusion or chaos: a study of the impact of church schools with particular reference to a parish in the diocese of Durham' (Univ. of Newcastle upon Tyne MA thesis, 1993).

Montgomery, A., 'Change in attitudes towards religion and religious education' (Polytechnic of North East London M.Ed. thesis, 1990).

O'Keeffe, B., 'A look at the Christian schools movement', in B. Watson (ed.), *Priorities in Religious Education* (London, Falmer Press, 1992), 92–112.

Pearson, P. R. and L. J. Francis, 'The dual nature of the Eysenckian lie scales: are religious adolescents more truthful?' *Personality and Individual Differences*, 10 (1989), 1041–8.

Pearson, P. R., L. J. Francis and T. J. Lightbown, 'Impulsivity and religiosity', *Personality and Individual Differences*, 7 (1986), 89–94.

Rhymer, J., 'Religious attitudes of Roman Catholic secondary school pupils in Strathclyde region' (Univ. of Edinburgh Ph.D. thesis, 1983).

Rhymer, J. and L. J. Francis, 'Roman Catholic secondary schools in Scotland and pupil attitude towards religion', *Lumen Vitae*, 40 (1985), 103–10.

Wilcox, C., L. J. Francis and S. H. Jones, 'Religiosity and happiness: a study among 15–16 year olds' (in press).

Bibliography

This bibliography cites the major studies referred to in the text, excluding those which employ the Francis scale of attitude toward Christianity. These studies are cited in the section headed 'References'.

Abrams, M., 'Demographic correlates of values', in M. Abrams, D. Gerard and N. Timms (eds.), *Values and Social Change in Britain* (Basingstoke, Macmillan, 1985), 21–49.

Acock, A. C. and V. L. Bengtson, 'On the relative influence of mothers and fathers: a covariance analysis of political and religious socialisation', *Journal of Marriage and the Family*, 40 (1978), 519–30.

Ajzen I. and M. Fishbein, 'Attitude–behaviour relations: a theoretical analysis and a review of empirical research', *Psychological Bulletin*, 84 (1977), 888–918.

Ajzen, I. and M. Fishbein, *Understanding Attitudes and Predicting Social Behaviour* (Englewood Cliffs, Prentice-Hall 1980).

Allport, G. W., *The Individual and his Religion: A Psychological Interpretation* (New York, Macmillan, 1950).

Annual Abstract of Statistics (London, HMSO, 1994).

Antill, J. K., J. D. Cunningham, G. Russell and N. L. Thompson, 'An Australian sex-role scale', *Australian Journal of Psychology*, 33 (1981), 169–83.

Argyle, M., *The Psychology of Social Class* (London, Routledge, 1994).

Argyle, M. and B. Beit-Hallahmi, *The Social Psychology of Religion* (London, Routledge and Kegan Paul, 1975).

Argyle, M., M. Martin and J. Crossland, 'Happiness as a function of personality and social encounters', in J. P. Forgas and J. M. Innes (eds.), *Recent Advances in Social Psychology: An International Perspective* (North Holland, Elsevier Science Publishers, 1989), 189–203.

Bannister, D. and F. Fransella, *Inquiring Man: The Theory of Personal Constructs* (Harmondsworth, Penguin, 1971).

Batson, C. D. and P. A. Gray, 'Religious orientation and helping behaviour: responding to one's own or to the victim's needs?' *Journal of Personality and Social Psychology*, 40 (1981), 511–20.

Batson, C. D., 'Religion as prosocial: agent or double agent?' *Journal for the Scientific Study of Religion*, 15 (1976), 29–45.

Belenky, M. F., B. M. Clinch, N. R. Goldberger and J. M. Tarule,

Women's Ways of Knowing: The Development of Self, Voice, and Mind (New York, Basic Books, 1986).

Bem, S. L., *Bem Sex Role Inventory: Professional Manual* (Palo Alto, Consulting Psychologists Press, 1981).

Bergling, K., *Moral Development: The Validity of Kohlberg's Theory* (Stockholm, Almqvist and Wiksell International, 1981).

Block, J. 'Advancing the psychology of personality: paradigmatic shift or improving the quality of research', in D. Magnusson and N. S. Endler (eds.), *Personality at the Crossroads* (London, John Wiley and Sons, 1977).

Blyth, W. A. L. and R. Perricott, *The Social Significance of Middle Schools* (London, Batsford, 1977).

Bouma, G. D. and B. R. Dixon, *The Religious Factor in Australian Life* (Melbourne, MARC Australia, 1987).

Bowlby, J., *Child Care and the Growth of Love* (Harmondsworth, Penguin, 1953).

Boyle, J. J., 'Catholic children's attitudes towards Christianity' (Univ. of Bradford M.Sc. thesis, 1984).

Boyle, J. J. and Francis, L. J., 'The influence of differing church aided school systems on pupil attitude towards religion', *Research in Education*, 35 (1986), 7–12.

Brierley, P. and B. Evans (eds.), *Prospects for Wales: A Report of the 1982 Census of the Churches* (London, Bible Society and MARC Europe, 1983).

Brierley, P. and V. Hiscock (eds.), *UK Christian Handbook: 1994/95 Edition* (London, Christian Research Association, 1993).

Brierley, P. and F. Macdonald, *Prospects for Scotland: Report of the 1984 Census of the Churches* (London, MARC Europe, 1985).

British Council of Churches, *The Child in the Church* (London, British Council of Churches, 1976).

Brown, G. and C. Desforges, 'Piagetian psychology and education: time for revision', *British Journal of Educational Psychology*, 47 (1977), 7–17.

Burghes, L., *Lone Parenthood and Family Disruption: The Outcomes for Children* (London, Family Policy Studies Centre, 1994).

Cattell, R. B., *The Scientific Analysis of Personality* (Harmondsworth, Penguin, 1965).

Chamberlain, K. and S. Zika, 'Religiosity, meaning in life and well-being', in J. F. Schumaker (ed.), *Religion and Mental Health* (Oxford, Oxford University Press, 1992), 138–48.

Coe, G. A., *The Psychology of Religion* (Chicago, University of Chicago Press, 1916).

Cohen, D., *Piaget: Critique and Reassessment* (London, Croom Helm, 1983).

Coleman, J. S., *The Adolescent Society* (New York, Free Press, 1971).

Coleman, J. S., 'Methods and results of IEA studies of effects of school on learning', *Review of Educational Research*, 45 (1975), 335–86.

Comber J. A. and J. P. Keeves, *Science Education in Nineteen Countries*, International Studies in Evaluation, vol.1 (Stockholm, Almqvist Wiksell, 1973).

Coopersmith, S., *The Antecedents of Self-esteem* (San Francisco, Freeman, 1967).

Coopersmith, S., *Self-esteem Inventories* (Palo Alto, Consulting Psychologists Press, 1981).

Cronbach L. J., 'Coefficient alpha and the internal structure of tests', *Psychometrika*, 16 (1951), 297–334.

Cruickshank, M., *Church and State in English Education* (London, Macmillan, 1963).

De Vaus, D. A., 'The impact of Catholic schools on the religious orientation of boys and girls', *Journal of Christian Education*, 71 (1981), 44–51.

De Vaus, D. A., 'The impact of children on sex related differences in church attendance', *Sociological Analysis*, 43 (1982), 145–54.

De Vaus, D. A., 'Workforce participation and sex differences in church attendance', *Review of Religious Research*, 25 (1984), 247–56.

Derrida, J., *Of Grammatology*, Eng. trans. G. C. Spivak (London, Johns Hopkins University Press, 1976).

Descombes, V., *Objects of All Sorts: A Philosophical Grammar*, Eng. trans. L Scott-Fox and J. M. Harding (Oxford, Oxford University Press, 1986).

Durkheim, E., 'The social foundations of religion', in R. Robertson (ed.), *Sociology of Religion* (Harmondsworth, Penguin, 1969).

Eastman, G., 'Scientism in science education', *The Science Teacher*, 36 (1969), 19–22.

Edwards, A. L., *Techniques of Attitude Scale Construction* (New York, Appleton-Century-Crofts, 1957).

Egan, J., *Opting Out: Catholic Schools Today* (Leominster, Fowler Wright, 1988).

Egan, J. and L. J. Francis, 'School ethos in Wales: the impact of non-practising Catholic and non-Catholic pupils on Catholic secondary schools', *Lumen Vitae*, 41 (1986), 159–73.

Eisenberg, N. and P. H. Mussen, *The Roots of Pro-social Behaviour in Children* (Cambridge, Cambridge University Press, 1989).

Eysenck, H. J., *The Psychology of Politics* (London, Routledge and Kegan Paul, 1954).

Eysenck, H. J., *Sense and Nonsense in Psychology* (Harmondsworth, Penguin, 1958).

Eysenck, H. J., 'Personality and social attitudes', *The Journal of Social Psychology*, 53 (1961), 243–9.

Eysenck, H. J., 'Social attitudes and social class', *British Journal of Social and Clinical Psychology*, 10 (1971), 201–12.

Eysenck, H. J., 'An experimental study of Freudian concepts', *Bulletin of the British Psychological Society*, 25 (1972), 261–7.

Eysenck, H. J., *Decline and Fall of the Freudian Empire* (London, Viking, 1985).

Eysenck, H. J. and M. W. Eysenck, *Personality and Individual Differences: A Natural Science Approach* (New York, Plenum Press, 1985).

Eysenck, H. J. and S. B. G. Eysenck, *Manual of the Eysenck Personality Questionnaire* (London, Hodder and Stoughton, 1975).

Eysenck, H. J. and S. B. G. Eysenck, *Psychoticism as a Dimension of Personality* (London, Hodder and Stoughton, 1976).

Eysenck, H. J. and G. D. Wilson, *The Experimental Study of Freudian Theories* (London, Methuen, 1973).

Eysenck M. W. and H. J. Eysenck, 'Mischel and the concept of personality', *British Journal of Psychology*, 71 (1980), 191–204.

Eysenck, S. B. G., *Manual of the Junior Eysenck Personality Inventory* (London, Hodder and Stoughton, 1965).

Eysenck S. B. G., 'Impulsiveness and antisocial behaviour in children', *Current Psychological Research*, 1 (1981), 31–7.

Eysenck, S. B. G. and H. J. Eysenck, 'The place of impulsiveness in a dimensional system of personality', *British Journal of Social and Clinical Psychology*, 16 (1977), 57–68.

Festinger, L., *A Theory of Cognitive Dissonance* (Evanston, Row Peterson, 1957).

Field, C. D., 'Adam and Eve: gender in English Free Church constituency', *Journal of Ecclesiastical History*, 44 (1993), 63–79.

Fishbein, M., 'An investigation of the relationships between beliefs about an object and the attitude toward that object', *Human Relations*, 16 (1963), 233-240.

Fontana, D., 'Some standardization data for the Sandler–Hazari Obsessionality Inventory', *British Journal of Medical Psychology*, 53 (1980), 267–75.

Forster R. and P. Marston, *Reason and Faith* (Eastbourne, Monarch Publications, 1989).

Francis, L. J., 'The psychology of religion: revived, not yet reborn', *Bulletin of the British Psychological Society*, 31 (1978), 44–5.

Francis, L. J., 'Psychological studies of religion head for derailment', *Religion*, 13 (1983), 127–36.

Francis, L. J., *Teenagers and the Church: A Profile of Church-going Youth in the 1980s* (London, Collins Liturgical Publications, 1984).

Francis, L. J., *Young and Unemployed* (Tunbridge Wells, Costello, 1984).

Francis, L. J., 'The personality characteristics of Anglican ordinands:

feminine men and masculine women?' *Personality and Individual Differences*, 12 (1991), 1133–40.

Francis, L. J., 'Male and female clergy in England: their personality differences, gender reversal?' *Journal of Empirical Theology*, 5(2) (1992), 31–8.

Francis, L. J. and J. Egan, 'Catholic schools and the communication of faith', *Catholic School Studies*, 60(2) (1987), 27–34.

Francis, L. J. and J. Egan, 'The Catholic school as "faith community": an empirical enquiry', *Religious Education*, 85 (1990), 588–603.

Francis, L. J. and A. Jewell, 'Shaping adolescent attitude towards the church: comparison between Church of England and county secondary schools', *Evaluation and Research in Education*, 6 (1992), 13–21.

Francis L. J. and Y. J. Katz, 'The relationship between personality and religiosity in an Israeli sample', *Journal for the Scientific Study of Religion*, 31 (1992), 153–162.

Francis, L. J. and W. K. Kay, *Teenage Religion and Values* (Leominster, Gracewing, 1995).

Francis, L. J. and D. W. Lankshear, *Continuing in the Way: Children, Young People and the Church* (London, National Society, 1991).

Francis, L. J. and D. W. Lankshear, 'Asking about baptism: straw polls and fenced fonts', *Modern Churchman*, 34(5) (1993), 88–92.

Freud, S., *New Introductory Lectures on Psychoanalysis* (London, Hogarth Press, 1946).

Freud, S., *Totem and Taboo* (London, Routledge and Kegan Paul, 1950).

Frisby, D., 'The Popper–Adorno controversy: the methodological dispute in German sociology', *Philosophy of Social Science*, 2 (1972), 105–19.

Gallup Report, *Political, Social and Economic Trends* (Princeton, Gallup, 1987).

Gaston J. E. and L. Brown, 'Religious and gender prototypes', *International Journal for the Psychology of Religion*, 1 (1991), 233–41.

Gee, E. M., 'Gender differences in church attendance in Canada: the role of labor force participation', *Review of Religious Research*, 32 (1991), 267–73.

Gibson, H. M., 'Adolescents' images of God', *Panorama*, 6(1) (1994), 104–14.

Gilbert, A. D., *The Making of Post-Christian Britain* (London, Longman, 1980).

Glock, C. Y., B. B. Ringer and E. R. Babbie, *To Comfort and to Challenge* (Berkeley, University of California Press, 1967).

Goldman, R. J., *Religious Thinking from Childhood to Adolescence* (London, Routledge and Kegan Paul, 1964).

Goldman, R. J., *Readiness for Religion* (London, Routledge and Kegan Paul, 1965).

Greeley, A. 'Religion in Britain, Ireland and the USA', in R. Howell, L. Brook, G. Prior and B. Taylor (eds.), *British Social Attitudes: 9th Report* (Aldershot, Dartmouth Publishers, 1992), 51–70.

Greer, J. E., *A Questioning Generation* (Belfast, Church of Ireland Board of Education, 1972).

Greer, J. E., 'The persistence of religion: a study of adolescents in Northern Ireland', *Character Potential*, 9(3) (1980), 139–49.

Greer, J. E., 'The persistence of religion in Northern Ireland: a study of sixth form religion, 1968–1988', *Collected Original Resources in Education*, 13(2) (1989), fiche 20, G9.

Grensted, L. W., *The Psychology of Religion* (London, Oxford University Press, 1952).

Guttman, L., 'The quantification of a class of attributes: a theory and method of scale construction', in P. Horst et al. (eds.), *The Prediction of Personal Adjustment* (New York, Social Science Research Council, 1941).

Guttman, L., 'A basis for scaling qualitative data', *American Sociological Review*, 9 (1944), 139–50.

Harding, S., D. Phillips and M. Fogarty, *Contrasting Values in Western Europe: Unity, Diversity and Change* (Basingstoke, Macmillan, 1986).

Hardy, A., *The Divine Flame* (London, Collins, 1966).

Harrison, J. *Attitudes to Bible, God, Church* (London, Bible Society, 1983).

Hay, D., *Exploring Inner Space: Scientists and Religious Experience* (London, Mowbray, 1987).

Hay, D., 'The bearing of empirical studies of religious experience on education', *Research Papers in Education*, 5(1) (1990), 3–28.

Hay, D., *Religious Experience Today: Studying the Facts* (London, Mowbray, 1990).

Hay, D. and A. Morisy, 'Reports of ecstatic, paranormal or religious experience in Great Britain and the United States: a comparison of trends', *Journal for the Scientific Study of Religion*, 17 (1978), 255–68.

Hearnshaw, L. S., *The Shaping of Modern Psychology* (London, Routledge and Kegan Paul, 1987).

Homans, G., *Social Behaviour: Its Elementary Forms* (New York, Harcourt, Brace, Jovanovich, 1974).

Hornsby-Smith, M. P., *Catholic Education: The Unobtrusive Partner* (London, Sheed and Ward, 1978).

Hyde, K. E., *Religious Learning in Adolescence*, Educational Monographs no. 7 (University of Birmingham, Institute of Education, 1965).

James, W., *The Varieties of Religious Experience* (Glasgow, William Collins, 1979).

Jencks, C., M. Smith, H. Acland, M. J. Bane, D. Cohen, H. Gintis, B. Heyns and S. Michelson, *Inequality: A Reassessment of the Effect of Family and Schooling in America* (New York, Basic Books, 1972).

Jennings, M. and R. Niemi, 'The transmission of political values from parent to child', *American Political Science Review*, 42 (1968), 169–84.

Jorm, A. F., 'Sex differences in neuroticism: a quantitative synthesis of published research', *Australian and New Zealand Journal of Psychiatry*, 21 (1987), 501–6.

Jung, C. G., *Psychological Types* (London, Kegan Paul, Trench, Trubner and Co., 1944). (First German edition 1920).

Kay, W. K., 'RE and assemblies: pupils' changing views', in L. J. Francis, W. K. Kay and W. S. Campbell (eds.), *Research in Religious Education* (Leominster, Fowler Wright, 1996).

Kay, W. K. and L. J. Francis, 'The seamless robe: interdisciplinary enquiry in religious education', *British Journal of Religious Education*, 7 (1985), 64–7.

Kay, W. K. and L. J. Francis, 'Well-being and its educational consequences', *Spectrum*, 26, 1 (1994), 8–14.

Keeves, J. P. (ed.), *Educational Research, Methodology, and Measurement: An International Handbook* (Oxford, Pergamon Press, 1988).

Kerlinger F. N. and E. J. Pedhauser, *Multiple Regression in Behavioral Research* (London, Holt, Rinehart and Winston, 1973).

Krech, D., R. S. Crutchfield and E. L. Ballackey, *Individual in Society* (New York, McGraw-Hill, 1962).

Lang, K. and G. E. Lang, 'Decisions for Christ: Billy Graham in New York', in M. Stein, A. J. Vidich and O. M. White (eds.), *Identity and Anxiety* (Chicago, Free Press, 1960).

Lawton, D., *Social Class, Language and Education* (London, Routledge and Kegan Paul, 1968).

Lazetwitz, B., 'Some factors associated with church attendance', *American Sociological Review*, 18 (1961), 301–9.

Lenski, G. E., 'Social correlates of religious interest', *American Sociological Review*, 18 (1953), 533–44.

Leuba, J. H., 'Religious beliefs of American scientists', *Harper's*, 169 (1934), 297.

Lifton, R. J., *Thought Reform and the Psychology of Totalism: A Study of 'Brainwashing' in China* (London, Gollancz, 1961).

Likert, R. A., 'A technique for the measurement of attitudes', *Archives of Psychology*, 140 (1932), 1–55.

Lipsitt, L. P., 'A self-concept scale for children and its relationship to the children's form of the Manifest Anxiety Scale', *Child Development*, 29 (1958), 463–72.

Luckman, T., *The Invisible Religion* (New York, Macmillan, 1967).

MacRae, D. G., *Weber* (London, Fontana, 1974).

Magee, B. (ed.), *Men of Ideas* (Oxford, Oxford University Press, 1982).

Martin D. A., *The Sociology of English Religion* (London, SCM, 1967).

Marx, K., *Capital* (Harmondsworth, Penguin, 1976). The first volume of *Capital* was published originally in 1867.

Maslow, A., *Toward a Psychology of Being* (New York, Van Nostrand Reinhold, 1968).

Miles, T. R., *Religious Experience* (Basingstoke, Macmillan, 1972).

Miller A. S., 'Conventional religious behaviour in modern Japan: a service industry perspective', *Journal for the Scientific Study of Religion*, 31 (1992), 207–14.

Mitchell G. D., *Sociology: The Study of Social Systems* (London, University Tutorial Press, 1959).

Moberg, D. O., *The Church as a Social Institution* (Englewood Cliffs, Prentice-Hall, 1962).

Mol, H., *The Faith of Australians* (Sydney, George Allen and Unwin, 1985).

Morgan M. Y. and J. Scanzoni, 'Religious orientations and women's expected continuity in the labor force', *Journal of Marriage and the Family*, 49 (1987), 367–79.

Morris, H. M., *The Biblical Basis for Modern Science* (Grand Rapids, Baker, 1984).

Morris, H. M., *A History of Modern Creationism* (San Diego, Master Book Publishers, 1984).

Morris, H. M. and J. Whitcomb, *The Genesis Flood* (Grand Rapids, Baker, 1961).

Murphy, J., *Church, State and Schools in Britain 1800–1970* (London, Routledge and Kegan Paul, 1971).

Murphy, J., *The Education Act 1870* (Newton Abbot, David and Charles, 1972).

Nelsen, H. M. and A. K. Nelsen, *Black Church in the Sixties* (Lexington, University Press of Kentucky, 1975).

Nelson H. M. and R. H. Potvin, 'Gender and regional differences in the religiosity of Protestant adolescents', *Review of Religious Research*, 22 (1981), 268–85.

Nelson, M. O. and E. M. Jones, 'Application of the Q-technique to the study of religious concepts', *Psychological Reports*, 3 (1957), 293–7.

Office of Population Censuses and Surveys, *Classification of Occupations 1980* (London, HMSO, 1980).

O'Keeffe, B., 'A look at the Christian schools movement', in B. Watson (ed.), *Priorities in Religious Education* (London, Falmer Press, 1992), 92–112.

Osgood, C. E., G. J. Suci and P. H. Tannenbaum, *The Measurement of Meaning* (Urbana, University of Illinois Press, 1957).

Piaget, J., *The Child's Conception of Movement and Speed* (London, Routledge and Kegan Paul, 1932).

Piaget, J., *The Moral Judgement of the Child* (London, Routledge and Kegan Paul, 1932).

Piaget, J., *The Principles of Genetic Epistemology* (London, Routledge and Kegan Paul, 1972).

Piaget, J. and B. Inhelder, *The Origin of the Idea of Chance in Children* (London, Routledge and Kegan Paul, 1975).

Poole, M. 'An investigation into aspects of the interplay between science and religion at sixth form level' (Univ. of London M.Phil. thesis, 1983).

Ramsey, I., *The Fourth R* (London, National Society and SPCK, 1970).

Reed, B., *The Dynamics of Religion* (London, Darton, Longman and Todd, 1978).

Reich, H., 'Between religion and science: complementarity in the religious thinking of young people', *British Journal of Religious Education*, 11 (1989), 62–9.

Roberts, M. B., 'The roots of creationism', *Faith and Thought*, 112(1) (1986), 21–36.

Robinson, E., *The Original Vision* (Oxford, Religious Experience Research Unit, 1977).

Robinson, E., *This Time-bound Ladder* (Oxford, Religious Experience Research Unit, 1977).

Robinson, E., *Living the Questions* (Oxford, Religious Experience Research Unit, 1978).

Rokeach, M., *The Open and Closed Mind* (New York, Basic Books, 1960).

Rubba, P. A., J. K. Horner and J. M. Smith, 'A study of two misconceptions about the nature of science among junior high school students', *School Science and Mathematics*, 81 (1981), 113–21.

Rutter, M., B. Maughan, P. Mortimore, J. Ouston and A. Smith, *Fifteen Thousand Hours: Secondary Schools and their Effects on Children* (London, Open Books, 1979).

Siegel, A. E. and S. Siegel, 'Reference groups, membership groups and attitude change', *Journal of Abnormal and Social Psychology*, 55 (1957), 360–4.

Signposts and Homecomings, *The Educative Task of the Catholic Community* (Slough, St Paul Publications, 1981).

Snider, J. G. and C. E. Osgood, *Semantic Differential: A Source Book* (Chicago, Aldine, 1969).

Spilka, B., R. W. Hood and R. L. Gorsuch, *The Psychology of Religion: An Empirical Approach* (Englewood Cliffs, Prentice-Hall, 1985).

Starbuck, E. D., *The Psychology of Religion: an empirical study of the growth of religious consciousness* (New York, Charles Scribner's Sons, 1899).

Stove, D., *Popper and After: Four Modern Irrationalists* (Oxford, Pergamon Press, 1982).

Tamayo A. and A. Dugas, 'Conceptual representation of mother, father, and God according to sex and field of study', *Journal of Psychology*, 97 (1977), 79–84.

Tawney, R. H., *Religion and the Rise of Capitalism* (Harmondsworth, Penguin, 1938).

Thompson, E. H., 'Beneath the status characteristics: gender variations in religiousness', *Journal for the Scientific Study of Religion*, 23 (1991), 381–94.

Thouless, R. H., *The Psychology of Religion* (Cambridge, Cambridge University Press, 1961).

Thurstone, L. L., 'Attitudes can be measured', *American Journal of Sociology*, 33 (1928), 529–54.

Thurstone, L. L. and E. J. Chave, *The Measurement of Attitude* (Chicago, University of Chicago Press, 1929).

Turner, E. B., 'Religious understanding and religious attitudes in male urban adolescents' (Queen's Univ. of Belfast Ph.D. thesis, 1970).

Turner, E. B., I. F. Turner, and A. Reid, 'Religious attitudes in two types of urban secondary schools: a decade of change?' *Irish Journal of Education*, 14 (1980), 43–52.

Turner, I. F. and C. J. Crossey, 'Stability and change over 21 years in the religious attitudes of adolescents', *British Journal of Religious Education*, 16 (1993), 58–64.

Vergote, A., A. Tamayo, L. Pasquali, M. Bonami, M.-R. Pattyn and A. Custers, 'Concept of God and parental images', *Journal for the Scientific Study of Religion*, 8 (1969), 79–97.

Vickers, B., *Appropriating Shakespeare* (London, Yale University Press, 1993).

Walter, T., 'Why are most churchgoers women?' *Vox Evangelica*, 20 (1990), 73–90.

Watts, F. and M. Williams, *The Psychology of Religious Knowing* (London, Geoffrey Chapman, 1988).

Webster, A. C. and P. E. Perry, *The Religious Factor in New Zealand Society* (Palmerston North, Alpha Publications, 1989).

Wilson, J., N. Williams and B. Sugarman, *Introduction to Moral Education* (Harmondsworth, Penguin, 1967).

Wright, D., *The Psychology of Moral Behaviour* (Harmondsworth, Penguin, 1971).

Wright, D. and E. Cox, 'Religious belief and co-education in a sample of sixth form boys and girls', *British Journal of Social and Clinical Psychology*, 6 (1967), 23–31.

Wright, D. and E. Cox, 'A study of the relationship between moral judgement and religious belief in a sample of English adolescents', *Journal of Social Psychology*, 72 (1967), 135–44.

Wright, D. and E. Cox, 'Changes in attitudes towards religious education and the bible among sixth form boys and girls', *British Journal of Educational Psychology*, 41 (1971), 328–31.

Wright, D. and E. Cox, 'Changes in moral belief among sixth form boys and girls over a seven year period in relation to religious belief, age and sex differences', *British Journal of Social and Clinical Psychology*, 10 (1971), 332–41.

Wulff, D. M., *Psychology of Religion: Classic and Contemporary Views* (Chichester, John Wiley and Sons, 1991).

Yinger J. M., *The Scientific Study of Religion* (New York, Macmillan, 1970).

Zeller, R. A., 'Validity', in J. P. Keeves (ed.), *Educational Research, Methodology, and Measurement: An International Handbook* (Oxford, Pergamon Press, 1988), 322–30.

Index